Advance Praise for
Rural Renaissance

Join these two delightful people on their modern-day journey back to the future, experiencing with them the joys and jitters of leaving the corporate cubicles of Chicago for the land, llamas, and rich lifestyle of a rural Wisconsin community. Also, this book is jam-packed with how-to's and resources in case you've been thinking of making your own journey into America's rural renaissance.

— JIM HIGHTOWER, radio commentator and author of *Thieves in High Places*

John and Lisa are a real inspiration, showing through their lifestyle, their Inn and their daily life how two people can make a real environmental impact now and for the future. Along with their personal story, they offer practical ideas and plenty of resources — and the reasons behind their choices. You don't have to move to the country to gain from their experience; there are lots of suggestions to help you put some of their ideas to work in your own life right now.

— NELL NEWMAN, co-founder of Newman's Own Organics

If you're like most North Americans, you want to live an ecologically sustainable life, but have not a clue about how to do it. Here's what you need: hundreds of wonderfully inventive and practical examples of "how to do it," based on real life, personal experiences. This well-organized book also shows you how all the parts fit together into a realistic, complete, and viable lifestyle.

— PAUL H. RAY, Co-author of *The Cultural Creatives: How 50 Million People Are Changing the World*

This book is for anyone wishing to improve their life by acheiving greater balance with the earth and their actions. The authors clearly trace the steps they took that continue to make a positive impact on their personal lives and community, while providing the resources readers need to follow suit.

— ALISA GRAVITZ, Executive Director, Co-op America

This inspired and inspiring book demonstrates that progress is not just the province of urban America. *Rural Renaissance* is the ultimate guide to reinventing individual lives and reinvigorating our shared future.

— DANIEL H. PINK, author of *Free Agent Nation*

Rural Renaissance does a wonderful job making sustainable living sound accessible, enriching and fun, while being realistic about the resources, skills and relationships necessary for getting started. John and Lisa's focus on being in and building authentic place-based community is a dimension too often overlooked in the sterner literature of simple living.

— KEITH MORTON, Associate Professor of American Studies, Providence College, Past Board Member, The Good Life Center

Fantastic! *Rural Renaissance* is inspiring, funny, and packed with information and resources for sustainable living; it thoughtfully presents the challenges and pleasures of living more sustainably. Add to that the practical advice and resources interwoven throughout the pages, and this book becomes a must-read for anyone wanting to tread more lightly on the planet.

— JAN JOANNIDES, Executive Director, Renewing the Countryside

Rural Renaissance is neither wishful thinking nor nostalgia. In fact it is utterly practical and can be as magical as serendipity for people looking for better ways to live.

— DAVID W. ORR, author of *Earth in Mind: On Education, Environment, and the Human Prospect*, and chair of the Environmental Studies program at Oberlin College

As part of the 1970s back-to-the-land movement myself, *Rural Renaissance* touched home. I chuckled as Lisa and John rediscovered many of the trials and tribulations that my peers endured. And I shared in their successes and celebrations. Their passion for who they are, what they do, their impact on the earth and society, and what they can offer the rest of us is contagious. The principles they live by will guide us all in a sustainable future. Lisa and John are, indeed, part of the solution.

— MICK SAGRILLO, President, Midwest Renewable Energy Association

About the Authors

John Ivanko and Lisa Kivirist are innkeepers, organic growers, and co-partners in a marketing consulting company.

John Ivanko is also an award-winning photographer, freelance writer, and author or co-author of numerous books, including the award-winning children's photobooks, *To Be a Kid* and *Back to School*, which help support the Global Fund for Children (www.shakti.org). He has contributed to *E/The Environmental Magazine*, *Mother Earth News*, *Scottish Life* and *Wisconsin Trails*, among many others.

Lisa Kivirist is a social and business entrepreneur, author of *Kiss Off Corporate America*, and an educator, reflecting her commitment to helping people create a more independent livelihood in harmony with the earth their personal passions. She's an inspiring example of the mushrooming self-employed/free agent workplace, where boundaries between work and leisure are dissolving, giving way to home-based enterprises and working parenthood, where the health and well-being of the family overrides strictly economic barometers of happiness.

Former advertising agency fast-trackers, the husband and wife duo are nationally recognized for their contemporary approach to homesteading, conservation and more sustainable living. Based in Browntown, Wisconsin, they share their farm and award-winning Inn Serendipity Bed & Breakfast with their son, a flock of free-range chickens and millions of ladybugs.

Visit Inn Serendipity on the Internet, at <www.innserendipity.com>.

❖ ❖ ❖

Ten percent of the authors' proceeds from this book will be donated to the Rural Renaissance Network, a program of the non-profit organization Renewing the Countryside, providing educational resources to foster more creative, healthy, and ecologically viable rural communities.

Visit the Rural Renaissance Network on the Internet, at <www.ruralrenaissance.org>.

If you have enjoyed *Rural Renaissance*, you might also enjoy other

BOOKS TO BUILD A NEW SOCIETY

Our books provide positive solutions for people who want to make a difference. We specialize in:

Sustainable Living ◆ Ecological Design and Planning ◆ Natural Building & Appropriate Technology
New Forestry ◆ Environment and Justice ◆ Conscientious Commerce ◆ Progressive Leadership
Educational and Parenting Resources ◆ Resistance and Community ◆ Nonviolence

For a full list of NSP's titles, please call 1-800-567-6772 or check out our web site at:

www.newsociety.com

New Society Publishers

ENVIRONMENTAL BENEFITS STATEMENT

New Society Publishers has chosen to produce this book on Rolland Enviro 100, recycled paper made with 100% post consumer waste, processed chlorine free, and old growth free.

For every 5,000 books printed, New Society saves the following resources:[1]

53	Trees
4,837	Pounds of Solid Waste
5,322	Gallons of Water
6,942	Kilowatt Hours of Electricity
8,793	Pounds of Greenhouse Gases
38	Pounds of HAPs, VOCs, and AOX Combined
13	Cubic Yards of Landfill Space

[1]Environmental benefits are calculated based on research done by the Environmental Defense Fund and other members of the Paper Task Force who study the environmental impacts of the paper industry.

NEW SOCIETY PUBLISHERS

rural renaissance

Renewing the
Quest for the
Good Life

JOHN IVANKO AND LISA KIVIRIST

foreword by Bill McKibben

NEW SOCIETY PUBLISHERS

Cataloguing in Publication Data:
A catalog record for this publication is available from the National Library of Canada.

Cover design by Diane McIntosh. Cover photos by John Ivanko.

Printed in Canada by Transcontinental Printing.
Second printing January 2007.

Paperback ISBN 13: 978-0-86571-504-2

To order directly from the publishers, please call toll-free (North America) 1-800-567-6772, or order online at www.newsociety.com

Any other inquiries can be directed by mail to:

New Society Publishers P.O. Box 189, Gabriola Island, BC V0R 1X0, Canada
1-800-567-6772

New Society Publishers' mission is to publish books that contribute in fundamental ways to building an ecologically sustainable and just society, and to do so with the least possible impact on the environment, in a manner that models this vision. We are committed to doing this not just through education, but through action. We are acting on our commitment to the world's remaining ancient forests by phasing out our paper supply from ancient forests worldwide. This book is one step towards ending global deforestation and climate change. It is printed on acid-free paper that is **100% old growth forest-free** (100% post-consumer recycled), processed chlorine free, and printed with vegetable based, low VOC inks. For further information, or to browse our full list of books and purchase securely, visit our website at: www.newsociety.com

NEW SOCIETY PUBLISHERS   www.newsociety.com

Books for Wiser Living from *Mother Earth News*

Today, more than ever before, our society is seeking ways to live more conscientiously. To help bring you the very best inspiration and information about greener, more-sustainable lifestyles, New Society Publishers has joined forces with *Mother Earth News*. For more than 30 years, *Mother Earth* has been North America's "Original Guide to Living Wisely," creating books and magazines for people with a passion for self-reliance and a desire to live in harmony with nature. Across the countryside and in our cities, New Society Publishers and *Mother Earth News* are leading the way to a wiser, more sustainable world.

To Uncle Phil and Aunt Judy

and

to all those who have joined in the journey.

Contents

Acknowledgments XIII

Foreword by Bill McKibben xv

Introduction XVII

CHAPTER 1: LIVING BY GREEN DESIGN 1
    Sustainable Living. 1
    How-to: Maintaining a Natural and Healthy Home 6
    Living With the Seventh Generation in Mind. 12
    How-to: Assessing Our Impacts: Ecological Footprints. 16
    Multiplicity of Small Changes 19
    How-to: Steps to Greening Our Life 23
    The Least Imperfect Path 26
    How-to: Appliances that can Make a Difference. 30
    Sustainable Woods. 33
    How-to: Buying Sustainably Harvested Wood 36

CHAPTER 2: FOOD AND FRIENDSHIPS 39
    Granolaheads Anonymous 39
    How-to: Living the Cultural Creative Dream 43
    The Forces of Spring 46
    How-to: Pick a Cuppa Sustainable Coffee 48
    Creative Kitchen Partnerships 50
    How-to: Supporting Local Farmers while Enjoying Good Food 52
    The Comfort of Potatoes 55
    How-to: Finding Our Place 57
    Ode to the Chickie 59
    How-to: Raising Happy Chickens 63

CHAPTER 3: GROWING AND GARDENING 65
  Planting Seeds 65
  How-to: Seeds and the Patenting of Life 71
  Organically Grown 72
  How-to: Organic Gardening Strategies 77
  Life Lessons in the Starter Garden 80
  How-to: Permaculture Design and Edible Landscaping 82
  Circle of Life 86
  How-to: The War on Bugs 88
  Free Canning Jars to a Good Home 91
  How-to: Basics of Food Preservation 95
  Perennial Magic 97
  Raised Beds and Raised Expectations 99

CHAPTER 4: ENERGY, INDEPENDENCE AND INTERDEPENDENCE 105
  Renewable Energies 105
  How-to: Energy Flows, Conservation and Efficiency 107
  The White Buffalo 113
  How-to: Solar Hot Water System Basics 116
  Apollo's Blessing 118
  How-to: Photovoltaic (PV) System Basics 120
  Interdependence Day 125
  How-to: Winds of Change: Generating Power from a Wind Turbine 129
  The Heart and Hearth of Fire 133
  How-to: Heating with a Woodstove 137
  Precious Water 139
  How-to: Water Conservation 142
  Personal Energies 144
  How-to: Walking and Designing a Labyrinth 147

CHAPTER 5: CREATING AND CARING FOR COMMUNITY 149
  Feeding Community 149
  How-to: Join the Anti-consumer Community 153
  Unappreciated Rhubarb 155
  How-to: Searching for Underrated Treasures 158
  That Interesting Couple on County P 161
  How-to: Thinking Outside of the Box 163

Cappuccino and Community 165
How-to: Supporting the Local Economy 168
A House of Straw 171
How-to: Building with Straw Bale 174

Chapter 6: Loving Our Livelihood 177
Right Livelihood 177
How-to: Work For Our Passion and Follow Our Bliss 181
Diversified Income-producing Portfolio of Work 185
Adopting a Different Measure of Wealth 187
The Bed & Breakfast Lifestyle 189
How-to: A Short Course on Starting a B&B 193
Home Sweet Office 195
How-to: Home Office Economics 197
Lifestyle and Workstyle: Blending Work and Leisure 199
How-to: Traveling as an Ecotourist 202
Blending Baby and Business 205
How-to: Nurture by Nature 209

Chapter 7: Leaving a Simple Legacy 213
Empty Hammocks 213
How-to: Creative Steps to De-cluttering 216
Growth Versus Development 219
How-to: Considering a Diversified Quality of Life Index (DQLI) 222
Bluebirds, Birch and Bass: Creating Wildlife Habitat 225
How-to: Building a Bluebird Trail 229
Eating Lower on the Food Chain 231
How-to: Going Vegetarian 234
Health and Wellness 236
How-to: Providing What a Body Needs 239
Freedom To and Freedom From 241
Leaving a Legacy 245
How-to: Leaving Biological Legacies 249

Epilogue: Independance and Interdependance Day 253
Index 255
About the Authors 267

Acknowledgments

Rural Renaissance: Renewing the Quest for the Good Life blossomed into being thanks to a multitude of people who graced its evolution. We are grateful to Chris and Judith Plant, our editor Ingrid Witvoet, and all the dedicated souls at New Society Publishers for sharing in our vision for this project and their commitment to creating a better society. Appreciation goes out to Bill McKibben for the tone he sets for this book, for the inspiration he shares, and for the love he demonstrates for the world around him.

Thanks goes to our community of friends who provided feedback, inspiration and energy throughout the manuscript's development (as well as in our quest for the good life), especially Ken Avery, Christopher Barth, Kara Belew, the Carus family, Tony Christini, Elizabeth Goreham, Marshall King, Amy Kremen, Dr. Jack Matson, Barb Meister, Jason Perry, Chris Sandvig, Claire Simpson, Mimi Tilmanis, Cheryl Toth, Matt Urban, Tom Walsh, Eric Welty, and Phil and Judy Welty. Related to John's photography, appreciation goes out to Maya Ajmera at The Global Fund for Children and Ron Nielsen at Photo Ink.

Rural Renaissance became a shared family project and could not have been pulled off without the loving grandparent support of Aelita and Walt Kivirist and Susan Ivanko, all eagerly watching Liam as Mom and Dad pecked away on the computer. Thanks to Liam Ivanko Kivirist for his abiding curious and happy demeanor while his parents massaged the pages of the manuscript between diaper changing and nursing.

Thanks, finally, to the many dedicated non-profit organizations that continually provide their resources and friendship, including, among many, the Midwest Renewable Energy Association, Co-op America, Renewing the Countryside, Inc., the Mississippi Valley Conservancy, the Michael Fields Agricultural Institute and the Monroe Chamber of Commerce and Industry. We are indebted to Inn Serendipity guests, the Reunion family, the Green County community — both the people and the nature-filled place — and to our rich network of friends across the globe who continually keep us connected, challenged and inspired.

Foreword

BY BILL McKIBBEN, AUTHOR OF *THE END OF NATURE*

Rural America, though in some broad sense in "decline" for a century, has seen several waves of back-to-the-landers — people who have given up mainstream contemporary American culture for a return to a way of life variously imagined as simpler, more natural, more rooted in community. One bible for an earlier wave was Scott and Helen Nearing's *The Good Life* — but there was something deeply Calvinist about their approach that probably discouraged as many prospects as it attracted. The hippies came next — no Calvinism there at all, but in many cases not much know-how either. Some stuck, but the cultural focus swung back to the fast-lane life of city and suburb.

Now, a generation later, the new returnees to rural America are exemplified — and will be inspired — by Lisa Kivirist and John Ivanko. They caught the gold ring on the merry-go-round of 1990s prosperity — ad execs in the big city, plenty of cash, small oceans of latte. But eventually they found it to be mere brass, deficient both in terms of their own satisfaction and in light of their dawning knowledge of the earth's environmental plight. They began asking the questions that are in the back of many millions of minds: If we live in the middle of the greatest economy ever known, how come I'm not happier and the planet is going straight to hell, or at least a place of a similar temperature?

And so they began their return to a world that seemed more real and complete, in their case a farmstead in southern Wisconsin. But because they were neither angry at the world nor stoned, they were able to travel in some kind of real balance. They didn't feel the need to become completely self-sufficient — in fact, they quickly figured out that one of the joys of rural life was finding all the other people who knew more than you did about something and would help you with it. (And who, in return, were interested in learning city lessons about coffee.) They invested serious time and money in alternative energy sources, but they tied their solar panels into the grid, instead of going it absolutely alone. They turned off the TV, but they kept their Internet connection. They encouraged their bed and breakfast guests to enjoy their organic vegetables, but they also realized American tourists were not going to share a bathroom down the hall.

They were, in a word, precisely the kind of "Cultural Creatives" that they hold out as the best hope for American renaissance. Now, Cultural Creative is the kind of phrase that only an adman could love — but there really does seem to be something happening with 40 or 50 million Americans who are educated and successful, but also out of tune with George Bush's America. They tend to be artistic, spiritual (but non-denominational), socially tolerant, interested in community, and concerned about the environment. They suspect, in other words, that the world they inhabit has more bottom lines than conventional wisdom would suggest. It's not that they want to be poor (or share a bathroom), but they don't put riches ahead of other items on their agendas. They suspect that some compromise is in order between money and time, between individualism and community, between personal conven-ience and protecting the planet. Most of all, they suspect that compromise is not the same as sacrifice; that in fact something like happiness lies down that middle path.

The real contribution of this book, and of Inn Serendipity, is to prove that, at least in the case of one family, those suspicions are correct. The descriptions of life at this bed and breakfast — of the vegetable gardens and the community celebra-tions and the hens laying eggs — are enough to make anyone wish to live such a life. And the frank acknowledgement of how little they knew going in is enough to con-vince anyone that, with a reasonable bank balance to get them started, such a life might truly be possible.

Those of us who have lived for a long time in the sticks value such newcomers, impressed by their energy and idealism. Especially when, like John and Lisa, they're wise enough to value their predecessors. A rural renaissance really might be in its early moments, as people start to rebuild the local institutions that would make beginning to disconnect from the global system a little easier.

An even more important test, however — and one I suspect that the Cultural Creatives will find themselves in the middle of — is whether this renaissance can spread to the suburbs and cities as well. It is only by changing the values and behav-iors of people in those places that we will start to see real shifts in the ways our soci-ety uses resources and produces pollution.

So Inn Serendipity need not be seen solely as a way station on the way to coun-try living, a stop on the Underground Railroad smuggling old ad execs out of the rat race. It — and this book — should also be a refuge where people can spend a few hours or a few days, refreshing themselves for the job of subtly remaking their lives, no matter where they are going to live.

By definition, that is, serendipity can happen anywhere and anytime. Surely it has struck in these pages.

The Quest for the Good Life

Since moving from downtown Chicago to a small farm in southwestern Wisconsin, our days have been richly flavored with discoveries and fresh opportunities to live more sustainably and closer to the land. Our journey has unfolded in a wooden bowl filled with a medley of lettuce leaves. It was one balmy July evening while sitting on our front porch eating dinner that we realized we were no longer just the owners of our farm; we were ingredients and participants. We shared a simple supper fresh from the garden: tender lettuce greens and ruby red tomatoes partnered with a warm and crusty loaf of homemade bread. We watched the summer sunset fade to a warm glow and fireflies begin their evening dance. Our souls merged with the earth through the fresh whole foods on the table, complimented by the starry light show.

Our quest for the good life entails more than a rural zip code and fresh produce savored slowly with firefly entertainment. It's a search for a life simpler in design yet richer in meaning, unearthing passion with every potato we plant. Living more sustainably and connecting with the crickets, coneflowers and community offers guidance, inspiration and even amusement with every failed zucchini crop. As our story continues to evolve around our country farmstead we hear more and more stories told by people living in urban enclaves and suburban homefronts, from big cities to remote Caribbean islands. We've discovered that the good life isn't dependent upon the goods of life.

This mutual desire for living authentically — and caring for all life — breathes through our everyday experiences by our approach to living, weaving together food systems, energy systems, living systems and livelihood. Nature is our model, our teacher and our healer. How we grow and eat our food is directly connected to how we produce and use our energy. The ecosystem we live in — nature's restoring cycles and the vital role biological and cultural diversity play — is inseparable from our life. How we earn income, in what we've come to embrace as right livelihood, is integrally linked to a restorative economy that is life-sustaining and soul-nourishing. These are the empowering themes found in our lives and throughout this book. We share a vision that celebrates diversity, fosters creativity, thrives on self-reliance and freedom, and respects nature. It sounds remarkably like life, liberty and the pursuit of happiness to us, complete with all the responsibilities as citizens that it entails.

Every day we're given a fresh start, a clean mixing bowl in which to create and concoct our life journey, if not also a fresh delicious salad. If we didn't get the blend right yesterday or things get too spicy with mustard greens today, we remind ourselves that tomorrow is a new, clean mixing bowl. The key is to keep learning as we go, to be open to new flavors, and keep connected to, grateful for, and nurturing of a sustainable lifestyle and a livelihood full of meaning and purpose.

About the Farmstead

Sketch of Inn Serendipity farmstead

A five-and-a-half-acre quintessential Wisconsin farmstead is home to Inn Serendipity Bed & Breakfast, our office, and our home. Perched atop a ridge, we're surrounded by rolling green fields, many of which have been worked by local farming families for generations. Outbuildings, flower beds and growing fields encircle the 80-year old farmhouse, creating places for us to wander, seek solace and inspiration, or come together in community. The dairy barn's second floor loft has bellowed with enthusiastic applause during open mic nights while downstairs, two curious llamas bed down. The granary is being transformed into a passive and active solar heated greenhouse made from strawbales. A hammock beckons guests, swaying in the breeze between two maple trees just west of the house. Surrounded by grapevines and

VALDEK KIVIRIST

next to the vocal frog population in the pond, this spot provides a dark, cool hide-away retreat on hot, sticky summer afternoons. Asparagus and strawberry beds, raspberry and black currant patches, and apple and cherry trees gift us with perennial crops, complimented by three fruit and vegetable growing fields east of the house. Chickens, cats, and our son Liam roam freely. A great horned owl occasionally hunts from atop the crest of the barn roof at night.

The farmhouse itself exudes its own energy and personality, a blending of tradition with modern times. We cook up hearty, farm-fresh eggs and vegetables for breakfast omelets, while B&B guests take a morning shower upstairs with water heated by the sun. Inn Serendipity beckons, bringing people together and growing community.

Restoration in a Living Economy

We plucked ourselves from the concrete jungle of Chicago and planted roots in a place where we could see stars and hear frogs, having faith that goodness would serendipitously blossom. A place where community could be cared for and nature could be nurtured. Could we rediscover who we are creatively, rekindle meaningful relationships, become more self-reliant and independent, and live a more healthy and harmonious lifestyle in greater balance with the earth? We wanted to live a life based on Mahatma Gandhi's philosophy of, "We must become the change we seek." The deeper our roots grow, the more we learn about and restore ourselves.

Back in our Chicago ad agency days, what we were doing was removed from our true passions and offered little authentic connection to the earth, to a healthy lifestyle, or to any feeling of community. Pulled into the money and image machine, with most of our daily hours and energy spent in a climate-controlled office, we failed to realize what was going on, that anything was amiss. It was only after we finally stepped out of that picture and began questioning our lifestyle that we started reconnecting with the genuine people buried deep inside ourselves.

The knowledge we gain by living closer to the land is real, providing steps that provide the purpose and meaning in our lives: going through the discovery of making raspberry jam for the first time; celebrating the results spread over a slice of crunchy whole wheat toast and sharing a couple half pint jars with our neighbors or friends; restoring the land with compost; replanting trees to help renew the health of a forest ecosystem; producing all of our own energy from the wind and sun; and learning to use that energy in wiser, more efficient ways. These are some of the many events and activities that shape and define our character and harmoniously reverberate through our souls. By renewing our lives based on ecological principles and with emphasis on relationships and connectivity, we arrive at a new, much more personal definition of success. We have transformed our business model into one that is life-sustaining, rather than life-destroying. In a living economy, rather than one that turns life into wealth in the form of products and services sold, we have crafted a livelihood full of enterprises that sustain us and the planet. Our work and leisure blend into a lifestyle and workstyle that reminds us of a time when commerce was still about community exchanges, relationships and local priorities.

Even with our clear vision, we've encountered moments of questioning doubt. It's natural. But our rural fumbles and bumbles were quickly balanced by those magical moments when the cornucopia of life overflows and you know you're where you should be, waking to that instant when the night stars and the pink of the sunrise slowly dance together.

While our story is rural, the repeating cycles of nature are ones we all share regardless of whether we're living in the country, city or suburbs. Many of the ideas presented could just as easily be done in the city or suburban subdivision — in fact, many have. We hope that our story and experiences provide kindling for the fires of your own dreams, and will help ignite or perhaps continue your personal quest for creating the good life, however you may come to define it.

CHAPTER 1

Living by Green Design

Sustainable Living

We aren't too concerned about what the neighbors think, or with keeping up with the Joneses. The neighbors aren't close enough to see us and those mythical, image-driven Joneses would probably take one look at the chicken poop on the sidewalk and keep on cruising by. This anonymity could give us carte blanche to do whatever, whenever, and however we like with no concern for the land. Nobody knows whether we put our recycling in color-coded bins on the curb once a week or burn it up in a fire pit out back, plastic, rubber and all. County roads don't have curbs, much less garbage or recycling pick-up. We schlep things to the dump, and recycling is voluntary. Whether we apply chemical pesticides and fertilizers in the garden or manage things organically is up to us.

But the frog croaking in the pond knows, as does the willow tree and the barn cat that gave birth to her second batch of kittens in the loft of the machine shed. Liam is directly affected by our relationship with and treatment of the earth. So we're determined to leave this land and farmstead, and this world, in better shape than we found it.

Nature observes and reflects our actions — and our inactions. Green design comprises our decisions about how we spend our time, the choices we make on products used, the lessons we learn, and our understanding of ourselves. It's is not a perfect, final result; rather, like nature, it evolves with new approaches, adaptations or creative innovations. Every day something has changed: the strawberry patch blooms; the lettuce goes to seed; a bluebird fledges from its nestbox. Our approach to green design has enabled us to better cope with and manage change in its many forms.

We moved to the farm for the freedom to live more ecologically, more independently, and with a greater sense of community. We've discovered that living by green design often refers to what we don't do and what we no longer need or want. Our commute no longer involves two bus routes, a monthly bus pass, and 20 hours a week. Lunch is not fast food with disposable everything. By working from home, growing our own food and living in a place where we can see sunrises and stars and breathe fresh air, a lot of the more consumptive or negative routines of our former corporate life are gone. That said, we also admire those living in the city and suburbs who have managed to carve out an ecological and socially responsible lifestyle, riding bikes to work, forming neighborhood groups to provide healthy and safe places to raise their families, figuring out how to cultivate crops on their rooftops. They, too, are pioneers in a new urban movement; one that includes community gardens, lawnless yards, rooftop solar panels, housing cooperatives and the like.

What is Sustainable Living?

Many definitions of "sustainability" exist today. In our case, we focus on a definition that emphasizes the self-reliant local community while recognizing the responsibility we have as global citizens. Sustainability is an ideal, a moving target, something we're always working toward. Sustainable living balances the economic, ecological and social needs of all life with that of our own, while enhancing those possibilities for future generations. Sustainable living values diversity, creativity and passion; it's not about growth of property, wealth or stuff. Rather, it's about creating livable communities and fostering greater social and economic equity while preserving and restoring the ecosystems we depend on for our very survival.

Our goals as individuals, global citizens and business owners are to plant more trees than we've used, help cultivate a bioregional and sustainable food system that is more secure for us and our community, completely offset the carbon dioxide emissions caused by our energy use (the largest contributor to global warming), live a fossil-fuel-free life, and feed the flames of our imagination. We have our lifetime to do it. While there are limits to growth (this planet can only sustain so many people), there's no limit to development of a better way of living, one filled with creativity, adventure, security, nature and meaning.

Much of our journey has been spent discovering solutions and ideas to describe what sustainable life could be. Our adaptive approach listens to our intuition and instincts while mindfully considering the vast amount of information, scientific research and personal experiences. There isn't one way or even a best way to approach sustainable living, since personal circumstances, location, climate and financial considerations are different for everyone.

Living green involves a constant passion for improvement, for challenging ourselves to tread more lightly on the Earth. Currently, the impact of one American over a lifetime is equivalent to that of more than ten people living in a sub-Saharan African country, based on the consumption of calories, energy, resources and a host of other variables. According to the non-profit organization Redefining Progress, "the average American uses 24 acres to support his or her lifestyle. In comparison, the average Canadian lives on a footprint 30 percent smaller (17 acres), and the average Italian on a footprint 60 percent smaller (9 acres)". Deciding to bring a baby into this world — another high-impact American — magnified these statistics even further for us. How can we live more sustainably *and* and raise our son? It's a question we're challenged by every day.

The farm helps us reconnect with the land. Our approach has been to question and evaluate each of our needs. If needed, what is the greenest, or most responsible, purchase we can make? Could we get it from a second hand store or must it be new? Answers to these questions are subjective. Lisa buys a jumbo pack of marshmallows for our annual summer season of campfire s'mores; John looks forward to upgrading to digital photography, to avoid film and processing. These are not survival needs, in the purest sense, nor are they particularly green. Still, marshmallows and film aside, there are plenty of other green trends we've tried to incorporate into our life.

Reuse

We try to re-use items whenever possible. When moving in, we didn't have a lot of furniture between us. However, we managed to completely furnish the 1,969 (182 m²) square foot house without having to purchase anything new, aside from mattresses for the bed & breakfast. It's amazing what folks have sitting around that they are happy to find a good home for — a chair and bookshelf from parents; a dresser from an old school buddy. We spent much of our first year, off-and-on, refinishing and painting, and our decor is admittedly eclectic. Comfortable is a word used to describe our place; a "put your feet up where you want to and hang out" kind of house, which we consider a compliment. We're tickled when our guests fall asleep on the living room couch or come down for breakfast in their pyjamas.

How some of these reused items end up here amaze us. About a month after we moved in, we decided to throw a holiday party, offering a good excuse for us to introduce ourselves to neighbors and invite them over for some holiday cheer. At this gathering, Carol, who shepherded us through the whole farm buying process as our realtor, gave herself a tour around the place and asked where we slept, noticing a lack of beds. We had not purchased the B&B mattresses yet, and our funds were too limited to buy our own mattress. We chuckled, admitting that we crashed in sleeping bags on the bedroom floor. This was no problem to us and part of our grand adventure, but Carol, always looking out for us, showed up the following morning with her son's extra futon in the back of her truck. "This has been sitting in the basement and I've been trying to get rid of it for years," explained Carol. Much appreciated and definitely used; we still sleep on it today.

Growing Our Food

With about seventy percent of our food needs met by our gardens, our grocery shopping is limited to the basic staples and purchased with a discriminating eye. We search out mostly organic items like flour, sugar, oats and pasta, and we've learned to read labels – helping us, for instance, to avoid anything with hydrogenated fat on the label because of associated health risks, selecting instead healthier expeller-pressed cooking oils, rather than oils extracted through use of solvents.

Non-toxic Cleaning

We clean the house with some of the same items that we might use in a meal. Baking soda is used as a cleanser and as a deodorizer in Liam's diaper bucket (for pre-soaking cloth diapers). A vinegar spray is used on mirrors and glass. Vegetable oil soap cleans just about everything else, although we do occasionally use commercially made non-toxic cleaners if necessary.

Power of the Purse

We make our purchase choices based on factors like the materials that are used to make the product (extra points when it's made with post-consumer recycled waste or organic materials); where it is made (the more local, the better); the store or producer's reputation related to the environment, quality and social issues (for example, their record on humane treatment of employees), and price. Sometimes these self-imposed criteria pose serious challenges. We can't just walk into Wal-Mart anymore and breeze out with a standard box of detergent, a gas lawn mower, or a birthday card. Is that detergent safe to use with a septic system? Is an electric lawn mower available? Is that card printed on recycled paper and if so, with what percentage of post-consumer waste? While our purchasing needs are few, the time it takes for us to make buying decisions has increased, requiring us to at times take our questions directly to the manufacturer. In the end, we try to choose retailers that care about the environment, about the communities in which they do business, and about how the goods they sell are made.

Sometimes our purchase decisions are less than ideal. Case in point are those new mattresses we purchased for the two B&B rooms. While organic mattresses were available at the time from a California manufacturer, we took another approach and purchased mattresses from Verlo Mattresses, a manufacturer of standard mattresses based in Wisconsin with a factory less than 60 miles (95 km) away. What is uniquely green about Verlo at the time was that they were the only US mattress company that practiced out-cycling, the recycling of materials found in old mattresses. Given the number of organic mattress manufacturers that have entered the marketplace in the past few years, we'll have many more options when it comes time to replace another mattress.

Sometimes our attempts to live by green design aren't green at all, they're blue. The need for new towels for the guest bathrooms led us to select a natural cotton towel with no synthetic dyes or colors. (At the time, there were few organic cotton options and none that we could afford.) Our country living naiveté surfaced after washing these towels when we discovered rust-colored stains. We called Carol, sure that something was wrong with the house plumbing or washing machine. Instead, she patiently explained that the well water, higher in mineral content, had been the culprit. Great for drinking, the water will sometimes leave its mark on light-colored materials when laundering.

What do we do now? We had invested a fair amount in these quality towels, and while we didn't want to have to use harsh stain removers, we didn't want our B&B guests thinking that we tried to reuse towels and sheets without washing them. Saving the day, Christopher, a textile-savvy friend in Monroe, suggested we dye the towels with a natural indigo dye, turning them blue. He offered to help us with this dying project, so one summer afternoon we dragged the towels, along with the vat of dye, to the laundry line, dipping the towels and hanging them to line dry. Unfortunately, we learned the origin of the old saying, "as crafty as a blue dyer." The indigo color appears when the wet material hits the air, meaning we needed to pull the towels out of the vat very fast and evenly — not something we were prepared for. So our towels have this blue tie-dye look to them, covering up the rust stains and befitting this eclectic, green-intentioned household.

How to

Maintaining a Natural and Healthy Home

With the understanding that everything is interconnected, we strive to select building materials, products, technologies and services that fall under an umbrella of energy conservation and socially and environmentally responsible manufacturing or design, and, to the extent possible, bioregionalism (purchasing products or services as close to home as possible). Although initial costs are often higher this way, we view our decisions cumulatively and long-term, much as we do our mortgage, which allows us to defray the economic cost over a longer term. And, as most people do, we live within financial limitations, moving forward with projects as they become financially viable.

THE HANNOVER PRINCIPLES:
Green Design Principles for Sustainability

by William McDonough

We've used William McDonough's Hannover Principles for Sustainability to help guide our projects, Written for the 2000 World's Fair, the Principles establish design parameters for sustainability, providing an ecology primer for designers and anyone else concerned with the intelligent use of natural resources. The Hannover Principles are considered a living document committed to transformation and growth in the understanding of our interdependence with nature, in order that they may adapt as our knowledge of the world evolves.

1. Insist on rights of humanity and nature to coexist in a healthy, supportive, diverse and sustainable condition.

2. Recognize interdependence. The elements of human design interact with and depend upon the natural world, with broad and diverse implications at every scale. Expand design considerations to recognize even distant effects.

3. Respect relationships between spirit and matter. Consider all aspects of human settlement, including community, dwelling, industry and trade, in terms of existing and evolving connections between spiritual and material consciousness.

4. Accept responsibility for the consequences of design decisions upon human well-being, the viability of natural systems and their right to coexist.

Our day-to-day operating decisions incorporate the adage: reduce, reuse, recycle. We added two more of our own — restore and redesign — while also considering William McDonough's Hannover Principles (see sidebar, *The Hannover Principles*). Reflecting this philosophy, we chose to remodel an existing farmhouse rather than build a new house. In a similar vein, we're transforming an old granary into a greenhouse, rather than burning it down and building a new structure. Buying the early 20th century farmhouse also helped us reduce our exposure to problems associated with the chemicals found in the materials often used in today's modern homes, such as chipboards, plywood, pesticide-impregnated timbers, vinyl flooring and plastic finishes. Other than the asbestos shingles around the farmhouse (best left alone), we've used our renovations as an opportunity to carefully remove many of the possible health dangers, such as the lead paint that was around the windows, and most of the carpet throughout the house.

5. Create safe objects of long-term value. Do not burden future generations with requirements for maintenance of vigilant administration of potential danger due to the careless creation of products, processes or standards.

6. Eliminate the concept of waste. Evaluate and optimize the full lifecycle of products and processes, to approach the state of natural systems, in which there is no waste.

7. Rely on natural energy flows. Human designs should, like the living world, derive their creative forces from perpetual solar income. Incorporate the energy efficiently and safely for responsible use.

8. Understand the limitations of design. No human creation lasts forever and design does not solve all problems. Those who create and plan should practice humility in the face of nature. Treat nature as a model and mentor, not an inconvenience to be evaded or controlled.

9. Seek constant improvement by the sharing of knowledge. Encourage direct and open communication between colleagues, patrons, manufacturers and users to link long-term sustainable considerations with ethical responsibility, and reestablish the integral relationship between natural processes and human activity.

Source: UVA Architecture Publications; © 1992 William McDonough Architects. Used with permission.

According to the US Environmental Protection Agency (EPA), indoor air pollution can sometimes be ten times worse than Los Angeles on a smog alert, no matter where we live. Around 1915, synthetic chemicals first started to show up; at present, there are over four million synthetic chemicals on record. It's not surprising that pollutants that impact human cells have been shown to accumulate in our bodies. Volatile organic compounds (VOCs) are chemically unstable, and readily turn into gas or combine with other chemicals which can then be inhaled. According to the EPA and other sources, doctors are beginning to recognize multiple chemical sensitivities and environmental illnesses. Allergic reactions are our body's way to signal exposure to toxic substances, some of which we used to welcome (remember "new car smell"?).

Rather than gambling with our lives and those of our family, friends and bed & breakfast guests, we've opted for safer choices. We wanted to feel vibrant and healthy, so we are working to make our house as healthy and safe as possible. The additional expense of ecologically safe products or materials is nothing when compared to spending years in and out of hospitals later in life from cancer or other diseases resulting from bioaccumulated toxins or poisons. The following products or services had a place in our journey toward living more sustainably and by green design. At times it's been a challenge to make informed decisions when limited information and labeling is available, and many of the companies offering ecologically sound alternatives are small-time operators, so perseverance and patience is sometimes needed.

Building and Construction Materials

Paint

Say "no volatile organic compounds," or "no VOC," and the paint store salespeople will often come back with: "you mean, low VOC." When shopping for our no-VOC paint, which we've now used throughout our house, we ended up asking for "hospital paint" to get what we wanted. Most major paint companies carry a no-VOC product line, but the names change frequently and sales staff seem to lack knowledge about this type of paint. American Formulating and Manufacturing (AFM) no-VOC Safecoat paint <www.afmsafecoat.com> and Bioshield <www.bioshieldpaint.com> are paint companies that offer ecological options. American Formulating and Manufacturing (AFM) also offers stains, sealers, cleaners and other safe products for building and maintenance.

Tile

Bathroom fixtures have yet to go green, but closing the recycling loop has never been more beautiful, stylish and functional with floor tiles made from almost 60 percent recycled automobile windshield glass and other post-consumer waste glass. Our tiles in our guest bathrooms and our first floor bath are made by Terra-Green Technologies <www.terragreenceramics.com>, and can be specially ordered through nearly any floor covering store. Terra-Green offers Terra Traffic tiles for flooring and Terra Classic tiles for walls. Eco Friendly Flooring <www.ecofriendlyflooring.com> offers many sustainable flooring products, including recycled glass tiles, linoleum, reclaimed and Forest Stewardship Council-certified wood, bamboo and cork.

Wood Floor Sealers (Poly-BP)

For our renovated kitchen floor and the main floor and hallway at the Inn Serendipity Woods cabin, we selected AFM Safecoat Durostain, a no-VOC stain and sealer, and followed it with AFM's Lock-In Wood Sealer. For a beautiful,

Indoor pollutants often found in the home.

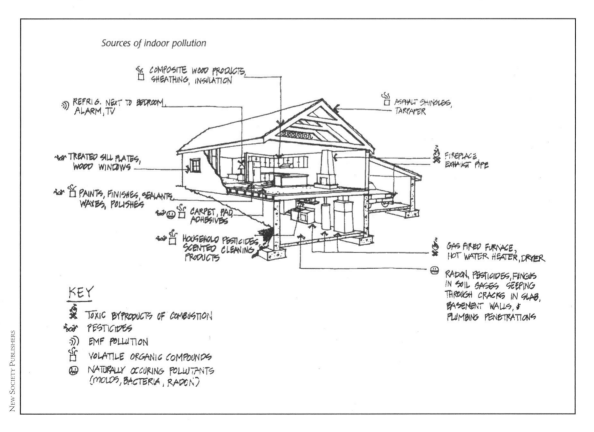

Sources of indoor pollution

COMPOSITE WOOD PRODUCTS, SHEATHING, INSULATION

ASPHALT SHINGLES, TARPAPER

REFRIG. NEXT TO BEDROOM ALARM, TV

FIREPLACE EXHAUST PIPE

TREATED SILL PLATES, WOOD WINDOWS

PAINTS, FINISHES, SEALANTS, WAXES, POLISHES

CARPET, PAD ADHESIVES

HOUSEHOLD PESTICIDES, SCENTED CLEANING PRODUCTS

GAS FIRED FURNACE, HOT WATER HEATER, DRYER

RADON, PESTICIDES, FUNGUS IN SOIL GASES SEEPING THROUGH CRACKS IN SLAB, BASEMENT WALLS, & PLUMBING PENETRATIONS

KEY

- TOXIC BYPRODUCTS OF COMBUSTION
- PESTICIDES
- EMF POLLUTION
- VOLATILE ORGANIC COMPOUNDS
- NATURALLY OCCURING POLLUTANTS (MOLDS, BACTERIA, RADON)

durable finish, we added the application of two coats of gloss and one coat of satin (best to mask scratches) Safecoat Polyureseal BP to protect the stained wood.

There are many options for safer, healthier homes, from non-toxic caulks to insulation made from shredded newspaper or roof shingles made from recycled materials. Even Gypsum wallboard, the mainstay of home improvement, is available in a type made from 18 percent recycled gypsum and 100 percent recycled paper backing.

The options are constantly changing, which can make locating a manufacturer more difficult. Complicating this further is the fact that contractors tend to be creatures of habit and use materials or products that they've grown accustomed to using and trust. Co-op America's Green Pages <www.greenpages.org> is a great place for tracking down healthier and greener alternatives, as are Gaiam Real Goods <www.realgoods.com or www.gaiam.com> and Healthy Home <www.healthyhome.com>.

In the Home

For around the house maintenance, cleaning, and laundry, we choose among an increasing array of non-toxic and environmentally safe cleaners and detergents, 100 percent recycled toilet paper and natural unbleached cotton linens, as well as fabrics made with organically grown fiber. Seventh Generation (www.seventhgeneration.com) offers a wide range of these household products that we've been using for years.

In the spirit of reusing furnishings, we used Citristrip <www.citristrip.com>, a citrus-based, non-toxic furniture refinisher, on the cabin property's ash dining room table and chairs, as well as on our antique lawyer's bookcase on the farm. Independently operated stores specializing in ecology-safe products, as well as larger commercial enterprises (such as Whole Foods Market, Wild Oats, or Trader Joe's), offer a wide selection of cleaning brands, often in more economical concentrated forms, that are chlorine and phosphate-free, unscented, biodegradable, and non-animal tested. Our oak coffee table came from Smith & Hawken, among the first to support Forest Stewardship Council-certified (FSC) sustainable wood use <www.smithhawken.com>.

SOURCES AND RESOURCES

Co-op America's Green Pages
Website: www.greenpages.org
The number of green businesses bringing socially and environmentally responsible goods and services to the marketplace is growing rapidly. Find wonderful products, values and savings - everything you need to put your economic power to work for change.

Sustainable Sources
Website: www.greenbuilder.com
Features everything from an on-line green building professionals directory to their sustainable building sourcebook, this website is a great place to search for green building resources and contractors.

Paul Hawken, *The Ecology of Commerce: A Declaration of Sustainability,* Harper Business, 1993.

Angela Hobbs, *The Sick House Survival Guide: Simple Steps to Healthier Homes,* New Society Publishers, 2003.

Editors of *E: The Environmental Magazine, Green Living: An E Magazine Planetary Resource Guide,* Plume, In Press.

John Schaeffer, *Real Goods Solar Living Sourcebook: The Complete Guide to Renewable Energy Technologies and Sustainable Living,* Real Goods, 2001.

Daniel D. Chiras, *The Natural House: A Complete Guide to Healthy, Energy-efficient Environmental Homes,* Chelsea Green, 2000.

David Pearson, *The New Natural House Book: Creating a Healthy, Harmonious and Ecologically Sound Home,* Fireside, 1998.

Nell Newman, with Joseph D'Agnese, *The Newman's Own Guide to a Good Life: Simple Measures that Benefit You and the Place You Live,* Villard, 2003.

William McDonough and Michael Braungart, *Cradle to Cradle: Remaking the Way We Make Things,* North Point Press, 2002.

Worldwatch Institute
Website: www.worldwatch.org
A non-profit research powerhouse, offering information and practical resources to assist in the transition to a more environmentally sustainable and socially just society.

Living With the Seventh Generation in Mind

Lisa is the self-appointed farm historian. Year round, you'll find her carrying her camera to document what's happening. While she does cover the bigger, expected events like birthdays and visiting friends, she really tends to focus on the rather obscure happenings that pass by quickly: bringing home a new batch of baby chicks from the feed store; that overbearing pile of zucchini we harvested in fifteen minutes flat last July; early spring chives peeking through the snow; John's inaugural apple pie of the season. These photos are chronologically organized in various scrapbooks and tucked in a corner shelf should interested guests wish to peruse them. Like the squirrel burying acorns under the oak tree, Lisa has always had this drive to preserve, to record our history for future generations.

Living with the seventh generation in mind takes this idea of concern for the future to a much deeper level. When making decisions today, we try to consider the impacts on many generations to follow. The concept of living for the seventh generation comes from the Iroquois Nation; every individual action is examined and evaluated based on how its effect may be felt seven generations into the future. It's one thing for us to take simple snapshots of how life is today. It's quite another to take responsibility for the quality of life future generations will inherit. Better yet, how do we go beyond just preserving today's status quo and instead improve things for our children's children, and beyond?

How we incorporate this philosophy into our lives is based on this: travel light. The less we leave behind, use up or burn up, and the less that collects at the landfill, the healthier our planet will be for future generations. Cutting back on wasteful ways is an ongoing goal that we've recognized as both manageable and tangible. We hope that, as economic market forces and entire worldviews change, we may be able to eliminate the very concept of "waste" altogether.

We're in direct control of what we bring to the Cadiz Township dump or recycling center. We separate cardboard, glass, plastic, paper, cardboard, and metal for recycling and the rest — about seven garbage cans a year — goes in the general bin and is transported to the nearest landfill. The Styrofoam that we've accumulated, as minimal as it's been, is in a pile in the garage until we can find a recycling home for it; we've used the peanuts as insulation in the greenhouse attic.

We're definitely the oddity when we do go to the Cadiz dump. First off, we rarely go — just a handful of times a year. At first, we had to keep reintroducing ourselves to the woman who staffs the dump because she didn't remember us. Now, she sets aside old chairs, pots and buckets for us. Our landfill-bound trash is so minimal for a couple of reasons:

- By growing our own fruit and vegetables, we've eliminated packaging. Our garden wastes are sent to the compost heap, with the chickens picking out the apple peels for snacks.

- When we do buy something, particularly food products, we select items with the least amount of packaging. Bulk food aisles satisfy a lot of our grocery needs, from dried beans to sea salt to couscous, and we bring our own containers to fill. The range of organic foods seems to get better every year locally, but we frequent the nation's largest food co-op, Willy Street Co-op in Madison, or Whole Foods Market for items we fail to find nearer home.

- For non-bulk items, we look to see what comes in recyclable containers made out of recycled material. Ideally, we prefer reusing rather than recycling the entire container. We collect empty mayonnaise jars throughout the year and use them for chocolate-covered pretzel gifts we make at Christmas. Cardboard cereal boxes are cut into sheets for flat mailings.

- When we do have an item that is broken beyond repair and landfill bound, such as an answering machine or fax machine, we methodically take the machine apart, adding the screws to the stash in the machine shed and separating plastic and metal parts for recycling. The actual landfilled item shrinks in size and we find the experience oddly relaxing.

Our dump visits are also odd because we often end up coming home with more than we arrived with. We've accumulated enough random chairs for sizable potlucks. Sometimes our "treasures" proved a bit more challenging. When Lisa was pregnant with Liam, John brought home a baby playpen that looked like it was just missing a couple of parts. He called the manufacturer, only to be told that for safety reasons it's illegal to fix broken baby gear and therefore parts were unavailable. In these situations, we grow even more determined to save something from the landfill. With some duct tape ingenuity, we reconstructed the playpen into a perfect home for our next round of baby chicks.

But the dump is nothing compared to the Superbowl of Dumpster diving: The annual clean-up days in Monroe. Many communities have this sort of annual ritual when folks can put out just about anything for garbage pickup that wouldn't normally be picked up during regular trash days — oversize items, appliances, miscellaneous lumber and other random oddities. Most folks in Monroe use clean-up days in early May as motivation to clean out the basement and garage.

We heard about clean-up days from our neighbors. The city garbage trucks come to pick things up on Monday, so that weekend before we join the other cars and pick-up trucks slowly trolling around the residential streets. "Curbside shopping," it's called — a borderline illegal activity since items on the curb for pick-up are technically on city property. But the city seems to turn a blind eye as long as folks don't make a mess of things or get hurt. Whether the city realizes it or not, it's a vibrant part of the local sustainability scene.

It's amazing to see what people throw out in what seems like a typical small town of 10,000 residents. Driving around town on clean-up days is a wild sociological sketch of what some consider unusable garbage. We found building supplies for the greenhouse and garden, including exterior doors, chicken wire, old windows, bricks, plastic buckets, a patio umbrella, multiple sets of roller blades, and sleds of all shapes and sizes. The spring before Liam was born we had a keen eye out for baby-related things and found his changing table, one of those plastic playhouses that we later realized retailed for over $200, and lots of assorted toys. Lisa polished the wood changing table, covered the shelving with contact paper, and sanitized the plastic items in a mild bleach solution. Some people can't say no to a puppy at the humane shelter; we couldn't say no to a wooden child's rocker, left on the curb for landfill pick up — another restoration project.

In the renovation work we've done, we've again tried to recycle or reuse as much as possible and, when new items are needed, buy as green as possible. We are fortunate to have connected with our contractor, Paul, early on in our renovation process. We have a lot of elbow grease and energy to devote to home projects, but our do-it-yourselfer building expertise is very limited. From our perspective, it makes sense to hire the experts, with the latest tools and expertise to do a job well.

Paul probably realized it wouldn't be business as usual working with us to add two bathrooms upstairs for the B&B. He routinely advised us to order a dumpster for the stuff that would be coming out of the renovation work: random wood pieces, old doors and windows, old tile, and plaster. New to construction, we already objected to the idea of creating a dumpster of waste through our attempt to eco-renovate. We told Paul we'd find a home for the materials that would have gone into the dumpster. He looked at us, giving us his now-infamous "I'll go along with it, I hope you know what you're doing" smile, and went back to whistling while he worked. Paul shook his head in amazement as John spent hours in the bathrooms pulling nails out of studs and stacking them neatly for future projects.

Perhaps we grew on Paul, who is a highly sought-after contractor, and hardly needs our work. Yet he keeps coming back for various projects, growing curious and supportive of what we were trying to do. In turn, he has developed an openness to green design and green materials. He worked with, sometimes for the first time, materials we special-ordered. Many contractors would have simply said no. He supported our vision of Inn Serendipity, and played an important role in making it happen. Paul installed the tile in the bathroom that was made out of 60 percent recycled auto windshield glass, put in the kitchen floor of FSC-certified wood, and applied a water-based stain, among other things. He'd chuckle and say he could find us something cheaper, and then stop mid-sentence and say, "But I know, you don't want that."

Together, we've come up with creative ways to reuse some of the items John salvaged during these projects. Studs in one wall were reused in our attic renovation. Old cabinet doors became entranceways to crawl space storage areas. Carpet pieces became weed barriers around newly planted saplings. Perhaps he didn't realize it at the time, but Paul already possessed green design instincts. He suggested laying the two new bathrooms on the second floor back to back, so we only needed one set of plumbing. Paul took out a kitchen wall to make room for the woodstove, which not only opened up the room flow, it efficiently utilized the heat. Paul's redesign ideas inspired us to think innovatively about other farm projects, leading to the redesign of the granary into a passive and active solar heated straw bale greenhouse, or creating a home for the llamas from space originally intended for dairy cows.

We may have exposed Paul to green design and materials, but he taught us lessons in quality and workmanship. It's become an ongoing joke: The two of us would be absorbed in some house project, Paul would stop by, take a quick look at what we're doing and say, "I wouldn't do it that way," then walk outside for a smoke. According to ritual, we'd set down our spackle, brush or whatever tool we were using and join Paul outside for a lesson in how to really do things right. Yes, it was quicker to just fill in the wall cracks with plaster before painting, but that won't last, advised Paul. Plus it will crack. So we placed fiberglass mesh on the cracks, then applied three coats of plaster, increasingly fanning out the layers and sanding between each application. Years later, our work is holding up, crack free.

And, to top it all off, Paul has turned into one of our best resources for reused materials. Working with a variety of remodeling projects in town, he's always aware of when people are pitching, as he calls it, "perfectly good stuff." Paul never really had a need or place to store these throwaways. Now we give him a running list of things we're looking for. It's kind of a warped form of a scavenger hunt: storm doors for the greenhouse, old fluorescent light fixtures, insulation. He shows up, unannounced, with a rescued item or two: a kitchen countertop for the greenhouse, a set of windows, wood hangers for the attic closet. We've learned that homemade cookies or piping-hot eggrolls are the best thank you for Paul.

How to

Assessing Our Impacts: Ecological Footprints

What if our planet couldn't sustain its human population? Many scientists already believe that we're experiencing an era known as the planet's sixth extinction, during which millions of plant and animal species are being wiped out forever. Millions of people go without food, safe drinking water and adequate shelter — daily.

According to Mathis Wackernagel and William Rees of Redefining Progress, if everyone lived the way we do, we would need 2.8 planet Earths to support our lifestyle. Wackernagel and Rees define an ecological footprint, measured in biologically productive acres, in their ground-breaking book, *Our Ecological Footprint*, as "the land and water area that would be required to support a defined human population and material standard indefinitely." Our personal total ecological footprint, which combines the impacts of our food needs, mobility, shelter and use of goods and services, is 12 acres (4.9 ha). In comparison, our footprint is about half of the average American of about 24 acres (9.7 ha) (that's the equivalent of about 30 football fields); an average Italian uses about 9 acres (3.6 ha). As our society encourages us more and more to be part of a "global economy," our bananas, clothing, furniture and cars come from increasingly far-off places, exacting an ever-increasing toll on the resources of the planet.

At present world population levels, the sobering reality is that only 4.5 biologically productive acres exist per person. Industrialized economies are considered to require far more land than they have, thus, through global trade, those economies impact resources and people in other countries. By better understanding our resource needs and being more careful in how we dispose of our wastes, we are working toward whittling down our footprint to a level that is life-sustaining. We realize that many of our actions and lifestyle and livelihood changes, such as adding a wind turbine system to produce electricity, could not be expressed in the easily completed ecological footprint quiz offered by Redefining Progress, but our Internet calculations serve as reminders as to how far we've yet to go.

Can the more than 6 billion people now on Earth possibly achieve what we commonly refer to as the American Dream — a house, car (or two), family, education, and healthcare — even if, in reality, many Americans never achieve it? The American Dream, for all its individualism, work ethic, and innovation that make its achievement possible for many, has increasingly serious costs to nature, our quality of life, and economic and social justice both here and abroad. The American Dream has come to embody a consumer culture above all else.

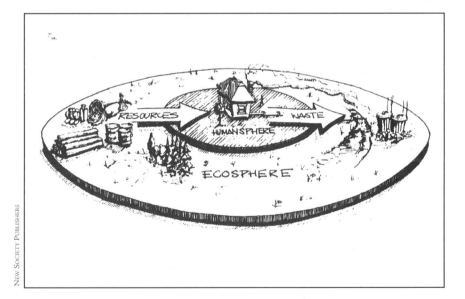

New Society Publishers

Our Ecological footprint

It's never been harder to edit out the word consumer in our conversation and daily life. We are not the possessions or services we consume. Yet we catch ourselves using the word, referring to people as consumers. But people are not consumers, as if it's our destiny to shop, buy, use, and throw things out. People are people — or citizens, humans, and among the animals in the animal world. While we have needs, our wants have gotten the best of us. It's the wants that compel us to work so hard to make so much money to try and satisfy what can't be satisfied through things.

Happiness is a state of mind – the intersection between mind, body sand spirit that occurs when we are doing what we love to do, and living in a way that is aligned with nature. That said, we recognize that there are things we purchase, like a computer or photovoltaic panels, that help us on our journey toward a more self-reliant, interconnected and sustainable life. Don't call us consumers; call us intentional humans, mindful participants in a living system, or carbon-based life form.

Our journey to the farm distanced us from the daily onslaught of the consumption culture, but didn't remove us from it. We are still, after all, citizens of this republic called the United States. As we began our restorative and more self-reliant journey, we discovered ways to navigate through choices we faced as active, participatory beings in the global world, even if much of what we did played out on the local scene and in a local economy.

Our response is to live creatively on the Earth at a level that can support other life. For those who live in cities, suburbs and small towns, reducing ecological footprints may take altogether different approaches. Our lives are filled with exciting possibilities — not endless trap doors. It's a matter of redefining progress, and happiness.

SOURCES AND RESOURCES

Redefining Progress
  Website: www.rprogress.org
  We examined our ecological footprint through this interactive and informative website.

American Forests' Personal Climate Change Calculator
  Website: www.americanforests.org
  To better understand how our lifestyle adds carbon dioxide to the environment, American Forests, a nonprofit conservation organization which promotes reforestation, provides an interactive website which offers a Personal Climate Change Calculator that allows us to track the impacts of the emissions resulting from our home energy needs and transportation.

Mathis Wackernagel and William Rees, *Our Ecological Footprint: Reducing Human Impact on the Earth,* New Society Publishers, 1996.

Gunter Pauli, *Upsizing: The Road to Zero Emissions, More Jobs, More Income, and No Pollution,* Greenleaf Publishers, 2000.

Sarah James and Trobjörn Lahti, *The Natural Step for Communities ,* New Society Publishers, 2004.

Multiplicity of Small Changes

Guests of the Inn often ask us what event prompted us to trade in city life and move to the country. It wasn't a singular, dramatic life-changing moment, as if we woke up one day, packed our bags and drove off into the sunset to find the lands of serendipity. Rather, it was a gradual process and a couple years of looking for a farm with potential. Our connection to this area started with casual weekend camping jaunts, and then, as technology and the Internet expanded home office options and the ability to work from anywhere, we started seriously considering the rural move. Every time we drove up to this area of Wisconsin from Chicago, we felt as if we were coming home. The rural life called to us. The thought of waking up to the smells of flowers wafting through the bedroom window, baking morning muffins for B&B guests, and biting into that first juicy strawberry of the garden season fueled our dreams as we planned and prepared for what came next.

With every step we took toward moving into the country, we acquired new knowledge, experience and confidence. When we started looking at farms, we were green in a very different way: we had no farming background, no clue as to how a septic system worked, and only a general sense of what living rurally might mean for us, economically and socially.

However, with each farm we visited, our questions improved: How old is the septic system? Has the well water been tested? When was the house rewired? Or more esoteric questions: Is the view from our office inspiring? How does the light fall in the kitchen? What was our first impressions when coming up the driveway? Likewise, while driving back to Chicago after touring farms, we talked about the whole experience and narrowed in on specific elements of our ideal future home: Not too much of a structural fixer-upper since we didn't have the funds or expertise; renovation requiring some elbow grease, clean-up, and decorating jobs were fine. We hoped for an older farmhouse, complete with squeaky hardwood floors and the character that comes with historic, solidly built homes. We needed to make sure we could logistically add bathrooms in the house for the B&B rooms and, ideally, we'd like to have a front porch, lots of trees, a spring or other water source on the property, and as much acreage as we could afford. We hoped for cathedral-like barns and practical outbuildings, even if they needed repair. The newer aluminum pole barns, while functional, did nothing for our souls.

The farm search evolved over about two years. We'd see places we loved but couldn't afford, with magnificent streams, woodlots or grand vistas. We saw places we loved and should have been able to afford, if the property was market-priced. We saw places about to fall apart in front of our eyes and places renovated in ways that couldn't have been more unhealthy. We made offers on a couple farms, but all were, in hindsight, fortunately rejected. Then we found our farmstead — somewhat short

FUNDING THE DREAM

The question often comes up among guests and visitors: "Life at Inn Serendipity sounds great but tell me, where did you get the money to do this?" Money. Intertwined between good intentions and hard work lies the inevitable reality that we live in a society where cash is a necessity. Money can create a double-edged sword when it comes to making a major life transition. You want to make sure you have enough savings and a financial plan, yet you don't want to obsess over it so much that you never make the change.

Some dream-funding strategies we adopted during our journey included:

- **Frugality rules.** The concept of saving hardly exudes sexiness, but it does provide an option that anyone can do at differing degrees, depending on circumstances. When we made the decision to exit the urban world, we went cold-turkey when it came to spending money. Dinners out, taxi rides, impulse shopping, and basically everything else except the basic needs disappeared. We learned to examine every purchase and question our true needs. The adventure of it all provided us with more positive energy and satisfaction than consumption did.

- **Staying within our means.** Cost of living and related real estate costs vary considerably across the continent. We chose our area of Wisconsin because of its affordability. The price of our five-acre farm was equivalent to the cost of a small studio condo in Chicago; however, it would have cost several million dollars if it was located in prime parts of California.

- **Safety nets help.** Through our transition, we continue to draw comfort and confidence from a range of friends and family that we could fall back on in tough times. We knew in our hearts that if all else failed, we had friends with open doors that we could turn to for a place to stay or a loan. This same group provided encouragement throughout our move, and sent customers, media contacts and care packages of our original criteria. We realized through the house hunting process that it was realistic — even desirable — to look at our situation from a different perspective. How would we bring into being what didn't already exist?

One thing we did not find on this particular property was a water source such as a stream or pond. We knew how beneficial water is to attracting wildlife, so we decided early on to add a small pond on the west side of the farmhouse. A tornado

of pistachio nuts our way. Having such a safety net in our lives gave us the support we needed to move forward. We, too, have enjoyed the opportunity to now extend our home to some of these folks as they begin to make their own changes.

- **Grants and incentives.** Take advantage of the variety of state and federal programs out there; with research, tenacity and some patience, opportunities can bloom. It took several years before we received a grant from Wisconsin Focus on Energy, which helped fund our wind turbine, but the end result was worth the wait. Putting acreage into CRP (Conservation Reserve Programs) can result in cost sharing and financial incentives for different conservation practices. With the rising costs of health care, many states offer insurance options for working families. Programs vary, but often premium payments are calculated based on household income. Visit <www.insurekidsnow.gov> for information.

- **Accounting for business.** Business development structures and incentives are established by government to foster entrepreneurship. For example, we are able to claim 24 percent of our house square footage as a legitimate business expense: two guest rooms and bathrooms plus a home office. In addition to a percentage of utility bills, the business, Inn Serendipity, pays us for the use of the second floor of the farmhouse.

- **Transforming inheritance.** It is estimated that trillions of dollars will be passed along to children of deceased parents over the coming years. Whether is it a few hundred dollars or many thousands, opportunity exists to use such windfalls to go beyond just paying living expenses or buying more stuff. By channeling such money toward various conservation efforts, we've been able to move along in the journey toward our dream and create a positive, lasting legacy in the memory of those who made it possible.

had passed through decades ago that downed several pine trees, leaving a low-lying area after the root systems rotted away: a perfect spot to create a pond. A relatively small restorative change to the landscape amazes us with how it positively affect the larger ecosystem. Meant for more than aesthetics, the pond attracted wildlife and serves as a cool microclimate to escape the sweltering heat of summer.

Most people use a back-hoe tractor to dig a pond, but since we didn't have one we figured we could make it work with some eager-to-help friends and borrowed shovels. On a hot July afternoon, we broke ground and dug until we came up with a kidney-shaped hole about eight feet in diameter and four feet deep. We lined the pond with thick rubber pond liner and gave it an initial fill with the water hose. Determined to not have to refill it with pumped water again, we connected one of the house gutters to the pond so that the pond water level would be replenished throughout the year. We added a small water pump to circulate the water, thus preventing algae growth and colonies of mosquitoes. Every spring, we expand the plantings around the pond with divided perennials and ground cover so that it's now a mini-Midwestern jungle during the summer months. A dead pin oak tree was left near the pond for year-round bird-perching until it finally fell, and some berry-producing holly was planted for wildlife food during the winter months.

Simple garden pond design

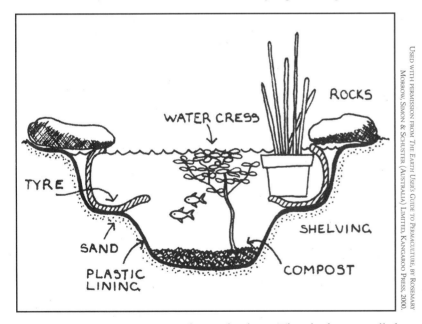

USED WITH PERMISSION FROM *THE EARTH USER'S GUIDE TO PERMACULTURE*, BY ROSEMARY MORROW, SIMON & SCHUSTER (AUSTRALIA) LIMITED, KANGAROO PRESS, 2000.

Our pond could hardly be confused with Lake Michigan by migrating herons. Still, almost overnight after we filled the pond, nature started lining up to use the facilities. The birds came for drinks or a quick bath splash: goldfinch, cardinals, bluebirds, sparrows, orioles, and robins. The chickens stroll down for afternoon tea. We've even seen a fox come for a spell mid-afternoon, seemingly so pleased with the water source that he was oblivious to the potential chicken lunch alertly watching.

And then came the frogs. We heard our first peepers, performing their annual choral series starting in mid-April, followed by bullfrogs, tree frogs and toads. They multiplied in such numbers that a couple of seasons later we can hear their nighttime singing a quarter mile down the road. Our frogs are so loud that a neighbor asked where we mail ordered them. While there isn't another water source around within half mile of agricultural land, somehow these frogs found our little pond and made a home, multiplying into the choral numbers that they are today. Small pond, big changes.

This rippling effect — the multiplicity of small changes — is something we carry over into our life. Between our various work pursuits and personal travels, we attend a fair number of meetings, conferences and workshops where we encounter that ubiquitous nemesis of green living: the Styrofoam coffee cup. Few outlets exist for Styrofoam recycling, thus billions of these coffee cups will be sitting in landfills for hundreds of years. It's shocking that Styrofoam cups appear at conservation or environmental conferences, but they do. Since we have a hard time saying no to coffee, we've learned to carry a mess kit in the car with a couple of plastic travel coffee mugs, sets of silverware and plastic plates. A small change to make, but the multiplier effect is huge.

Other small changes include bringing our canvas bags to the grocery store. We're considered odd at the check-out counter; we need to grab our groceries before the bagger perfunctorily starts stuffing them into plastic or paper bags. We're trying to minimize our use of battery-operated stuff and for those times when batteries can't be avoided, we've invested in rechargeable batteries and a recharger unit.

The taking of small steps collectively is what will change the world for the better. Whether restoring a farm, replanting a field, building a new place with an eye toward beauty, energy conservation and green design — or even just writing our grocery list on the back of the telephone bill envelope — green steps add up to a greener world.

How to

Steps to Greening Our Life

Remember that heartwarming story about a kid who tosses a starfish back in the ocean to extend the life of the starfish, and make a difference? Greening our life is a lot like saving that tiny starfish in a troubled sea; it can transform the world, especially if it takes place in conjunction with other actions by other people, by a community, by a state, by a nation.

To green the many everyday things we do, day in and day out, we joined a visionary organization called Co-op America. This non-profit shares how each of us can decrease our impact on Earth, advance social justice and strengthen our communities, and it provides many of the resources and contacts to do it. (See Resources, below.)

We've adopted a strategy from Co-op America: prioritizing our actions by taking items we use or consume the most and make them more socially or environmentally responsible. It's become an ongoing challenge to discover new ways to make more responsible purchases, such as buying Recycline toothbrushes made from recycled Stonyfield Yogurt containers <www.recycline.com>. We stopped squeezing the advertised brands and started wiping with 100 percent post-consumer waste toilet paper. A few of our discoveries include:

- **Clothing.** Shoes, underwear, shirts, pants we wear everyday, but only until recently did we understand how widespread exploitative child and adult sweatshop labor is. Co-op America's website <www.sweatshop.org>, keeps us up to date on the latest information about companies employing unfair and exploitative labor practices. Increased use of synthetic fibers and the immense use of pesticides in growing cotton has resulted in our increased interest in organic fibers, or at least in fibers that are natural and unbleached. Now, some of Liam's diapers, two sets of B&B linens, and a growing collection of our tee-shirts are organic and produced by ecologically and socially responsible manufacturers. We avoid Disney paraphernalia made in well-documented exploitative factories and buy a Patagonia fleece jacket made in the US from recycled plastic pop bottles. We wear Timberland shoes and, of course, Birkenstocks (our next pair will be their leather-free alternative). Everything is done incrementally and on a shoe-string budget. Because of this, we also find ourselves attracted to vintage clothing shops and used clothing stores. Reused clothing cuts down on raw materials, energy and the transportation costs of newly manufactured clothing.

✦ **Saving trees.** We set out to eliminate wasting an immensely precious resource: trees. Elimination of junk mail (and avoidance of the dinner-time telemarketers) can be accomplished by writing to the American Direct Marketing Association, asking to be put on the "do not mail" and "do not solicit" lists. We do it every year and seem to have disappeared off most marketer lists.

To be removed from mailing lists, send a note including your address to: Mail Preference Service, Direct Marketing Association, P.O. Box 9008, Farmingdale, NY 11735-9008. And for a blissfully silent dinnertime telephone, send a note including your telephone numbers to: Telephone Preference Service, Direct Marketing Association, P.O. Box 9014, Farmingdale, NY 11735. To make a dent in unwanted e-mail solicitations, "opt out" at <www.dmaconsumers.org>.

For those solicitations we do field, we take the opportunity, in the case of a mailed solicitation, to send everything back, enclosures and all, with our refusal of credit, subscription or other offer. In our office, we use the clean side of once-used paper for our fax, printer, and for notes. For the limited printing of our B&B literature and newsletter, we've found 100 percent post-consumer waste paper and remind companies like Kinko's and Staples to keep stocking it. We reuse mailing envelopes and the self-addressed stamped envelopes sent by companies or organizations after we completely blacken out the bar codes and address information. We haven't purchased envelopes in years.

✦ **Telephone long distance service.** Working Assets provides long distance telephone service that supports social and ecological organizations as well as providing free calls to communicate with our Congresspersons. They donate 1 percent of our monthly charges to non-profits we help select. <www.workingassets.com>

✦ **Bank check printing.** Message! Products offers printed bank checks that support social and ecological organizations, as well as making sure the checks themselves are printed on recycled paper. <www.messageproducts.com>

The Least Imperfect Path

"Do you have any bugs?" asked the guy at the other end of the phone line. Before Lisa could answer, he quickly couched his question with, "I realize that is a strange question but my wife, well, she has stayed at some B&Bs that didn't exactly meet her standards, if you know what I mean. Me? I'm fine with anything."

Good thing he offered an explanation since Lisa had been about to answer, "Sure, we have bugs. How many and what kind would you like?"

Don't get the wrong idea. We take pride in our home and keep things clean. We're licensed as a B&B and inspected by the state. We go into B&B-mode when we have guests and spiffy the place up, but it's fair to say that even then, our place might not be perfect by foo-foo standards. We live in it. There's a perpetual competition among spiders looking for the best corner for their webs, laundry on the lines, and always more weeding to do. Living on a farm, we've learned that bugs will crawl or fly into the house every opportunity they get.

> "The trick is to realize that the only true perfection is finding peace and balance in an imperfect world."
> — Maria Rodale, Editor of *Organic Style* magazine

Insects are an accepted, desirable, part of the farm. They're part of the living community which we share and we've enjoyed noticing the beneficial insect population increase. A diverse insect population indicates healthy soil and a strong ecosystem. Every autumn we tolerate an "invasion," when the ladybugs and Japanese beetles migrate into the house. On the first cold day of fall they fly in through open doorways, windows or any crevice they can find. They make themselves at home on top of warm light bulbs, in a house plant jungle, and huddled together in the furthest reaches of the kitchen cabinets. The onslaught is annoying in October, but it's a welcomed sign of life in February when a ladybug lands on the open page of a book as the snow falls outside.

So, yes, we have bugs, and some creaky floorboards too. It's a part of who we are; our imperfect, unpolished selves. We're rural "wabi-sabi." The Japanese wabi-sabi philosophy is based on the concept of slowing down, a shifting from always doing to being, to appreciating things as is, rather than trying to perfect everything. We celebrate the beauty inherent in what is flawed or worn. Wabi-sabi prompts us to sometimes choose the least imperfect path, rather than frustrate ourselves by never achieving perfection.

We find our wabi-sabi selves on a perpetual quest to creatively make do, to see how we can recycle and reuse what is already around us, rather than buying new. Four years after we got married, we're still reusing wrapping paper from wedding gifts, and we've discovered that tissue paper looks brand new with a quick, cool ironing. We use a piece of duct tape to hold together a waffling seam on slippers. We collect heart-shaped Valentine chocolate boxes and refill them with our homemade truffles.

Quirky habits, but they creatively make do. There may be a more perfect, greener way to do something sometimes, but in our attempt at a balanced approach to life, we allow space for the wabi-sabi perspective of productively using what already exists. Sure, we could buy new organic hemp slippers, but with a little duct tape, our old ones are just fine. John's mom's mending skills keep expanding, thanks to the challenging projects she keeps graciously accepting from us. Torn pants, unravelled sweaters and time-worn quilts are renewed under her patience and expertise.

Using an old slab of concrete, a life-size chess set and board was created at Inn Serendipity

Trying to live by this creatively-making-do philosophy, we have collected an assortment of imperfect things. We have a hard time saying no to things that might have some use left in them. In our basement, we have a ten year supply of those little soaps found at motels. John's dad was quite a collector, and when he passed away we uncovered his extensive soap collection. These are not the naturally-made soaps we preferred to use, but had we not dragged this soap back to Wisconsin from his home in Michigan, the pile probably would have been pitched; this was the least imperfect action we felt we should take.

When there is something we need that we can't locate in our basement or closet, we've learned it makes sense to first ask around and poke in other people's closets (if they let us). A perfect example is the creation of our life-size outdoor chess set. We found the inspiration for this chess set during our travels. In the creatively make-do wabi-sabi tradition, we found the perfect spot for this chess board: an old 20 by 24-foot (about 6 m x 7 m) cement slab on the south side of the former granary (now a greenhouse).

Woodworking is not our forte. Creating this chess set turned out to be one of those projects that we jumped into a little blindly, not exactly knowing how long it would take, and realizing months later what we'd got ourselves into. We started with our regular-sized game board chess set, as a model. A friend helped hand sketch each piece to life size on paper. We then cut out the pattern, bought some plywood from the local lumberyard and started tracing and cutting out each piece with a jigsaw. Two kings. Two queens. Four knights, and so on. Thirty-two pieces later, we cut out round bases for all of them and mounted each piece, then added three coats of paint. We painted the checkerboard pattern on the cement slab, and stood back to admire our work. Sure, it took most of the winter, but we were smug in the knowledge that this was a creation uniquely our own.

Well, sort of. While chatting with some folks at our local Monroe Arts Center (MAC) during the middle of the cutting and sanding stage of our chess set project, we discovered the idea wasn't so unique in Green County.

"Oh, yeah, we have one of those," said Lori, the program director at MAC. "Been sitting in the closet for years. We've been trying to get rid of it. Do you know anyone who might want one?"

We quickly replied, "No, you don't know what we mean. We're talking a life-sized set, each piece is about three feet tall. You know, like what they play with in Europe."

"Yeah, that's what we have," insisted Lori. "Nate made it years ago for the Cheese Days Festival. We marked off playing squares on the lawn for folks to play."

Our faces went flush. Not only did MAC have such a chess set, but Nate made it, which meant it was the epitome of craftsmanship. We asked to see a piece out of curiosity. Sure enough, it was classic Nate: each piece was three-dimensional, sculpted wood and an individual masterpiece. Nate is a local legend. Retired from running the local lumber yard and hardware store, he's a man of many talents and trades, his most noteworthy is woodworking. At one of our holiday gatherings, Nate brought us two of his hand-carved wooden mixing spoons. One is designed for left-handers, the other for right-handers. He wasn't sure which we were and, kind-hearted as he is, wanted to make sure we had the right equipment. Today they are Liam's favorite toys, in addition to stirring many muffin batters.

Back to Nate's chess set. We realized the power of asking around about what's in another person's closet. In our case, we probably could have had that set in the

MAC closet for a small donation. But we assumed that no one had what we hoped to create, so we jumped right into buying supplies and building. Now we know better. At that time, we were too far along in our chess set project to justify stopping and acquiring MAC's chess set. So we pressed on and finished up the project.

Our house renovations also presented numerous opportunities to incorporate green building materials, green design principles and, when replacing appliances, more ecologically-sound options. We committed ourselves to buying and restoring an existing farmhouse. Sure, building a new house from scratch would have given us the opportunity to be super energy-efficient and, in many cases, more environmentally friendly, employing such techniques as in-floor radiant heat or passive solar design. However, if we'd built a brand-new house, we'd be leaving yet another historic farmhouse to fall into disrepair and taking yet another divot from the rapidly shrinking farm lands or open space. We felt drawn to preserving and reusing what existed, albeit in an imperfect sort of way. For example, our farmhouse came with asbestos siding, an environmental nightmare in dust form should it ever be inhaled. As the hard siding for the house, it wasn't going to be a problem unless we removed it, and the house is well-built, so the siding isn't going anywhere.

We've found living by green design does call for commitment to a long-term view, particularly when it comes to the financial side. Green appliances cost more at the outset than conventional ones, but we need to keep reminding ourselves of the long-term payback and that ecological costs are rarely factored in to prices in our society. Since a refrigerator's electricity needs make up 12 percent of an average electricity bill, the energy-efficient Sun Frost we purchased would reduce our bill by about $50 per year, paying for itself in about 40 years. Less energy use translates to lower utility bills and less impact on the environment.

Over the years since we purchased the SunFrost, the EPA's Energy Star program has made huge inroads in energy efficiency for Energy Star refrigerators, offering comparable models and efficiency at more competitive prices. The retail market is slowly discovering the buying power of the green market — those people who make purchase decisions based on environmental impacts in addition to quality and price. In the meantime, brands change and companies come and go, and we continue to recreate our lives in the least imperfect, wabi-sabi ways possible. Give or take a chess piece or two.

Appliances that can Make a Difference

A little applied technology can go a long way to living more sustainably on earth without chucking too many of the conveniences and comforts we're used to. After all, we never set out to live in a log cabin and read by oil lamps. We've learned that flexibility and creativity are essential to incorporating green products and appliances into a more sustainable lifestyle, and that such changes come incrementally, and often at a premium. As we see it, that premium is the dividend reserved for the silent stockholder: the environment.

Advances in technology have given us energy-efficient and water-conserving appliances, which we've incorporated into our household and business wherever possible. We realize that we cannot talk about generating our own electricity before we've nearly exhausted our energy conservation efforts. Energy conservation is the most cost-effective first step. In the long term, investments made toward energy conservation will help us save money, time, and resources. As Ben Franklin said, money saved is money we don't need to earn.

The growing number of efficient appliances and green products provided an opportunity to green our home, office, or our cabin in the woods. One of the things we've used to guide our decisions is the EPA's Energy Star label. This logo identifies products that have been evaluated and qualify for the Energy Star seal for energy efficiency. Before any purchase, we also review *Consumer Reports* magazine for relevant articles, and we consult the best-selling *Shopping for a Better World: The Quick and Easy Guide to all your Socially Responsible Shopping*, by the Council on Economic Priorities. Long-lasting, well-made products with good warranties indicate a commitment by the company to stand by their product. Here are some of the areas we examined and researched for green options:

+ **Refrigeration and freezing.** Before we finally replaced our old GM-made refrigerator (it was still operating when we moved in), we thought about basic principles of green design. We thought back to fifth grade, when we learned that heat rises. Why would an engineer design a refrigerator and place the heat-producing compressors on the bottom or back of the appliance? In our search for the replacement refrigerator, we found Sun Frost and more recently, Energy Star refrigerators, to offer significantly more energy efficient alternatives. Our super low-energy SunFrost refrigerator — with the compressor up top! — sits in our kitchen, operating at a whisper. High humidity compartments keep our fruits and vegetables fresher for a longer time, and with 3 inches (7.5 cm) of insulation on all sides and 6 inches (15 cm) on top, the hot stays out and cold stays in.

• **Washing machines.** With a small child and constant comings and goings by guests and visitors, doing the laundry could take up a lot of time, energy and water. However, our front-loading Maytag uses 50 percent less water than the average top-loading machine and about 37 percent less electricity per year. While the house came with a clothes dryer, we use it only in the chill of winter or to fluff the towels for our B&B guests. We've become increasingly adept at using a dry rack in the front-room when we're not hosting B&B guests. Wasting water or energy moves us away from our goal of balancing our needs with those of the Earth.

• **Dishwasher.** According to the EPA, Energy Star dishwashers save money and the environment by using both improved technology for the primary wash cycle and by using less hot water to clean. Construction includes more effective washing action, energy efficient motors and other advanced technology such as sensors that determine the length of the wash cycle and the temperature of the water necessary to clean the dishes.

The water temperature in a dishwasher should be at least 140 degrees Fahrenheit (60°C) to clean dishes, but these special models come with internal water heaters that boost water temperatures inside. This allows us to turn down the thermostat on our household water heater to 120 degrees (49°C), reducing our water heating costs by 20 percent. By using our dishwasher's air drying option, we save additional energy.

• **Computers, printer and fax machine**. Like any home office, ours has several computers, a printer and a fax machine. The computers have energy-saving modes and the Sony Trinitron monitor, Hewlett-Packard Laserjet printer and Brother fax machine are Energy Star products. Energy Star fax machines are equipped with a power-management feature that can reduce energy costs associated with the use of the machines by almost 50 percent. When we leave home for extended periods, we turn off the power-strip to which they're connected.

- **Air conditioners.** For our home office space, we added an Energy Star Panasonic room air conditioner with the an Energy Efficiency Ratio (EER) of 10.0 (the highest rating). According to the EPA, an oversized air conditioner is actually less effective than a correctly sized unit. Air conditioners remove both heat and humidity from the air; if the unit is too large, it will cool the room quickly, but only remove a portion of the humidity. This leaves the room with a damp, clammy feeling. A properly sized unit will remove humidity effectively while it cools. Running a smaller unit for a longer time will use less energy to completely condition a room than running a larger unit for a shorter time.

  For the rest of the house, we usually do what worked before the advent of air conditioning: open the windows at night when it's cool and close them during the day. With our "low E" double-pane windows, the cool nighttime air is trapped in the house. Deciduous trees to the south and west of the house offer protection from the sun during the hottest parts of the day, and the small pond immediately to the west provides a cool microclimate.

- **Dehumidifiers.** Like many houses, our basement perspires in the summer, creating both unhealthy and structurally problematic issues resulting from moisture build-up and entrapment. Fans move the air, but they don't remove the humidity, which by the end of the summer can turn the walls into breeding grounds for fungus and mildew. Our dehumidifier, the most energy efficient one we could find, collects gallons of water every summer, which we then use to irrigate the perennial beds outside.

- **Farm equipment.** While growing beautiful flowers and healthy, delicious foods, we found ourselves having too much of a footprint during the planting season. To mow the lawn, we primarily use a gas-powered lawn mower, but are committed to using our electric mower more. At the cabin, to avoid various doses of herbicides around our newly planted native hardwoods, we've employed a brush mower for weed management. We buy only the equipment that we know we'll use regularly; we borrow or rent the rest. We might still use fossil fuels, so we take steps to mitigate the global effects of our local use.

By planting trees on our lands, supporting tree planting programs and minimizing our use of the equipment, we try to offset our impact on global warming. Mowing the lawn is not a leisure activity or something we do for exercise; it's something we hope to avoid doing altogether one day, by planting "no-mow" grass and other ground covers to replace the grass.

SOURCES AND RESOURCES

EPA Energy Star program
  Website: www.energystar.org
  Website includes a complete listing of Energy Star products, including fans, electronics and air conditioners. The website also lists examples of EPA Energy Star Small Businesses — including Inn Serendipity. This is a free, voluntary program aimed at helping business owners cut their energy costs and reduce their environmental impacts.

Inn Serendipity is among the nation's small businesses that have joined EPA's Energy Star Small Business, a free, voluntary program that helps small business owners cut their energy costs and reduce their impact. For a complete listing of Energy Star products, including fans, consumer electronics, and dehumidifiers, visit them online.

Alex Wilson and John Morrill, *Consumer Guide to Home Energy Savings*, American Council for an Energy Efficient Economy, 2000.

Sustainable Woods

Though she is our official historian when it comes to documenting events, Lisa couldn't bring herself to take photos when the towering farmyard elm tree succumbed to Dutch elm disease and had to be cut down. That is our only event that brings back memories of loss. The tree, well over 100 years old, greeted everyone driving up the gravel. Its branches seemed to cradle the farmstead, protecting the land and all who came here, offering a swing to children and the young at heart. We didn't talk about it when one spring a section of the branches didn't green. The majority of the tree died out the following year. We knew the tree had been hit by Dutch elm disease; there was nothing we could do to save it. We felt painfully powerless.

Before the dead limbs started rotting away, we hired a local tree service to cut down the tree. As the piercing sound of the steel saw blade made its first cut, we made an excuse to head into town. When we came back that afternoon, the elm lay in a dozen large chunks on the ground. What took decades to grow came down in a couple hours. Like *The Giving Tree*, this diseased elm kept giving. Even when the elm came down, a full season of fuel for our woodstove came from this tree, keeping us warm and cozy on long winter nights.

This interest in protecting the trees and more mindfully using wood led us to look for some wooded property about two hours north in Vernon County, Wisconsin, a less developed, more rugged and remote area, home to a strong Amish farming community. In Green County, where the Inn is located, only sporadic wood lots remained and most of those were being divided up for new homes.

With two feet of January snow on the ground, we first visited a 30-acre (12 ha) parcel of land that would eventually become Inn Serendipity Woods. Even as the trees lay barren and the acre pond frozen, our hearts warmed while walking the land, about 20 acres (8 ha) of which were mostly wooded. Birch trees jutted white and black against the clear blue sky on the north side of a steep ridge that protruded into the center. A hawk circled overhead as we tromped through the snow below a stand of hickory and maple.

View across the one-acre pond at the Inn Serendipity Woods cabin property.

We discovered an old vineyard that needed care, sandstone outcroppings, what promised to be lots of wild blackberry patches, and some elm trees signaling possible morel mushroom hunting grounds. The property also had an A-frame cabin which could sleep up to eight people. It was sold as a functionally furnished cabin, down to the toaster and popcorn popper. Our original intent was to find some wooded land without buildings, but we started thinking that this cabin made sense from a business perspective. We could run rentals through the B&B guest base we had already developed, using proceeds from the cabin rentals to help fund our conservation and restoration work.

As we moved ahead in the purchase process, we encountered some harsh lessons in the realities of business and life. The seller of this property was a local entrepreneur, who owned and managed several properties as rental units. Owning this property for only a couple of years, he seemed determined to take as much profit out of the sales transaction as possible. Fair enough, we hardly expected any financial sacrifices from him because of our conservation motives. Still, as we went through the real estate game, he played a wild card we failed to anticipate. He heavily harvested about 50 trees from the back part of the woods, many of which were quite large, and sold them to the local saw mill. He had apparently decided to squeeze as much cash out of the land as he could.

We're hardly oblivious to the fact that wood is a necessary commodity. Wood is a renewable resource we use to heat our farmhouse, and it's among the more popular building materials. While new to the concept of forest management at the time, we understood what he had done was less than ecologically sound. Sustainable forest management involves having a long-term plan, identifying mature trees for harvest, and replanting new trees, ensuring a diversity of native varieties. Harvesting is done without the scars his hired timber harvest crew had left on both emergent trees or the forest floor. Even now, we're still watching for exotic plants that may invade the areas he cut and left vulnerable.

With the damage done, there wasn't any point to discussing the matter further. Trees can't be put back on their stumps. As we walked the land for a second time after the timber harvest, we realized that his harvest had further motivated us to purchase this property. We felt compelled to reach out and protect the 30 acres, to help heal these scars, to replant and restore.

The purchase was one of those endeavors where nothing was final until the ink on the sales contract was dry; we crossed a lot of hurdles before making it to the closing. The house inspection found water damage and cracks in the cabin foundation. The first water test came back with problems, but another test conducted by a licensed plumber came back fine. We jumped through hoops with the mortgage company since we didn't fit into their cookie-cutter application boxes. For one, we worked in the non-profit world and voluntarily accepted significantly less pay than a decade before, when we worked at the ad agency. We knew we had enough money for a down payment and monthly payments because we had such minimal living expenses; we grew much of our own foods, and we bought scrap lumber from the local lumber yard to fuel our wood stove for $15 a pick-up load.

Our two used cars were owned free and clear, and we used a credit card like a one-month interest free loan from the bank, never carrying a balance. None of these facts seemed to matter to, much less impress, the mortgage company. The fact that we did live such a frugal, debt-free lifestyle only complicated matters, since we were not the norm, and required more work on their part. Thankfully, we connected with an agent at the mortgage company who was intrigued enough with our story to give our paperwork a second, approving look, which finally brought Inn Serendipity Woods into fruition.

Inn Serendipity Woods is an opportunity to learn sustainable forestry and restoration. We no longer had to imagine walking the land and planting trees like Aldo Leopold, we could do it ourselves. Within the year, we enrolled 2.5 acres adjacent to our stream in the USDA's Conservation Reserve Program (CRP), and designated 20 acres of mostly woods under the Wisconsin Managed Forest Law as a privately managed and conserved forest. We integrated Inn Serendipity Woods cabin rentals into the existing B&B business. Both offered guests an opportunity to take showers with water heated by the sun and gather around an EPA-certified woodstove in the cooler months.

We occasionally use the cabin property for our own recharging. We love the farm, but Inn Serendipity Woods provides a strong contrast, both in landscape and pace. We sometimes joke that we should sell parking passes on the farmstead, since the driveway can get crowded with B&B guests, interns, visiting friends and other folks stopping by. We relish such creative activity and energy, but at the cabin we can lounge naked on an inner tube floating in the pond with little likelihood of encountering other humans in the forest. Time at the cabin provides us with a creative re-charge, undoubtedly fueled by the diversity of the surroundings. And yes, Lisa has a photo album fully dedicated to documenting the evolution of and our restoration efforts on this land, including shots of John working on his full-body tan.

How to

Buying Sustainably Harvested Wood

Silviculture is a fancy name for supporting healthy and biodiverse life in a forest ecosystem and, from time to time, selectively harvesting timber. According to the World Wildlife Fund, forests are the great storehouses of natural life, home to more than half the world's terrestrial species. But the exploitation of forests — for timber, fuel, agricultural land, and other needs — has wiped out more than half of the world's original forest cover. More careful preservation of remaining intact forest ecosystems and the sustainable management of productive forests are critically necessary.

As conservation entrepreneurs, we recognized our opportunity to make a difference at the cabin property by replanting native trees in a field once planted with corn, and restoring a 20-acre stand of mixed hardwood and softwood timber that had been conventionally harvested prior to our purchase. Burying our noses in sustainable forestry literature and developing a management plan in partnership with a forester from the Wisconsin Department of Natural Resources, we found implementing silviculture principles presented a practical reason for us to finally learn to identify trees and understand the complex relationships between them in a healthy forest ecosystem. It was also a way to jump-start a possible livelihood for Liam, who will inherit the Inn Serendipity Woods property one day.

While learning responsible forest stewardship practices, we decided to support sustainable forestry through our more immediate wood purchases by buying Forest Stewardship Council-certified (FSC-certified) wood directly from a nearby sustainable-woods cooperative. The FSC oversees the independent third party review of forestry management and harvest practices, and serves as an information clearinghouse for companies selling FSC-certified wood products. While locating FSC-certified wood at our local lumberyards was a challenge, companies like Home Depot are beginning to include some products in their inventory. However, prices can be higher than non-FSC products. We supported the bioregional economy and met our building needs without sacrificing the environment by purchasing our FSC wood directly from the closest sustainable woods cooperative we could find, which was about 60 miles (97 km) away.

Growing members across the continent, private landowners and companies are designing a new forest management model by managing their woodlots under SmartWood-certified sustainable forest management plans. Sustainable forestry protects and restores the biological diversity of woodlands, preserves air and water quality, and stays within the ecological carrying-capacity of the land. The Forest Stewardship Council and SmartWood certification standards provide sound guidance to landowners, foresters, and loggers working to protect and improve the long-term health of our woodlands.

We have used FSC-certified oak flooring for the farmhouse kitchen floor, elm hardwood flooring in the hallway and front room of the cabin, rough cut aspen dimensional lumber for the greenhouse, and one-inch stock aspen boards and black locust for window trim.

SOURCES AND RESOURCES

Alan Drengson and Duncan Taylor, *Ecoforestry: The Art and Science of Sustainable Forest Use*, New Society Publishers, 1997.

Co-op America's Woodwise Consumer Guide
   Website: www.woodwise.org
   Providing practical tips and resources to use forest products more wisely.

Forest Stewardship Council (FSC)
   Website: www.foreststewardship.org
   The Forest Stewardship Council is a non-profit organization founded in 1993 by a diverse group of representatives from environmental and conservation groups, the timber industry, the forestry profession, indigenous peoples' organizations, community forestry groups and forest product certification organizations from 25 countries. Information on their website includes lists of vendors and suppliers that sell FSC-certified wood.

World Wildlife Fund
   Website: www.worldwildlife.org
   Known worldwide by its panda logo, the World Wildlife Fund (WWF) is dedicated to protecting the world's wildlife and wildlands. WWF directs its conservation efforts toward three global goals: protecting endangered spaces, saving endangered species, and addressing global threats. According to WWF, the average American citizen consumes seven times as much commercial wood and paper as citizens in other countries; their Global Forest Program offers resources to help preserve and restore the remaining forests.

CHAPTER 2

Food and Friendships

Granolaheads Anonymous

In December, 1997, *Newsweek* published a trend article entitled "Sell In, Bliss Out," which talked about the new yuppie class, young professionals who are exiting the corporate treadmill and doing their own thing, prioritizing quality of life over size of salary. We were interviewed by phone for this article, which mostly reflected positively on us, but from which *Newsweek* ultimately concluded that Lisa was "taking her granolahead philosophy too far" by suggesting that Americans should sell their TVs.

When visiting Inn Serendipity, however, many of our guests and visitors are left with a sense of contemporary country life, from a photovoltaic system that generates solar electricity to a home office complete with multiple computers, fax line and an Internet connection. One journalist wrote that one half expects to find '60s musician Mama Cass crooning in the fruit cellar; when friends from Monroe journey out for a Scottish night and potluck, they're not surprised to be entertained by a bagpiper.

We're not scheming to put TV companies out of business — it's just that TV isn't a priority for us. We're happy with our old TV offering fuzzy local reception, and it works fine for viewing videos.

We like to make and eat granola. We also enjoy eating many local artisan-made cheeses, like Gruyere, Havarti and Swiss. Guess that makes us both granolaheads — and cheeseheads. As we understand the term, we're different from the stereotypical granolaheads. We don't smoke pot, but we do brew our own raspberry ale. We don't own any John Lennon albums, but we're all for peace, love and skinny dipping. The granolahead characterization is what caught Lisa by surprise in the *Newsweek* piece. The reporters assumed that our goal was to convince Americans to live the way we do. They concluded that we were running away from the establishment and setting up our little organic B&B in rural Wisconsin. But that's not the case.

MAKING INN SERENDIPITY GRANOLA

While we're a new generation of homesteaders, we are deeply appreciative of the Nearing era pioneers, and yes, of granola. Our symbolic way of honoring them and digesting that *Newsweek* comment with humor is by crunching on granola. Often made in big batches where the whole house is blanketed in the sweet smell of honey, granola is one of those can't-miss recipes, since it's easily adaptable to what's on hand in the cupboards. Because we regularly cook by taste and use what ingredients are in the house, no two batches are the same. We like to make granola for the holidays, pouring it into recycled canning jars and giving the granola as gifts. It's difficult to go back to the store-bought stuff after making our own.

Ingredients (yield: 8 cups)

6 c. rolled oats	1/2 c. honey
1 c. chopped nuts	1/2 c. packed brown sugar
1/2 c. flaked coconut	2 T. water
1/2 c. sesame seeds	1 1/2 t. vanilla extract
2/3 c. canola oil	

Preparation

Preheat oven to 275 degrees. In a large bowl, combine oats, nuts, coconut and sesame seeds. In a saucepan over medium heat, simmer oil, honey, brown sugar and water and until well mixed (do not boil). Remove from heat and stir in vanilla. Pour honey mixture over oat mixture and stir to coat evenly. Pour into two greased 13-inch x 9-inch x 2-inch baking pans. Bake for 50 to 60 minutes or until golden brown, stirring every 15 minutes. Keep a careful eye on the granola during the final baking period — it can easily burn! Cool, stirring occasionally. Store in an airtight container.

The truth is, what we and many others are doing is creating a more sustainable lifestyle by living closer to the land in an ecologically and socially mindful way. We're anything but lone rangers in our quest, and we enjoy the diversity of perspectives and approaches we learn about from our guests, friends and others with whom we cross paths. Many of the "hippies" who have stuck with renewable energy are now teaching and sharing how practical energy conservation and renewable energy generation can be. But times and technology have changed. For us, reviving, renewing and restoring a homestead steeped in history made more sense than building a new home. Our challenge has been to selectively use certain elements that can enhance our lives, such as computers, while avoiding elements that cause unnecessary clutter or conflict with our values, like fast food. Sustainability is not about subsistence. Rather, sustainability is about constant innovation and creative expression.

This movement toward sustainable and more simple living, a movement that has assumed many different forms depending upon where and how the movement is being realized, is in its infancy. But it's growing. In the country, a rural renaissance is underway, particularly in counties with the greatest scenic value and amenities. Entire small town main streets are being rebuilt and restored. Swaths of the countryside are being set aside in perpetuity as farmland, open space or conservation lands. Entire neighborhoods in suburbs and large cities have experienced grassroots sustainability initiatives, in places like Seattle and Prairie Crossing, a suburban development north of Chicago, where a whole new approach to living with nature is being cultivated within the

RURAL RENAISSANCE

For the first time in over three decades, a net migration back to the country is occurring, resulting in over 20 percent of the US population living in rural areas. While America is hardly a nation of farmers anymore, the allure of the rural life is attracting many to more pastoral roots in small towns, farms, even wooded properties. Increased wealth, technological advancements in telecommunications and computers, and improved transportation have facilitated these changes. And the allure is hardly surprising, since most Americans are less than two generations away from a rural community.

Additionally, new home construction is mushrooming, as is the number of second homes or vacation homes. According to Mary Umberger with Knight-Ridder News, it's estimated that Americans will be buying about 1,000 second homes per day over the next decade, bringing the total of second home ownership to about 10 million. This doesn't include the millions of acres of private property — without homes — that often have an assortment of conservation efforts underway. Migration to rural areas is further compounded by an aging population thinking about retirement and a move to a community which better meets their preference for climate, pace, amenities and scenery.

The countryside is dotted with farms and homesteads not unlike our own, giving new life and perspectives to life in the country. In our area, for example, hobby farms are flourishing while traditional mid-size family farms go under. Across the nation, this same pattern is emerging, with the new, thriving hobby farms blending income from on-farm and off-farm sources. For example, our neighbors Claudia and Ryan manage an apple tree orchard, run a B&B, have dairy cows, a craft store and give farm tours to area schoolchildren. To help cover expenses, Ryan works for a local engineering firm.

community. From large-scale, city-wide initiatives to tomato plants popping up in window sill gardens; from new eco-enterprise start-ups to compost bins under the kitchen sink, this movement freshly challenges the status quo with a revitalized passion for sustainable living and an awakened imagination.

While past homesteading generations tended to live in more isolated locales, often building cabins in the woods alongside others with similar values, we thrive on keeping connected to a diversity of people on a global basis, and today's technology enables us to do this. Between faxes, voicemail, and international couriers, we can literally set up shop anywhere.

Connectedness is the element that makes this 21st-century sustainability movement unique; e-mail and the growth of the Internet are key players in what we've come to call a rural renaissance. We've communicated with an international board of directors for a conservation organization, sent out query letters to editors, and tracked the B&B reservations by e-mail. On a social level, e-mail helps us maintain our friendships. While we have a locally based coffee-table community, we also have a wide web of connections which keep us wired to the global community.

Perhaps due to greatly dispersed family structures, friends are rising to the same level as family in importance. Our relationships among our network of friends offers greater mutual support, involvement, communication and love than many blood relations. It assures a connection to a strong community wherever we plug in our laptop, and allows us to live where we feel most drawn. Of course, e-mail and other forms of technology are no substitute for face-to-face communication; but it does help keep us connected between visits.

Working from home has become increasingly accepted. When we first left the ad agency to hang out our small business shingle, we got caught in trying to appear bigger than we were, hiding the fact that we were working in sweats and a tee-shirt on a laptop at home. Apartment numbers became suite-so-and-so, and with voicemail we tried to create the illusion of a cubicle environment; "we're on the other line or in a meeting," rambled the outgoing message. That masquerade is over now.

We've found that a chicken clucking in the background or a milk truck rolling down the road can be a competitive advantage. People are curious. Talking to us on the phone, editors from New York City ask how the llamas are doing. We chat about how we gathered fresh eggs or made a dinner salad with fresh tomatoes from the garden. "That's fascinating," they say. We've noticed, too, that we end up sharing recipes or gardening stories, as many of these urban and suburban dwellers are making connections of their own through rooftop gardens or solar electric systems. Technology has expanded the frontiers of the home office, and we're relishing those new, wider boundaries.

A balanced approach to using technology allows us to more readily connect with our garden as well. A food processor makes it a breeze to blend leeks, potatoes and butter into leek soup. The microwave more quickly and efficiently blanches broccoli. The ongoing challenge is to use technology in a balanced way so that it helps us connect with our food source, rather than insulating us from it.

A strong reconnection with our food sources digs deeper than planting tomatoes. We find ourselves sharing a passionate quest for what is raw and real in an overprocessed world. We want to feel some dirt under our fingernails, make our own strawberry jam, share an afternoon and a pitcher of lemon balm iced tea with a friend.

We're often asked how we find the time to do all this, the planting, the picking, the processing. The answer can be found in the tenets of moving back to the land: we're selectively connected. We may religiously e-mail friends in the Big Apple, but we rarely watch TV. Our shopping trips are quick and specific, as our needs are few. We've de-cluttered our lives, exited the earn-and-spend cycle of consumption, and halted the hour-long commute in bumper-to-bumper traffic. We're gifted with time — to can cinnamon applesauce, call mom, and renew our connection to and our passion for the world around us. But this isn't just for back-to-the-landers — it's for people anywhere who want to experience a renaissance in their lives.

How to

Living the Cultural Creative Dream

Do we actively pursue an ecologically-minded approach to living, working, playing, or raising our child, while others contemplate $100,000 renovations on their already comfortable 2,000-square foot (186 m²) home while the nanny takes care of the kids? Are we turned off by politics as usual? Are we experimenting with new models of living and working, seeking to transform our economics away from serving the few to serving the many, while restoring nature? Yes. And we're not alone. We're among the many so-called "Cultural Creatives".

According to their 13 years of research, sociologist Paul H. Ray and psychologist Sherry Ruth Anderson estimate that there are 50 million adults in the United States who have the worldview, values and lifestyle of what they call the Cultural Creatives. (They estimate about 80 to 90 million Cultural Creatives in Europe as well.) This group of people is creating a practical and grounded culture centered on realigning life with personal values.

Among the many ways we identified with the depiction of life by those who are Cultural Creatives include our nature-based lifestyle and our deeply felt concern about the condition of the planet that our son will inherit. Our exodus from a culture that spends as quickly as it gets has landed us in a simpler way of life that is rich in meaning, relationships and friendships. Among our luxuries are the time spent with Liam, each other, and the enjoyment of sunsets.

One of our toughest departures was letting go of the control of "the market" over our daily experiences, pursuing instead, meaningful and creative activities that meet our annual financial obligations and offer countless developmental dividends. We believe in commerce, but distrust the large corporations and their never-ending quest for ever larger profits, seemingly blind to the havoc it causes people and the environment. And we've joined many Americans who want to support political leadership that addresses a new view; one that might include universal health coverage, and a department of peace. We often meet this same group of people at youth hostels around the world; they share our thirst for a better understanding of the world's rich diversity of cultures and people. In the end, our life is about building more ecologically sustainable communities and living truer to our calling.

According to Ray and Anderson, Cultural Creatives are redefining and reframing what success means, away from success at work and making a lot of money, and toward a more soulful life focused on personal fulfillment, social conscience, and a better future for the planet. Cultural Creatives are the people who are helping support a multibillion dollar industry in the US called the Lifestyles of Health and Sustainability (LOHAS). Many of these people fill our B&B beds, join us for open houses, or share John's multicultural books with their children. Cultural Creatives are also creating new kinds of businesses and non-profits, focusing on the issues and concerns they hold dear.

What we found most revealing about those Cultural Creatives we've gotten to know is their awareness of what is happening around the world and in their communities, and their attempts to change course. Despite the mainstream media spinning stories to the contrary, the emerging dream among Cultural Creatives is beginning to take hold, forever changing our worldview.

SOURCES AND RESOURCES

The Good Life Center
Website: www.goodlife.org
Building on the philosophies and lifeways exemplified by Helen and Scott Nearing - two of America's most inspirational practitioners of simple, frugal and purposeful living - the Center promotes active participation in the advancement of social justice; creative integration of the life of the mind, body and spirit; and deliberate choices in living responsibly and harmoniously in an increasingly complicated world.

BackHome: Your Hands-on Guide to Sustainable Living
Website: www.backhomemagazine.com
This bi-monthly how-to magazine covers everything from renewable energy to family activities and vacations, with the purpose of helping people do more for themselves.

Countryside and Small Stock Journal
Website: www.countrysidemag.com
With an emphasis on food production at home, this bi-monthly magazine offers rural homesteaders practical information, much of it contributed by its readers.

Helen and Scott Nearing, *The Good Life: Helen and Scott Nearing's Sixty Years of Self-sufficient Living,* Schocken Books, 1990.

Paul H. Ray and Sherry Ruth Anderson, *Cultural Creatives: How 50 Million People are Changing the World,* Harmony Books, 2000.

Wendell Berry, *Sex, Economy, Freedom, and Community,* Pantheon Books, 1994.

John Storey and Martha Storey, *Storey's Basic Country Skills: A Practical Guide to Self-reliance,* Storey Books, 1999.

The Forces of Spring

When is an in-box truly empty? A calendar clear? The pantry shelves barren? Rarely. New computers inherit old files, next year's fresh calendar is quickly stuffed with obligations before New Year's Eve. Even when moving to a new house, it quickly fills with boxes packed with old baggage and belongings. Yet something is different each year when spring arrives. With a whoosh of Mother Nature's magical wand, we're gifted with a blank canvas of possibility. It's not necessarily a pompous ushering in at the chiming of the vernal equinox. But rather, spring slowly rolls in with every baby green chive peeking through the snow until we are drenched in its possibilities. Any dark winter impedimenta is miraculously absolved and we're giddy with hope, drive and spirit. Fresh asparagus appears.

We've rediscovered the seasons, tart May rhubarb; juicy July tomatoes; crisp fall skies; comforting squash curry soup enjoyed around the woodstove in winter. But the season of spring tends to fall into a special class of inspiration. Spring is a fresh start, a booster shot of confidence wrapped in a dose of giggly bliss. Spring is Earth's gift of renewal, a launching pad of rejuvenation and faith.

The challenge in today's modern world is to connect with this raw power. Spring is more than a new pastel wardrobe, Easter greeting card commercials and washing salt grime off the car. Spring is an espresso jolt sending us scurrying off in exciting new directions. We peel down to the essence of what this gift entails, remembering that spring doesn't come from a strip mall, can't be put on layaway, and doesn't need to be exchanged for an extra-large.

Spring ushers in a fresh start, a clean slate on which to start anew. The weeds have been winter-killed and the potato beetles missing in action. Call it Earth's confessional booth – past sins forgiven and washed away in the melting snow. We feel this fresh palette most when planning the garden. Inspiration rises like yeast during the early spring, as we contemplate the rainbow of seed catalogs that land in our mailbox. Last year's failed carrot crop is forgotten. Whining about last season's weeding is a blurry memory as we ambitiously plot this year's garden. Double the snow peas! More tomato varieties! Yes, the watermelon we've planted every year has resulted in absolutely no watermelon, but who's to say this isn't our year? And while we're at it, let's add a perennial bed, extend the asparagus patch, and paint the barn in one afternoon. We try to avoid letting spring's ambition spiral too much out of control. If our creative spirit can't grow with the blossoming flowers we helped nurture – perhaps because we are so exhausted from weeding – then what's the point?

Spring isn't just the name of a season. As our farm years fly by, and we learn to live closer to the cycles of the land, we realize that spring is an attitude of spicy and sassy confidence. Sometimes these early boosts of confidence can get us into trouble, like when we pack the blustery woollies away in the attic cedar chest too soon, in our haste to strip down to shorts, and our pudgy, winter-white legs turn to popsicles in the cool spring breeze. We have an annual debate over when to clear the deadweight off the perennial flower beds and expose the new green shoots to the forces of nature. Our last frost date is around May 15, but by early April, even late March in some years, we're having bursts of warm spring afternoons that can melt any wintry souls, teasing us that summer is a stone's throw away.

Spring rejuvenates. We itch in ways that can't be scratched, as if we're waking from hibernation, a bit stiff from winter slumber but reinvigorated and ready to get off the bench and into the game. We jump on life's diving board, our knees a bit wobbly but reach to spring forth and cannonball jump off with gusto.

Spring is cyclical and seasonal, gently and naturally following the flow of winter. Winter's hibernation is a good thing in its own right. Long dark nights around the woodstove fuel ideas, provide time to catch up on indoor projects, and allow us to make a dent in our reading list. Then comes spring and its blooming rejuvenation, and our energies are invigorated in different directions.

Lastly, spring implants playfulness. Regardless of our age and otherwise mature demeanors, we demand recess. We want to fly kites, eat ice cream for dinner, stay in bed and make love Monday morning. Details of nature are magnified and magically enhance us: fuzzy baby chicks; silky buds on the pussy willow tree; gentle spring rain caressing our faces. As nature awakens the soil, our bodies feel stimulated. Senses magnify, heartbeats flutter, midriffs reveal.

One afternoon we were clearing the bed of irises that surround a maple tree on the east side of the house. Iris roots lay very close to the ground, so we gently loosen any encroaching weeds and try to pull them out without damaging the flower root. As Lisa moved in with her trowel to weed around another iris plant, her arm froze. Nestled in between the tender green iris shoots were five baby bunnies, no more than a couple of days old, each a couple inches long. Lisa didn't want to move, afraid to break the magical spell of sharing the garden with these adorable fur balls. But she silently, hurriedly, motioned to John to come see. Watching such raw, new life induced us to step back from our daily to-dos and lie next to each other atop the soft spring grass carpet, legs intertwined. We bonded with the bunnies and each other, warmed by the golden setting sun. Sure, we were supposed to be clearing flower beds, but we never heard the recess bell ring.

Despite living on the farm, we spend most of our time doing typical office activities: typing on the computer, conference calls on the phone, and reading trade journals. Whether we're in a cubicle or somewhere else is irrelevant if we're oblivious to Earth's changes around us. But spring prompts us to take the time to go barefoot in the grass, crunch on fresh greens, and act on fresh goals.

How to

Pick a Cuppa Sustainable Coffee

Among our steps toward living a more sustainable lifestyle was through our coffee cup. Coffee is our beverage of choice and the sound of coffee beans grinding in the morning is music to our ears. As coffee connoisseurs, we use our purchasing dollar to support sustainable coffee production. When purchasing coffee beans, we look for the following:

- **Is it shade-grown?** Conventional coffee plantation practices typically involve clear-cutting forests for monoculture coffee plantations. This destroys the ecosystem and requires fertilizers and pesticides which then adversely affect both the health of farmers and local wildlife. Shade-grown coffee is made from sustainably harvested beans from coffee plants that grow in the shade of the existing forests, without destroying the natural ecosystem. Coffee plants grown this way do not need to be subjected to a regime of pesticides or fertilizers; thus, most shade-grown coffee is also organically grown.

- **Are the farmers equitably compensated?** Historically, companies from developed countries such as the United States have set the terms for the pricing of world commodities, including coffee. This has resulted in a huge inequity in developing countries, where coffee farmers have little choice but to accept the terms offered. While a pound of gourmet coffee may sell for $8-$10, only 35 to 50 cents of that goes to the farmer.

Fortunately, there is a growing number of progressive coffee companies that not only offer organic coffee, but do so in a way that support fair trade, striving to ensure that sustainable growing practices and equitable pay scales are offered to farmers. Most sell coffee through direct mail order or at local food co-ops and independent coffee houses. Among the leaders are Equal Exchange and Thanksgiving Coffee. Dunkin' Donuts, Starbucks Coffee and Albertson's supermarket chain have also agreed to sell Fair Trade Certified coffee.

Beside coffee, the fair trade movement has grown in response to the increasing awareness of sweatshop labor, unfair labor practices, environmental degradation, and other social issues. Today, there are fair trade certified teas, chocolate, bananas, oranges and a wide range of hand-crafted products, revenues from which support —not exploit — the communities that make them.

SOURCES AND RESOURCES:

Fair Trade Federation
   Website: www.fairtradefederation.org
   Provides information on fairly traded products and a listing of companies supporting the fair trade movement.

TransFair USA
   Website: www.transfairusa.org
   A non-profit that regularly reviews and certifies the business and growing practices of coffee, tea and cocoa (chocolate) producers to insure that they meet fair trade conditions.

Co-op America
   Website: www.sweatshops.org (to avoid supporting sweatshop labor)
   Website: www.responsibleshopper.org (for information on resposible shopping)
   Website: www.fairtradeaction.org (for information on fairly traded goods)

Rainforest Alliance
   Website: www.rainforest-alliance.org
   As one of its initiatives to protect the rainforests and the people who live

in them, this non-profit organization certifies cocoa, oranges, coffee and bananas grown according to environmentally and socially responsible criteria. Look for the Rainforest Alliance Certified label.

Equal Exchange
251 Revere Street, Canton, MA 02021, 781-830-0303
Website: www.equalexchange.com
Offers fairly traded coffee, tea and cocoa by mail order.

Thanksgiving Coffee Co.
P.O. Box 1918, Fort Bragg, CA 95437, 1-800-462-1999
Website: www.thanksgivingcoffee.com
Offers a wide variety of fair trade-certified and organic coffees, also by mail order.

Creative Kitchen Partnerships

We're not psychologists. But we do have a nugget of love advice that may be so basic that it's chronically overlooked by pop psychology: the more interconnected the lives of two people, the deeper and stronger the relationship bond. That stirring of souls, that blending of dreams, can often be found in our kitchen.

We have very different cooking styles. John is the cook preferred if stranded on a deserted island; he can whip up something ingenious with whatever happens to be around. His most important cooking utensil is his palate. His tastebuds constantly override whatever the recipe ingredient list may command.

Lisa's kitchen style is the direct opposite, but she is the one you would want to cook a Thanksgiving dinner for twelve. She writes out detailed shopping lists for needed ingredients and considers tablecloth color a vital culinary decision. She measures quarter teaspoons and uses a knife to level off exact cups. Substituting yogurt for sour cream makes her very nervous.

The way we individually decide what to cook is also quite disparate. Lisa gleans through recipe books as if they were the steamy sections of a romance novel. She can readily eyeball a recipe and determine if it has potential, then files it away for future reference. She's a gleeful baker; hearty, country-cooking sweets and dessert items are usually high on her list of recipes to concoct. John, however, first craves something, usually an ethnic entree. Then he looks for a specific recipe, adapting what is locally in season, or in some cases, left over in the refrigerator. John's taste for travel has translated to a talent for hummus, pad thai, and spanakopita.

These distinctive cooking approaches rise to a new level when we cook breakfast for B&B guests. We have a couple of staple menus which we vary based upon what's in season and available. We quickly developed distinct production roles in the morning kitchen, with Eggs Florentine the best example of our partnership in the kitchen. John does the poached eggs, keeping an eye on the cooked density of the eggs and making sure that some turn out a bit runnier while others are on the firmer side. He fries up the hash browns, seasoning with a bit of rosemary, chives or whatever strikes his morning mood. Lisa washes the spinach, John sautés. Lisa is in charge of the hollandaise sauce. On mornings when Egg Florentine is served there's even a well-defined boundary in the kitchen: John's turf is on the east side of the kitchen and he controls the range top. Lisa manages the sink and oven on the west side. Rarely do the two sides meet until the celebratory plating, complete with nasturtium flower garnish or a sprinkle of paprika for color.

The descriptions of our culinary perspectives and romps in the kitchen don't seem to symbolize compatibility. Or do they? While we may have dissimilar approaches to the culinary arts, we are deeply rooted in the same vision and values. We share a passion for food and a love of cooking together. We have a mutual mission to bring our fresh produce to the table in a way that highlights flavor, color and nutrition. After all, cooking is creating.

Creativity in the kitchen is artistic expression. Our senses craft and guide our end result. We touch the leathery skin of the potato and hear the crisp crack when snapping carrots. Too often, at the grocery store, food is a commodity designed for filling a stomach. Portability, shelf-life, and most of all, profitability for agribusinesses (not most farmers) are key traits of carrots, crackers and canned salsa. When we used to eat gourmet entrees at trendy eateries, we had little knowledge or interest in where our food came from, how it was grown, when it was in season, or the condition of the growers who harvested it for the meal. That pattern changed when we started to grow our own fruits and vegetables and cracked open fresh eggs from our chickens. We came alive in the kitchen, artistically blending the foods created from the miracle of what nature had provided for our sustenance and eating pleasure.

We didn't have a master plan for balancing our relationship. Rather, it serendipitously evolved. The more we talked about and better refined our values, the deeper the love grew between us. The more partnership connections we created, the stronger we became as a couple. Independently pursuing our goals also tightened our bonds. The farm, the kitchen and our pursuits offered the necessary creative foundation for a solid, loving and nurturing partnership.

Traditional definitions of work and play now blend as smoothly as the stick of butter melting into the egg yolks of the hollandaise sauce, so that we can't easily identify one from the other. When we philosophize into the night around the campfire with B&B guests, is that work? When Lisa e-mails a fellow writer friend about a project she is currently working on, is that leisure? Who knows? Who cares? We like the work and leisure blend, of losing traditional boundaries and definitions and mixing our days serendipitously.

On those Sunday mornings when we're both in the kitchen wearing our B&B aprons as the welcoming morning light taps on the kitchen window above the sink, we silently merge into our Eggs Florentine dance pattern. As we go about our accustomed roles and quietly plate the dish, we are reminded that there is something more going on than feeding the hungry people sitting at our dining room table. Cooking together, balancing in the kitchen, blends more than wet and dry ingredients. Our souls tango in the frying pan, creating a bond to the food on the table, to each other, and to the farm and the world around us.

How to

Supporting Local Farmers while Enjoying Good Food

According to the US Department of Agriculture, half of agricultural production in the US comes from about one percent of farms, mostly corporate mega-farms. Thankfully, several options exist for us to reconnect with our food purchases. Buying local or growing our own insures that our food is fresher, tastier and more nutritious; and when we buy directly from area farmers, we also support a stronger local economy.

1. Community-Supported Agriculture (CSA).

A CSA farm allows individuals or families to become members of and direct investors in a farm, purchasing shares of what the farm will produce during the growing season. CSA members pay at the beginning of the season for their share; this gives farmers the capital they need to buy the seeds and grow the food, and also means that shareholders share some of the growing risks. CSAs cater most to people residing in urban or suburban locales who crave fresh fruits, veggies, flowers and herbs. An accessible weekly drop off point is generally set up for CSA members to pick up their weekly share. Increasingly, CSAs also offer other value-added products such as honey, cheese and eggs. For a directory listing a local CSA and other direct from the farm options, contact the Robyn Van En Center <www.csacenter.org>, Local Harvest <www.localharvest.org>, or read *Sharing the Harvest: A Guide to Community Supported Agriculture*, by Elizabeth Henderson (Chelsea Green Publishing, 1999).

2. Farmers' Markets

Farmers' markets are mushrooming across the continent. Not only do farmers' markets provide direct access to locally grown fresh foods and products, they are often fun, carnival-like events that help create community and bring growers and those who love agricultural products together. They're the perfect spot for leisurely strolling with a market basket, taking in the sights, smells, relationships and, of course, fresh foods. There's no extra packaging, no preservatives, and no fancy advertising campaigns. For updated listings of farmers' markets in the US, visit <www.ams.usda.gov/farmersmarkets/map.htm>.

Becoming an active participant at a local farmers' market can be accomplished in the following ways:

- Engage the farmers at the market by asking them how they decided on the kinds of crops they are growing: whether they grow organically; how long it took to harvest; what time they got up that day to make it to market. A conversation and a cantaloupe later, a new community grows through local foods.

◆ Bring re-usable canvas bags, baskets or boxes. The farmers will offer thanks, since it'll be one less thing for them to collect and cart from the farm.

◆ Be open to new seasonal offerings, like swiss chard, beets, watercress and green tomatoes. These were all new to us. After a little research and some good recipes, they top our garden favorite list. During harvest bounty time at the farmers' market, try bringing home one new vegetable or fruit to experiment with each week.

3. Growing Our Own

The Madison Famers' Market, among the largest in the US.

Regardless of whether we live in an urban highrise or on a countryside hobby farm, growing our own fresh fruits, vegetables, herbs and flowers can be done with a modest amount of money and know-how. In the country, we now have the space for three growing fields to meet about seventy percent of our annual food needs.

But had we been more creative and engaged in Chicago, we could have grown fresh tomatoes, strawberries and basil in containers on our patio. Friends we've visited who live in urban or suburban areas astound us with their effectiveness at growing a wide range of produce in limited backyards or on rooftop gardens. The key is starting small and expanding as your expertise grows (see Chapter 5).

The Comfort of Potatoes

It has all the makings of the quintessential, crooning country western ballad: "You didn't know how much you loved her till she was gone like cotton candy blowing away in a hurricane." It's about a neglected relationship; no cozy romantic Saturday night dinners, no sentimental appreciation on Valentine's Day … then one day she freezes up, and the comforting relationship has vanished. And then comes the familiar lonesome twang of the F-sharp guitar chord as you wail into the wistful refrain: "Oh, take me back to last year, when my little potato was still here; I treated her bad, she got mad, and left me crying spudless tears into my beer."

Well, no, Hank Williams hasn't warbled his hankering for french fries lately. But we have been through the relationship wringer when it comes to taters. As a result, we never miss an opportunity to sing praises to the potato. We've learned that spuds are more than cheap and easy carbohydrates. Potatoes ground us to everyday reality and cultivate a continual appreciation for the little things we tend to take for granted.

We started out as gardening insurgents, championing the spud. We were adamant about planting potatoes, despite good intentioned neighbors tendering advice like, "You know, kids, you can get a 10-pound bag of potatoes at the grocery store for $1.49 on sale." Ignoring their counsel, we tilled the soil by hand that first early April afternoon, planting twenty pounds of seed potatoes, ten pounds each of White Russet and Irish Red. Our relentless planting of the potato is probably due to our desire to rebel against common wisdom. It took a few more years before we realized the potato's deep merits.

Our first potato crop was invaded by Colorado potato beetles, resulting in three crates of runts. The following year we came better prepared, rotating our rows and hand-picking the malefic beetles. The potato gods generously rewarded us with a bumper crop of potatoes. We dug them up in early September, then packed them into old plastic crates, storing them on the front porch covered by a few sheets.

September quickly faded into October, then November. We ceremoniously ate a couple of baked potatoes to celebrate our victory over the potato beetle, but after that initial taste, our palates were bewitched by other harvest produce: blazing squashes, ruby apples, succulent grapes fresh off the vine. The spuds sat alone in storage on the porch.

The whirl of the December holidays rolled through with an entourage of festive goodies. Our front porch is enclosed but not heated, so by this time of year it

MAKING BAKED POTATO PANCAKES

Potatoes can be used for meals at any time of day and are frugal food options, whether home-grown or purchased at a local farmers' market, co-op or grocery store, and potato pancakes are the epitome of morning comfort food. We serve these in the fall, accompanied by sour cream and homemade applesauce. These potato pancakes are a healthier twist on the traditional Jewish latkes, which are fried in butter or oil; we bake them, giving them a crisper, lighter texture. Leftover baked pancakes are great warmed up in the toaster.

Ingredients (serves 4)

2 t. cooking oil

2 pounds (4-5 medium) potatoes (unpeeled)

3/4 c. onion, finely chopped

1/4 c. all-purpose white flour

1 t. salt

1/8 t. black pepper

2 eggs, lightly beaten

Preparation

Set oven racks at middle and lower positions. Preheat oven to 400 degrees. Prepare 2 baking sheets by brushing each with one teaspoon oil (or use non-stick pans). Grate potatoes with a hand grater or the shredding blade of a food processor. Place in a large bowl and add onions, flour, salt and pepper; toss with 2 forks to mix well. Add eggs and remaining 1 teaspoon oil; toss to mix (it is easiest to mix using clean hands). Drop heaping tablespoons of this mixture onto the prepared baking sheets and press with a spoon to make a flat pancake. Bake approximately 15 minutes or until pancake is nicely brown on the bottom. Turn the pancakes over, switch positions of baking sheets and bake for about another 10 minutes or until pancakes are nicely brown on both sides.

Presentation

Serve pancakes with a dollop of sour cream, sprinkled with finely cut fresh chives. An interesting recipe variation is making these pancakes with sweet potatoes.

was too cold to hang out in, but it's the perfect temperature for a walk-in refrigerator, which came in handy for the holiday leftovers. Next to the decadent mocha cake and embellished gingerbread men sat the stacked crates of lonely potatoes.

Then one day shortly after New Year's Day, we noticed a pool of water dripping out from under the potatoes. After we unstacked the crates and poked fingers into the mushy, wet potatoes, it became clear what happened: The potatoes had frozen during a deep cold spell the week before and then had defrosted into this state of mush. We had known that eventually the porch would be too cold for potato storage and we would need to move them down to the basement. Distracted by the chocolate covered pretzels that needed dipping and mulled cider spilling over on the counter, we forgot. Overrun by other holiday priorities and homemade gift-making, we had left our homegrown potatoes out to freeze.

We attempted to quick-fix the situation, but nature is not always forgiving of neglect. We sorted through the potatoes and managed to excavate a buried crate that didn't freeze. We learned that while we could eat the mushy potatoes (which would taste awful), we couldn't use them as seed potatoes in next year's garden, since freezing kills the germination. We settled on sharing them with the hogs at a neighboring farm. The pigs gladly feasted, and we savored the potatoes we did manage to rescue, swearing never to mess up like this again.

Starting fresh the following year, we achieved repeat victory over the potato beetle and harvested a decent crop. Back to the potato crates, back to the porch, and back to holiday chaos. And back to, you guessed it, another crop of frozen potatoes, inadvertently left out on the porch too long. Winter's freeze had come early. Knowing what happens after a third strike, we are confident that we have been hit enough times on the head to get our act together.

Our potatoes remind us to appreciate the everyday simplicities that surround us that we take for granted: a grandmother's stories; nursing a baby to sleep; a typical Wednesday night supper at home with the family. Sometimes, we fall into the trap of longing for what isn't there, dreaming of tropical islands as the snow falls. Those crates of potatoes teach us that we can find strength in familiarity. It's our responsibility to nurture the proverbial potatoes in our lives, to give gratitude for everyday simplicities, and never take a spud for granted.

How to

Finding Our Place

How do we know where we live? When do we know we are where we need to be – whole, alive, at peace, happy? What sets our country road address apart from the next one down the road? At first glance, our four-square farmhouse, two barns and agricultural lands seem to be just like our neighbors. Our farm is just like the others.

But it's not. We know where the rabbits like to hide out from the barn cats, which gutters overflow in heavy rains. We feel more a part of our gardens because we are, literally, a part of them through the foods we harvest and eat. The sunlight falling on our faces outside heats our water and generates some of our electricity.

Cloudy days mean something now. Wendell Berry writes that if you don't know where you are, you don't know who you are. Before we arrived to this place, we didn't understand what he meant.

In Chicago, we knew the street names, the bus line numbers and addresses for our home, office and favorite coffee house, but we were fundamentally disoriented.

Our connection to place was based on dining, shopping and amenities. Nature was the lakeside park system, and community was what we called Saturday nights out on the town with friends. We found our way to work and back home again every night just fine, but our relationship to the land, our food, shelter and livelihood was all but miss-

Sketch of Inn Serendipity farmstead.

ing. As a result, we didn't care about stormwater runoff, chemicals in our food or the impacts of the products we helped advertise. We operated without navigation.

Rediscovering a sense of place is one of life's best-kept secrets. When we arrived, we became keenly aware of the smells of the country, and how they change through the seasons: moist decay of early spring; parched fragrance of mid-summer; crisp tartness of harvest time in autumn; breathtaking chill of winter. The cycles of rain, wind and dry spells delicately weave themselves into a wildlife tapestry of comings and goings. Bluebirds arriving, followed by the hummingbirds passing through. Frogs singing riotously, followed by the soothing sounds of crickets and grasshoppers through summer. Then suddenly, with an autumn cold spell, they're gone, along with the leaves, flowers and apple harvest.

If we can miss seeing the Wal-Marts and McDonald's in our community, and instead ferret out the cheese factory that still makes Limburger cheese and the tavern that has hosted daily euchre games for decades, we'll find that these features that offer a sense of place can also provide insight into the soul of the community. Often, the greater the sense of place, the more the community feels a responsibility to care for what makes their home unique: historical buildings like our Monroe

Arts Center, natural areas like Honey Creek, and cultural heritage, whether it's a cheese factory or the Turner Hall with its Swiss architecture. We work together for the long-term health of the community because we understand what's so important about these places. They're where we live; who we are. We care for the environment, because at the end of the day, we go to sleep with whatever pollution or garbage we've created. Unlike the anonymous time we spent in our neighborhood in Chicago, our time — and knowledge — of our community today is empowering. It leads us to act in restoring and protecting what it is that first attracted us to the area. We indeed aspire to keep Green County green, in all senses of the word.

Ode to the Chickie

They say the teacher appears when the student is ready to learn. We've encountered many lessons, but what we didn't plan on was that the teacher leading us to many insights would be the feathered puff balls out in the coop.

We decided to raise chickens on a pompous tail wind after a modestly successful gardening season. We declared mastery of tomato growing, since we consumed, canned, froze and gave away so many we lost track. Carry on, then, to poultry! In reality, we had only climbed the first couple of rungs up the ladder of gardening wisdom, but farm confidence ran high so we embarked on a research project on how to raise chickens.

There is no best method of doing anything in the country. Everyone has their method and opinion, typically a result of years of family wisdom and experimentation. This concept is what probably fuels the quest for a blue ribbon at the county fair. Go into the home economics exhibit tent and what do you see? A row of seemingly identical canning jars of pickles, fresh zucchini or cinnamon rolls. But look closer. It's almost like an advanced adult version of that puzzle on Sesame Street – one of these things is not like the other. Look closely. This jar of pickles has, interestingly, some carrots floating in between the cukes. "For extra crunch," it says on the entry description propped next to the jar. These cinnamon rolls are made with nutmeg. And the gardener who nurtured this monster-sized zucchini swears that you need to wait until May 21st to plant summer squash seeds.

Our chicken-raising research project was surprisingly confusing. Few people raise chickens for home use any more, and while many an old-time farmer remembers raising chickens as a kid, each seems to have a different version of how it was done. Let the chickens free-range during the day, but close the coop door at night. No, don't close the coop door; foxes aren't a problem. The chickens should start laying at about four months, or maybe that was eight months?

So, we asked a lot of questions, cross-referenced various answers and checked out, renewed and re-renewed *Storey's Guide to Raising Chickens* from the library. We hoped for the best and invested about $3.30 at our local feed store for an order of ten baby leghorn chicks (called pullets) in early spring. At 33 cents a pop, we calculated that even if we didn't have all the answers, our risk wasn't too steep and we would lavish unheard-of love on them while they were here.

We had a chicken coop among our existing outbuildings. The coop hadn't been used by chickens in a couple of decades, but required only minimal work to ready it for the next generation. We decided on creating a chicken convent (no rooster), since our main goal was egg production and, given the B&B, we rationalized that folks up for a weekend of quiet and rest might appreciate sleeping in past dawn's early light without the rooster's incessant wake-up calls.

Turns out, bringing home baby chicks gave us a preview of what it would be like to be parents, long before Liam came onto the scene. We bring these living creatures into our home that are totally dependent on us. We try our best to keep them warm, fed, and watered. They scream (or, as with chicks, peep at operatic decibels), and we wonder if their world might be coming to an end. After desperately flipping through the poultry guidebook, we rest assured that this is, indeed, normal. And, oh, how quickly these chickies grew. When we picked them up, they were about two days old. Cute little yellow pom-pom puffballs that looked ready to be cast in a chocolate Easter egg commercial. At about two months they entered the poultry version of that gawky, awkward teenage phase. Adult feathers started growing in, jutting out in all directions like a perpetual bad hair day.

At around four months the chicks seemed ready to venture outside the coop during the day. We opened their little coop door and took a seat on the grass to watch what happened next. Like having a private screening of a show on the Discovery Channel, we watched these chickens discover life outside their coop. Their coop door is about a twelve-inch wide square opening a foot off the ground, with an old wood board serving as a ramp to the ground. We sat and watched as one chicken immediately assumed the leadership role and stuck her head out the door. And then quickly ran back inside the coop. Ah yes, we silently agreed. Reality can sometimes be a bit overwhelming, take your time. Another chick came to the door and nibbled on some long grass growing up against the side of the coop. Slowly, all the chicks poked their heads into the sunlight and eventually jumped completely out the door. Then, their discovery takes on the tone of a National Geographic

Happy free-range chickens at Inn Serendipity.

adventure special, with the chicks going on safari, exploring the farm grounds, pecking, tasting and clucking along the way. We could relate to the chicks' discovery experience. The biggest leap is moving through that door, keeping ourselves open to new experiences, humbled by all we don't know.

The chickens remind us of the miracle of life and the circle of life. Finding the first egg was a prodigious encounter during one of the last, relatively mild early November days. We had been putting away the patio furniture and getting the garden ready for winter, mulching and such. The chickens were then a bit over five months and, according to that poultry book (the library was about ready to give us the book), the chickens should start laying eggs any day. We were anxiously looking for anything white and round. We were bringing a load of laundry out to hang on the clothesline when we passed the lilac bush, its branches bare and the grass beneath withering. Regally, sitting on a throne of grass was an egg. Not an average egg, but a rather jumbo-sized one. Since the Leghorns look pretty much identical, we couldn't figure out which one to officially congratulate, so we took a photo of the first egg for the posterity scrapbook and fried up a memorable one-egg omelet for dinner that evening.

After a couple of days, all the chickens were dutifully laying an egg a day inside the coop. After finding that first egg outside, we were a bit concerned that egg gathering may turn into an ongoing hunt. But someone gave us some good advice: if we only open the coop door and let them outside late morning, they might complete their egg-laying inside. It worked.

We're reminded of the power of the circle of life whenever we let the chickens outside and go into the coop to collect eggs. We pick up a fresh egg from the straw nest and it is warm to the touch. You can't help but hold it for a couple of seconds. Like our gardens, the chickens brought us closer to our food source. Our previous egg encounters involved purchasing Styrofoam cartons full of twelve pure white eggs from the dairy case at the supermarket. Sometimes we could buy them on sale for under a buck. We never gave eggs, let alone the chickens, any more thought. That game quickly changed with the arrival of our chickens and their eggs.

Not all eggs are the same. Mother Nature doesn't buff and whiten eggs until they are all clones. Humans — or rather large agribusinesses — do that. Somewhere along the line, someone, or more likely a marketing research group, decided that eggs need to be white and uniform. So imagine our shock to realize that in reality, eggs can be bumpy and rough on the outside, not to mention oblong and oval. The insides of fresh eggs make store-bought eggs look like a generic second cousin of Eggbeaters. The color of our chickens' egg yolks is the vivid orange of the early morning sun, the egg whites are a thick, transparent yellow. We learned that our farm eggs, before washing, can stay fresh for several months. It's the commercial processing that wears down the shell to the point where it's quite thin and can't preserve the insides of the egg nearly as long.

The chickens have not only connected us with a food source, they have enriched our lives through integrating us with the circle of life. We take from our world by being alive in it; there's no way to avoid that. Everything and everyone is someone else's lunch. So the question remains: if we can't avoid taking, how can we minimize the take, maximize what we give back, or minimize what we leave behind? What actions can we take and what things can we do differently to collectively leave the world a better place than when we found it?

Here's where the chickens provide a good example of the give and take exchange. The chickens eat our food scraps, clucking whenever they get a banana peel or stale bagel. The chickens forage the garden for insects and weed seed, supplemented with feed. The chickens poop nitrogen-rich organic fertilizer throughout the garden, enhancing the soil fertility. We've not, yet, figured out a way to keep them away from our back door and the main walkway that leads to the house; we're probably the only bed and breakfast that offers year-round hop-scotch. We eat the eggs for nourishment, composting the egg shells or sometimes using them as an added calcium nutrient by burying them around the tomato plants. The tomato from the tomato plants wind up as pasta sauce, which the chickens seem to like because they get to eat the tomato peels and scraps when we make a batch of sauce.

We now maintain a flock of about twenty chickens, each laying an egg a day (give or take a slacker or two). We started with six leghorns, followed by various varieties in succeeding years to include barred Plymouth Rock, white Plymouth Rock, Rhode Island red, Columbian Rocks, and our favorite, Araucanas which lay eggs with blue and green colored shells. The chickens remind us to keep a participatory, giving role and to give special thanks before every omelet.

Raising Happy Chickens

Eggs produced from happy chickens can be good for you, from both a health and an environmental perspective. The challenge in today's mass-produced food economy is to filter out the mass-produced eggs and purchase free-range and, where possible, organic eggs. Factory-farm eggs involve overcrowding of pens, short life spans for chickens, and painful routine procedures like debeaking or forced molting (starvation) that don't need more detail here other than to say they hardly make a chicken happy.

Free-range chickens have access to the outdoors and may also be certified organic, which means they are fed 100 percent certified organic feed and are produced without hormones and antibiotics.

On the health side, free-range eggs offer some of the highest-quality protein available. Egg protein is often called high quality protein, or complete protein, because it contains the essential amino acids (building blocks of protein which the body needs but cannot make) that we require.

Raising chickens is relatively easy, and in fact, we've met many urban and suburban residents who raise a couple chickens in even the largest of cities. (Most cities have specific ordinances specifying how many hens homeowners are allowed.) We started with chickens because they were low maintenance, fit well within the interconnected farmstead, and produce something usable and salable.

Healthy chickens need water, a food source, shelter from wind, and space to move around. We were fortunate to have an old chicken coop that we restored, but simple plans exist to readily build chicken coops and pens. If predators, such as foxes or coyotes, are a problem, it would be wise to create a pen that could be closed at night. Other than a hawk killing one hen on Halloween day, our flock size has been most impacted by domestic dogs wandering onto our farm. Keep the feed and water inside the coop, and the chickens will naturally return there at night to roost and, in the morning, lay their eggs.

CHAPTER 3

Growing and Gardening

Planting Seeds

We plant a collection of seeds every spring, sowing them in tidy raised beds, sprinkling them with water, and having faith that good things will germinate. We plant seeds of relationships with our neighbors and others in our community with hopes and intentions of growing roots. We scatter the seeds of various entrepreneurial endeavors, from operating the B&B to completing contractual work for non-profits, trusting that our ideas and efforts will generate enough operating income to pay the mortgage and be satisfying, enriching, and fun. And we plant seeds within ourselves and together as a couple, aspiring to grow and vigorously flourish in this place we call home.

The concept of planting seeds, whether literal or figurative, took on a deeper meaning during our first growing season. Our first harvest from those teeny seeds reminded us of what real food is: the strawberries are different sizes, tomatoes sometimes resemble plump buttocks more than perfect spheres, and carrots will never be completely clean. That's okay.

For the first time in our adult life, we had decided to stay put, ending more than a decade of moving and traveling. Our mobility — always searching for the better job, more dynamic city-life, more spacious living space — seemed to get us no further along, since our perspective and the terrain kept changing. Once we settled down, however, the whole natural world unfolded. We became grounded in the familiar, connected to a naturally occurring cycle, and at peace with not moving and going.

> Though I do not believe that a plant will spring up where no seed has been, I have great faith in a seed. Convince me that you have a seed there, and I am prepared to expect wonders.
>
> — Henry David Thoreau, *The Dispersion of Seeds*

When we started growing and eating our own food from seeds we planted, this quest for authenticity oozed into the rest of our lives and evolved into a passionate mantra. In addition to filling our bodies with real food, we now wanted the rest of our lives to be true to our values. We embarked on a quest for the authentic; however, we quickly began to learn that living an authentic life is much more challenging than shopping the organic food aisle. Living authentically requires determining what our central calling and deepest passions are, then taking the time and thought to ascertain what we value and follow through with intentional actions. Living authentically is personally defined and when achieved, offers immense satisfaction - but it's an ongoing challenge to put into practice. We say we value our family and friends, the planet and our food sources, just to name a few. But do our daily actions reflect and reinforce these values? The honest answer is: it's a balancing and blending act.

For us, authentic living causes us to focus on those relationships in our lives that inspire us, people who understand and support the life we try to live; who keep us connected and challenge us with their own passions and missions.

Living authentically means questioning our purchasing dollar, asking ourselves if we really need an item, and if so, taking into account where and how the item was made. It means paying a premium — often necessary — for recycled or other more sustainably manufactured material. We call this premium "nature's share" — the value so often missing in the price tags of so many other products. Recycling can only work if we buy recycled products as much as we recycle. And sometimes, the quest to be real leads to difficult, often imperfect decisions —

AN AUTHENTIC LIFE

Solid words of advice on leading an authentic, or real, life sometimes comes from unlikely sources, like the well-worn book collection in Liam's room.

"Does it hurt?" asked the Rabbit.

"Sometimes," said the Skin Horse, for he was always truthful. "When you are real, you don't mind being hurt."

"Does it happen all at once, like being wound up," he asked, "or bit by bit?"

"It doesn't happen all at once," said the Skin Horse. "You become. It takes a long time. That's why it doesn't happen easily to people who break easily, or have sharp edges or who have to be carefully kept. Generally, by the time you are Real, most of your hair has been loved off and your eyes drop out and you get loose in the joints and very shabby. But these things don't matter at all, because once you are Real you can't be ugly, except to people who don't understand."

— From *The Velveteen Rabbit*, by Margery Williams Bianco

SEED CATALOG AND DRIP IRRIGATION RECOMMENDATIONS

While there are many seed catalog companies across the continent, only a few remain committed to offering a wide selection of heirloom seeds, many of which are organic, some noted below. For more local recommendations, we ask our favorite farmer at the farmers' market, seed buyer at a CSA, or a food cooperative. An added bonus to asking local farmers or growers would be their recommendations for seeds that they grow best in the regional climate.

FEDCO Seed Company
PO Box 520, Waterville, ME 04903
Telephone: 207-873-7333
Website: www.fedcoseeds.com
Offers quality seeds inexpensively, including organically grown seeds and a wide selection of heirlooms. Flowers, vegetables, bulbs, trees, seed potatoes, garden supplies. No color photos.

Johnny's Selected Seeds
955 Benton Avenue, Winslow, ME 04901
Telephone: 207-861-3900
Website: www.johnnyseeds.com
Colorful catalog, good quality seeds and supplies, catering to home and production gardeners since 1973.

Peaceful Valley Farm Supply
P.O. Box 2209, Grass Valley, CA 95945
Telephone: 1-888-784-1722
Website: www.groworganic.com
Catalog committed to sustainable agriculture, tools and supplies for organic gardeners and farmers since 1976. Organically grown seeds, irrigation supplies, tools and machines, seed mixes for lawns, vermiculture, organic fertilizers, and natural pest management.

Jordan Seeds, Inc.
6400 Upper Afton Rd., Woodbury MN 55125
Telephone: 652-728-3422
Seeds, supplies, irrigation. No color photos.

Seeds of Change
1 Sunset Way, Henderson, NV, 89014
Telephone: 1-888-762-7333
Website www.seedsofchange.com
Founded on the philosophy of preserving biodiversity and promoting sustainable agriculture. Informative website.

Drip Works
Igo Sanhedrin Circle, Willits, CA 95490
Telephone: 1-800-522-3747
Extensive inventory of everything needed to set up a garden drip irrigation system, or set up a small pond.

we buy some pretty toxic super glue so that we can fix, rather than landfill, the pitcher, coffee mugs and the ceramic flower vase.

Authenticity isn't perfection; it constitutes effort. Every seed in the packet won't germinate; we need to remember to plant multiple seeds, and then water, weed, mulch and patiently wait. Likewise, our desire to live authentically tests our patience and commitment.

One year we planted a small patch of zucchini in the garden. Now everyone knows how prolific zucchini is. There are cookbooks, festivals and a litany of jokes devoted to the fruitful zuke. Just about any gardening idiot can grow zucchini, right? We didn't harvest any zucchini that fateful year, and humbled by our ineptitude, graciously accepted grocery bags of extra zucchini from a neighbor's garden throughout the summer.

Why, exactly, did those handfuls of zucchini seeds fail to produce? we asked ourselves while planning our crops for the following year with an order for a fresh packet of seeds. Maybe it was due to low rain levels, depressed nutrients in the soil or perhaps the chickens snacked on the seeds before they could germinate. Hard to say, but for whatever reason, those zucchini seeds did not have the right environment in which to thrive that summer. Similarly, our ideas and aspirations, and our efforts to live authentically, need the right environment to flourish. Support, patience, resources and information are but a few of the variables leading to success.

Seeds also remind us of the importance of diversity. Flip through any seed catalog and one banner theme quickly blooms: strength in diversity. Reading through the actual varietal descriptions is akin to drooling over the menu at our favorite Chinese restaurant: each option is different and more intriguing than the next.

It's this collective diversity of seeds that builds vitality in both our garden beds and in our lives. In diversity is stability; if one seed doesn't germinate due to a late spring frost, heavy rain or because it became lunch for the chipmunk, other seeds will carry the day. Diversity in nature reinforces species helping and connecting with one another. The chickens molt and shed feathers which the chickadees use in nest-building. The llama droppings add rich nutrients to the soil. Purple coneflowers provide a bumblebee banquet.

Unfortunately, authentic and diverse seeds are quickly becoming an endangered element, much as human cultural diversity is being lost to fast food, television, and corporate imperialism. Monocrops, genetically modified organisms (GMOs), and corporate-owned industrial-based agriculture scream the "bigger, better, mechanized, one-size-fits-all" motto.

This is evident when we drive down our county road. Yes, the rolling green hills are dotted with postcard picturesque fields. But look closer. Row after row, field after field, are the same rows of Bt (Bacillus thuringiensis spliced) corn with some Roundup-Ready soybeans contoured in — crops grown for animal feed, not food for human consumption. Ironically, we live in the heartland of American agriculture, yet we'd struggle to make a healthy, balanced meal out of anything grown on many of the surrounding farms. The Rockwellian image of farmers sitting down to hearty home-cooked fare, freshly picked from the farm garden, has become only that — a painting. Instead, folks around here eat much the same as folks in the rest of the US, purchasing their prepackaged foods at the supermarket.

Until the middle of the last century, farms were diversified, integrated family-based enterprises. Chickens pooped and naturally fertilized the garden; surplus chicken eggs were sold for extra income. Seeds were saved for next year's garden or crop. Chores were shared and the family was fed by the food grown on premise. Our farmstead once reflected such diversity, and it's something we are trying to gradually recreate, on more sustainable terms for today's times. Our chickens

BACKYARD BIODIVERSITY

According to Kenny Ausubel, founder of Seeds of Change and author of *Seeds of Change – The Living Treasure: The Passionate Story of the Growing Movement to Restore Biodiversity and Revolutionize the Way We Think About Food*, backyard biodiversity is becoming the prime territory for the conservation of life. The gardens, small row crops, and the seed saver exchanges are where the fate of life-sustaining biodiversity rests. Taking this to heart and to task at Inn Serendipity and also at Inn Serendipity Woods, our over-arching goal is to intentionally foster plant, animal and fungal diversity, while considering how the land can also meet our needs and be used as a tool for others to reconnect with nature. While new to the biodiversity business, we've already noticed increasing bird populations and the arrival of frogs. Our pursuits offer us the opportunity to grow and learn about the life forces around us, and become better caretakers.

have taken up residence in the coop, after an absence of about forty years. The old granary is now a strawbale-insulated greenhouse. An easy-access herb bed is right out the back door, vigorously greeting guests with a whiff of basil and chives. Llamas reign over the former alfalfa field and are the new tenants of our dairy barn.

We are often inspired by stories from our neighbor Burnette. A retired farmer, Burnette has lived his whole life in this area and has seen farming evolve from his parent's generation to today. Burnette remembers the healthy soil when he learned to farm from his father. Nobody did things specifically organic back then; it was just the way things were done, and it made sense. Call it sensible agriculture. Rebuild soil nutrients with compost and manure; be self-sufficient in meeting your family's food needs from the garden; selectively use farm equipment; cultivate cooperation with neighboring farms. As Burnette came of age in the 1950s, the United States government created the Future Farmers of America (FFA), which promoted the use of nitrate (left over from the war), and other chemicals, allowing the farmer to grow more, bigger and quicker. Burnette, as most farmers of his generation, spent the majority of their working years conventionally farming in this new-fangled manner.

In the years since his retirement, Burnette has seen the quality of the soil around him degenerate, and nutrient rich top soil disappear down rivers and streams. Meadowlarks no longer sing and water tables and wells become increasingly contaminated with high nitrate levels. Rains do not replenish quickly enough the water used for agriculture, in homes, or for other purposes. Today, farmers have one of the highest rates of cancer and other illnesses.

Burnette has changed his mind on the use of chemical pesticides and fertilizers; he now gardens organically in his own vegetable plot, taking pride in his bountiful and beautiful potato harvest. He's lived through the changes of modern agriculture and has come full circle. We have much to learn from him as we plant our seeds for a more sustainable future. Today, it's the retired farmers like Burnette or the new generation of farmers and homesteaders who are recognizing sensible agriculture as one of the many solutions to restoring balance on Earth.

THE SIXTH EXTINCTION

The planet is presently undergoing an epoch of the sixth extinction. Unlike the first five that have covered the earth and of which the disappearing Dinosaurs is the most famous, the sixth extinction is primarily a result of human activities and happening at a geological pace far faster than any other period of mass extinction.

Widespread habitat destruction, human over population, climate change, rampant disease, and the uncontrolled introduction of exotic, or non-native, animals and plants have contributed to the loss of biodiversity and unprecedented extinctions, threatening the very basis of evolution itself. While extensively documented by the World Watch Institute, United Nations Environmental Program and many other scientifically-based research organizations, the current level of extinction has yet to reach the critical threshold, beyond which restoration will no long become viable. That said, millions of people globally are struggling for their survival — to meet basic food, water and shelter needs — while every ecosystem is clearly in decline.

Seeds and the Patenting of Life

There are many types of seeds available in the marketplace. At Inn Serendipity, we're striving to plant organically-propagated, heirloom and traditional-based (open-pollinated) hybrid seeds.

- **Heirlooms and traditionals (open-pollinated).** According to the Seed Savers Exchange, if you want variety, superior flavor, unusual colors and shapes and unique histories, heirloom gardening is a wonderful alternative to growing the F1 hybrids (see below) featured predominately by many large seed companies. Most home gardeners and growers don't need tomatoes with skins tough enough to withstand cross-country shipment, or potatoes that will pass the fast food's uniformity tests.

Since the 1940s, hybrid seeds have been the most-marketed varieties to home gardeners. Choices grew increasingly smaller as the seed companies discarded those varieties that did not fit the factory-farm, monoculture mold. As a result, an entire generation has grown up believing that all tomatoes are red, round and identical in taste — we're among this generation. Heirloom gardening has changed attitudes and discriminatory tastes. There are hundreds of different tomato varieties, and although some are red and round, there are many others with incredibly complex flavors and a virtual rainbow of colors!

- **Hybrids (multiple generation).** Hybrids are seeds based on the genetic offspring of two patented parent crosses, which are often patented by a seed company. These hybrids that are open-pollinated will reproduce, allowing seeds to be saved from one year to the next. As far as hybrid seeds go, these are the seeds that we also support.

- **Hybrids (first generation – F1).** F1 hybrids are seeds based on the genetic offspring of two parent crosses. These hybrids do not reproduce true to form, which results in growers having to reorder seeds every year. We try to avoid these seeds.

• **Genetically modified organisms (GMOs).** Also called GE (genetically engineered) or transgenic plants, these are the newest entry in the seed market and perhaps the most dangerous, since so little is known about their long term effects or their impact on the environment. GMOs take the genes of different species and splice them to create an entirely new plant-plant — or plant-animal. Animal or fungus genes have been spliced into plant genes to create a new plant. We never plant GMOs.

SOURCES AND RESOURCES

Seed Savers Exchange
   3076 North Winn Road, Decorah, IA 52101
   Telephone: 563-382-5990
   Website: www.seedsavers.org
   Non-profit organization dedicated to saving heirloom (handed-down) seeds from extinction.

Native Seeds Search
   526 N. 4th Avenue, Tucson, AZ 85705
   Telephone: 520-622-5561

Website: www.nativeseeds.org
Non-profit organizations that seeks to preserve the crop seeds that connect Native American cultures to their lands.

Suzanne Ashworth, *Seed to Seed: Seed Saving Techniques for the Vegetable Gardener,* Seed Savers Publications, 2002.

Organically Grown

"Is that what you call organic gardening?" asked a neighbor, gazing at our lawn.

Since arriving, entire swaths of the tidy grass lawn the former owners had meticulously mowed are being torn out by us. Our goal was to replace grass with various native perennial ground covers and other shrubs and bushes, so that we wouldn't need to spend time pushing a lawnmower around. We wanted to surround ourselves with a habitat that would readily flourish on its own without the need for pesticides and fertilizers. But this is a work in progress, and at one point — noticed by our neighbor — our lawn looked like a wild Wisconsin jungle as we battled the weeds that tried to overtake the newly planted perennials.

We explained our plans and long-term vision to our neighbor. He didn't mean harm, he just saw something that from his viewpoint ran wild and unkempt, therefore organic, something some folks were into nowadays. It may have appeared that by growing organically we were doing nothing, allowing things to amble and grow as they may. But this wasn't the case. Rather, we quickly learned that growing organically takes time. Enriching the soil naturally takes longer than spraying an annual fertilizer dose. Yet we realized through this experience that using the organic label in describing ourselves and our growing practices would require commitment, current information and an amiable attitude.

Multiple reasons motivate us to grow and eat organically. Health factors play an overriding role. The more research coming out linking various diseases and conditions to modern toxicity, the greater our incentive to be careful of what we put in our bodies. Safety to growers is a concern as well, as we see senior retired farmers around us afflicted with cancers and other ailments possibly caused by years of chemical spraying in the fields.

Whenever we return home after being away for a couple of days during the growing season, we'll almost immediately head outside to reconnect with the garden to see what's new. We marvel at how quickly that fresh bed of perpetual spinach added a few inches. We tie a sweet pea vine back to the trellis and tenderly touch a yellowing zucchini vine, concerned that it may be an invasion of the squash vine borer. Water the lettuce greens, weed around the raspberries, nibble on a strawberry. The bee balm show off their new blooms, preening in the breeze; the cherry tomatoes offer Liam their first fruits of the harvest, which he readily devours.

Our relationship with the garden is reciprocal, like two old friends connecting over a pot of tea. Such an intimate, hands-on relationship with our food source lets us bond out there with the basil and black currants. These garden homecomings reconfirm our desire to grow organically. Once we learned to see the land as a friend, how could we treat it any other way than with the utmost respect and care?

Our organic gardening approach parallels our lifestyle philosophy: healthy plants thrive in healthy soil. If the growing medium is rich in nutrients and provides the plants a healthy environment, seeds readily germinate, roots form and plants thrive. Rather than wait for a problem to erupt, such an approach stimulates preventative practice. We sow clovers in our garden pathways and dormant fields to increase nitrogen and protect the soil. A fall application of compost enriches the beds with the soil's equivalent of Thanksgiving dinner, a buffet of nourishment to replace what we ended up harvesting and eating the previous season.

MAKING HOMEMADE FERTILIZER: COMPOST

Large piles of organic material make up our compost heaps. Inside the piles, bacteria, fungi and insects are at work breaking down layers of kitchen scraps, plants, straw, chicken manure and weeds. Heat, a by-product of decomposition, helps destroy harmful microorganisms and weed seeds. Temperatures can rise to as high as 160 degrees Fahrenheit (71°C) within the piles as they age, though our slow compost piles are much cooler and therefore take longer to produce rich humus. (Fast compost is created by frequent turning of the pile, producing a rich, crumbly humus in about three months.) The piles can be occasionally watered, to keep moist. Aeration of the pile can be done to speed the decomposition process by turning the compost pile with a pitchfork or potato fork. When added to garden beds, the humus replenishes nutrients removed when the crops were harvested. Humus also improves soil structure and creates a spongy texture that helps the soil absorb and hold water efficiently. At Inn Serendipity, our slow compost is ready every six to eight months.

Making compost is easy. Dry, coarse vegetation, such as twigs and corn stalks, forms the bottom layer of the compost pile; this is covered with kitchen scraps and green vegetation, including weeds, grasses, and leaves, and topped with soil and a source of nitrogen, like chicken manure. These alternating layers are formed until the pile reaches a height of about three or four feet. The walls of the compost heap can be constructed by matting loose straw. Bacteria use the nitrogen as they break down the vegetation into a nutrient-rich humus. Worms also help speed up the process of decomposition by digesting the organic matter, leaving nutrient-rich castings.

As long as the pile allows air to move through and aid in the decomposition process, the compost pile will not smell foul. Keeping meat scraps out of the pile also helps, keeping away scavengers and avoiding possible pathogens. This active, aerobic decomposition process stands in direct contrast to the infamous — and smelly — decomposition process that occurs in an outhouse, which is anaerobic. The best compost pile is one that doesn't smell!

When spreading the humus, a little compost goes a long way; application should be done evenly and sparingly. Sifting the humus helps separate particles and any clumps that exist. Ideally, the humus should be worked into the first couple inches of soil.

Adapted in part from the publication *Self-Guided Tour of the Farm*, from the Center of Agroecology and Sustainable Food Systems at the University of California at Santa Cruz.

This was a new approach for us, the idea of focusing on the soil — the foundation of life — rather than troubleshooting plant problems. Conventional farming and gardening typically blankets entire crops with a clever cure: Spray the corn with pesticide; dust the flower beds with a fungicide.

We tended to take the same quick fix mentality in other parts of our life, so we could appreciate the lure of the spray-and-solve-it solution created by advertisers. Make the crisis of the moment go away and move on.

As we used an organic approach to gardening, we witnessed how tomatoes bloomed and bumblebees buzzed. We started thinking big picture, stepping out of our day-to-day details, envisioning plans for wind turbines, writing projects and having a baby. We started gleaning ways to improve our daily routines: how can we work in more exercise, green vegetables and down time alone for just the two of us? Like the gardens, the more we prioritize nurturing the quality of our lives, the greater we thrive.

LIFELINES

If all else fails, we can always go back to the cubicle.

This was — and still is — a refrain in the back of our minds, a coping technique when life at the farm teeters on the edge. The well pump dies, real estate taxes increase, a spring lightning storm surges through and fries the fax machine — again.

There is empowerment in the knowledge that we could go back to the life we once had, even if we dread the thought. We could clear the cobwebs off the suits and update our resumes. Returning in some capacity to the corporate routine would yield more regular paychecks. Just knowing that we could go back to where we've been provides enough of a sense of a safety net to allow us to keep going, a confidence boost to take risks in new directions. Of course, a good dose of sarcasm also helps us deal with these trying times, usually followed by another dose of good humor and a big bowl of ice cream.

A deeper sense of inspiration helping us to weather those tough times comes from our community of friends and family. They're our lifelines, keeping us connected, encouraging us to remain on course to reach our dreams.

We tap into these lifelines in different ways. When Lisa needs a boost, she may vent through e-mail to girlfriends across the country, knowing she will receive back re-affirming, butt-kicking, "you go girl" replies. John anticipates the larger-scale events where we are surrounded by a large group of like-minded people, such as a weekend at a renewable energy fair or our July 4th Reunion, a gathering of friends, family and community.

Other lifelines, ways we keep plugging away through tough times, include:

- **Keep income project focused.** During those times when it feels like we're overwhelmed with problems and stress, it's sometimes challenging to keep focused on the bigger picture. We need to remind ourselves that an important slice of this reality is the need to continue generating income. This means prioritizing and focusing on current income-generation opportunities to keep the cash flowing, and not getting caught up in projects and issues that don't need to be handled right away. Finishing a magazine article on deadline takes priority over making strawberry pies with the buckets of berries overloading the refrigerator. If they sit too long, we'll just make wine instead.

- **Keep diversified.** A continual life theme that magnifies during tough times: the greater the number of options and ideas we have in the hopper, the more opportunity and inspiration we have.

- **Keep up relationships.** We all have times when we need to lean on family and friends — be it for emotional, financial or physical support. But we've learned that, like so many other elements of life, such support comes from relationships that are mutually fostered over time, inviting folks over for supper or dropping by some of our zucchini surplus is important; when those tough times roll around, we'll have a foundation of support from which to draw. Living more independently does not exclude letting in the community of friends and neighbors; in fact, we've found that greater independence seems to thrive most when interdependence is fostered.

- **Keep communicating.** It's a rough day: the phone keeps ringing, a neighbor's dog just nabbed a chicken, we're out of coffee, Liam is whiny, and a cloud of deadlines are hanging over our heads. Hardly the ideal environment for some blissful good-life experiences, but we'll regularly connect, perhaps later in the evening or early the next morning when things quiet down, to regroup. Collaboratively and cooperatively, we determine what needs to be done and who is responsible for what, making sure to quickly place an order for more coffee.

Of course, despite healthy environments, there is still day-to-day pest and crisis management in the garden just as there is in our lives. Cucumber beetles attack the pickle patch and need to be hand-picked off and squished. Liam's new teeth are breaking in and he's grumpy and in need of attention. We book a last minute B&B reservation and quickly need to get the house guest-ready. The back-up furnace won't start, the refrigerator motor won't stop. In the garden, and in life, we can weather these daily hurdles more readily when our foundations are strong.

How to

Organic Gardening Strategies

Natural ecosystems are self-regenerating; nutrients continually recycle through ecosystems when plants and animals die and decompose. But agricultural systems work differently: their products — crops — are not returned to the soil. Rather, the products are shipped off to market along with the nutrients and organic matter. To enrich the soil, conventional farmers apply chemical fertilizers. These inputs provide crops with an abundance of nutrients, but these nutrients can also leach away, often into drinking water sources, rivers, and lakes. This is happening at such a rate, for example, that a dead zone in the Gulf of Mexico the size of the state of Massachusetts is being caused by nitrates washing down the Mississippi River and spilling into the gulf. Conventional agriculture also depends on synthetic pesticides to control insects, diseases and weeds, and on heavy equipment to cultivate and harvest crops. In addition to burning non-renewable fossil fuels, heavy equipment also causes soil compaction and erosion. Instead of following this damaging cycle, we have embarked on a long-term journey to rebuild the soil on our land and foster ecological diversity. The following are just a few of the many organic gardening strategies possible (adapted in part from the Center for Agroecology and Sustainable Food Systems at the University of California at Santa Cruz).

+ **Beneficial Insect Allies.** Although insects are often thought of as garden pests, many insects are actually allies. Some of these beneficial insects help keep pest populations in check; others pollinate plants. Beneficial insects found in the gardens include ladybugs, which feed on aphids and other small, soft-bodied insects; many types of wasps, whose larvae feed on such pests as leaf miners and various caterpillars; and lacewings, which also eat aphids.

- **Variety, Diversity and Polyculture.** In natural ecosystems, many different plants and animals live together, each with its own ecological niche. This diversity creates a balance of predators and prey, and inhibits the outbreak of pests or diseases. The garden mimics nature's greater diversity by including many different types of vegetables, fruits, flowers, and herbs; these provide a variety of habitats for birds and beneficial spiders and insects. We try to plant or encourage the growth of as many different plants as possible in our food gardens as well as on the rest of the farm. In contrast, conventional agricultural practices rely on the efficiency of monocrops, which tend to attract large numbers of pests and fewer beneficial insects, thus requiring vast amounts of chemicals to control and combat pests and stave off diseases.

- **High-Density Planting.** The rich, well-aerated soil conditions created by adding compost and raising the beds can support a high density of plants. In some beds, the seedlings are spaced so that the leaves of the mature plants will touch the adjacent plants; the canopy they create reduces evaporation from the soil and inhibits weed growth.

- **Crop Rotation.** To help minimize insect pressures and to maintain high soil nutrient levels, crops are rotated, which means the same crop is never planted in the same place as it was the previous season. Often, crops are rotated based upon which families they're from; for example carrots (root crop) might follow lettuce or spinach (leaf crop).

- **Intercropping and Interplanting.** Growing more than one type of crop in the same plot, or growing crop and non-crop plants together, may limit pest problems and in some cases, increase the yield from each crop. This is called intercropping or interplanting. Deep- and shallow-rooted plants can be grown together because they draw water and nutrients from different soil layers. Shade-tolerant vegetables, such as lettuce and radishes, can be grown beneath trellised cucumbers or peas, which prefer sun.

• **Mulching.** Mulching is the process of adding several inches of organic matter such as straw, grass clippings or leaves, on top of the soil. This helps preserve moisture in the soil and inhibits weed growth. Additionally, as the mulch layer decays, it adds nutrients to the soil. However, some types of mulch, such as wood chips, can tie up nutrients as they break down, thus temporarily decreasing soil fertility.

• **Green Manures and Cover Crops.** Rather than having compacted soil or woodchipped pathways, we planted Dutch white clover, to serve both as a green manure and as a cover crop. Serving much the same purpose as composted manure, cover crops of this green manure help hold the soil in place and provide nitrogen through the nitrogen-fixing bacteria in their roots. When tilled into the soil, they decompose and release this nitrogen.

• **French Intensive Raised Beds.** We also use French intensive organic techniques in our growing beds. Such techniques include spacing plants close together in raised beds that include application of compost and other natural fertilizers and nutrients. This practice is used by French market gardeners to maximize yields from small plots of land.

SOURCES AND RESOURCES

Center for Agroecology & Sustainable Food Systems
  Website: www.zzyx.UCSC.edu/casfs/
  Many of the farming definitions and gardening technique descriptions we've used here we owe to the Center for Agroecology & Sustainable Food Systems, University of California Santa Cruz; for more information, visit them online.

Gardens Alive!
  Website: www.GardensAlive.com
  From helping preventing powdery mildew on phlox to improving our apple crop, this mail order catalog offers biological control options to deal with common garden problems.

Eliot Coleman, *The New Organic Grower: A Master's Manual of Tools and Techniques for the Home and Market Gardener*, Chelsea Green, 1995.

Fern Marshall Bradley and Barbara W. Ellis, *Rodale's All-New Encyclopedia of Organic Gardening: The Indispensable Resource for Every Gardener*, Rodale Press, 1992.

Life Lessons in the Starter Garden

A garden is a mirror to your soul; that dark, chocolate-brown soil may seem non-reflective, but the amount of dirt under our fingernails is directly proportional to the insights we learn about ourselves through gardening. We didn't fully realize the power these garden plantings would have — that our rows of sugar snap peas would add more to our lives than just the crunch in our salads.

We originally regarded the garden as something we were in charge of, something we created and controlled to serve our own desire to feed ourselves fresh fruits and vegetables. We skimmed our library of gardening books and radiated a smug, naive attitude. With each passing season, however, we realized we were the pupils under the garden's tutelage. The garden as teacher, as a compass providing direction and insight into our modern lives, became a refrain throughout each growing season.

Our three main gardening fields stretch east of the farmhouse, expanding to take care of our needs over the years. We enter the garden area by walking past the perennial bed and under an arched white wooden trellis.

Walking under the trellis to enter the garden is like walking through cathedral doors, crossing over into our sacred growing space. Most of the time we speed under the trellis without any thought for the sanctified. Still, the trellis silently and proudly honors the raspberry patch, the tomatoes ripening on the vine and even the bunny pilfering lettuce leaves. It's a constant reminder that we are no more than temporary custodians of this place, privileged to be blessed by the beauty of the flowers and nourished by the vegetables, fruits and herbs that grow here.

Our planting criteria in the garden is rather simple: plant what we like to eat, balanced with what grows well given our soil and relatively short growing season, although we try to experiment a little every year. The core of our growing focus is what we personally relish on our plate: various greens, potatoes, onions, broccoli, beets, cabbage, squashes, and an abundance of tomatoes and sugar snap peas. The garden came with perennials: raspberries, asparagus, rhubarb and a hearty horse-radish plant for which we haven't yet developed an appreciation; we've also added several strawberry beds that have taken off to the point that if you say the word June, we start to salivate and fantasize over that first fresh strawberry of the season.

Still, particularly during those early growing seasons, we harbored some unrealistic images of the quintessential, neat and tidy garden with nary a weed in view. Well, that idea went straight to the compost heap around late June, when everything, including those chronic weeds, were growing in multiple directions. Quack grass ambushed the lettuce bed. Wild morning glory vines strangled the tomato plants. On an organic farm, especially in the first transitional years, weeds will be a part of the garden and will need to be regarded as a lingering part of the natural ecosystem. We have learned about the value in taking preventative measures, such as using mulch for weed control. Hoeing weeds a few times a month without disturbing much of the surface of the soil avoids the more labor intensive task of pulling weeds later (or forgetting about the weeds and letting them go to seed). Cutting down weeds at this "white root" stage allows us to leave them to decay where they lay, thus increasing the organic matter in topsoil.

More than just the planning and planting, weeding and mulching, the garden reminds us to not take ourselves — and life — too seriously. Let berry juice dribble down our chins and let our pant knees get dirty. Living is fun, or at least it should be most of the time. We're OK with laughing at ourselves; there's power in humor. We're never going to control the marionette strings of life, nor are we going to capture every potato beetle and pick every strawberry before it falls to the ground to rot. We can name our farm Inn Serendipity, but the gardens still remind us to live it.

A prime example was when our friends in town, John and Mary, gave us a brown paper bag stuffed with soybean seeds. The dried soybeans were still in their shells, so we cleaned out a handful of the beans and planted them in a tidy row in the garden. We waited and watered and waited some more. Not a single plant came up. We tossed the still large bag of unshelled soybeans into the junk drawer by the backdoor and promised to research planting how-to's more thoroughly next season.

The following spring we were back planting the garden. We had put in a long but productive day with the help of many friends, and had planted most of the garden, crouched over those neat little rows again. It was late in the afternoon and we were racing to finish before a rainstorm hit. We planted the last seed packet and were about ready to usher in quitting time when we found that bag of soybeans in the junk drawer. Our energy was waffling. Gone were the neat little rows and to hell with shelling those bean pods: we ran outside as the rain started to cascade down and scattered the beans in an open corner of the garden. We didn't even push them down into the soil. Just tossed them and kicked a bit of mulch on top. The brown paper bag was left on the ground to slowly decompose. We ran back inside and promptly forgot about those soybeans.

How does the story end? That part of the garden that we had invested the least amount of time and effort proved to be the most prolific of the season. Those soybean plants popped up like jack-in-the-boxes.

It took an army of little green soybean plants to remind us to savor serendipity. We're not advocating gardening without plans, clearly delineated rows, crop rotations, or any of the other time-proven organic strategies. For healthy soil and healthy plants, such an approach is a must. But sometimes, if you're open and willing to throw caution to the wind, take a detour, and try broadcasting seeds randomly under foreboding skies, these actions can flavor our lives with fate and chance, resulting in a bumper crop of life. Or in our case, soybeans.

How to

Permaculture Design and Edible Landscaping

Permaculture was developed by Bill Mollison and David Homgren in Australia during the 1970s. As clearly explained by Rosemary Morrow in *The Earth User's Guide to Permaculture*, it came about in response to soil, water and air pollution resulting from agricultural and industrial systems; the increasing loss of animal and plant species; decreased natural non-renewable resources, and an increasingly destructive economic system.

Based on the principles of ecology — the study of interrelationships and interdependence of living creatures — permaculture is about designing sustainable human settlements. It is a flexible approach which encourages us to become a conscious part of the solutions to the problems we face, both locally and globally, and requires keen observation and a commitment to work with, not against, nature.

Permaculture has been developed around a set of ethics and principles which serve as guidelines for a truly diverse set of strategies and techniques, uniquely appropriate for the locale. Permaculture can be applied just about anywhere that can sustain life. At Inn Serendipity, we aim to live this approach.

Because permaculture is a holistic, system-based approach, it helps preserve genetic diversity, respects the right to life for all species, and uses species and habitats sustainably to preserve life-sustaining processes. In creating a permaculture plan, our farm is broken into zones, each with interrelated purposes and ecological connections, although not all zones are needed to use permaculture; in many cases, the zones blend, overlap or combine.

PRINCIPLES OF PERMACULTURE

- **Everything works at least two ways.** Example: chickens clean up pests and weeds, and provide eggs.

- **See solutions, not problems.** Example: Mollison saying: "You don't have a snail problem, you have a duck deficiency."

- **Co-operation — not competition — in work, communications, and economics.** Example: share information and ideas so people can learn to live sustainably.

- **Make things pay.** Example: recycle gray water and compost organic waste.

- **Work where it counts.** Example: only weed if you plan to replant immediately, otherwise you'll be weeding again within the month.

- **Use everything to its highest capacity.** Example: use sunlight to grow your plants, warm your house, heat your hot water and cook your lunch.

- **Bring food production back to the cities — and backyards.** Example: grow your own vegetables and fruit and raise chickens and bees in the backyard.

- **Help make people self-reliant.** Example: collect your own water and generate your own electricity.

- **Minimize maintenance and energy inputs to achieve maximum yields.** Example: locate garden beds where they are easily accessible and use a drip irrigation system.

Source: Adaped in part and used with permission from
The Earth User's Guide to Permaculture, by Rosemary Morrow,
Simon & Schuster (Australia) Limited, Kangaroo Press, 2000.

The permaculture zones for Inn Serendipity are summarized below:

- **Zone 0: Living space.** Our house. By retrofitting with renewable energy and implementing water and energy conservation measures, we preserve the Earth's resources. Adopting more ecologically sound natural materials in our home helps us achieve greater health and well-being.

- **Zone 1: The home kitchen garden.** The diversity of vegetables and small fruits in the north, south, and far south raised beds, as well as herbs found in our back door bed, all of which can be visited frequently and are located conveniently near the house. For most of the food we eat, we rely on what grows well in our gardens — and what we enjoy eating. We care for three main growing fields just east of our house: the north field, measuring 40 by 70 feet (12 x 21 m); the south field, measuring 50 by 82 feet (15 x 25 m); and the far south field, measuring 40 by 48 feet (12 x 15 m). In these fields are thirty raised bed rows of tomatoes, potatoes, spinach, beets, beans, peppers, cabbage, lettuce, strawberries, pumpkins, zucchini, broccoli, cucumbers, onions, carrots, and a variety of "experimental" crops, such as collard greens and swiss chard. Similar to the Victory gardens of the 1940s, our gardens consistently provide fresh fruits and vegetables, for which we don't have to leave the farm.

- **Zone 2: The orchard area.** Our food forest located further away from the house, consisting of red, golden and snow apple trees and a dwarf cherry tree, visited when the fruit ripen. We added grapes along the driveway and planted black currants adjacent to garden beds as part of edible landscaping.

- **Zone 3: Crop fields.** This zone features larger scale food crops like oats, corn, potatoes; or a large scale orchard or area for growing nuts; or used as forage for animals (cows, sheep, or goats). In our case, Zone 3 is used as an alfalfa field and llama pasture.

- **Zone 4: Woodlot or forest.** While a woodlot is not practical for our small acreage, we planted pine and spruce trees along the perimeter to serve as windbreaks. They will also provide wildlife with shelter and movement corridors.

- **Zone 5: Natural forest.** While this is absent on the farm property, the focus at the 30-acre (12 ha) Inn Serendipity Woods cabin and wildlife sanctuary is reforestation and silviculture, the sustainable management of forests.

Edible landscaping means designing with nature; cultivating plants that provide needed foods for ourselves as well as for wildlife in our area. We find ourselves grazing while walking around the farm, since so many fruits and vegetables ripen at different times of the year. And because no chemical insecticides, fungicides or herbicides are used, we can nibble away right in the garden.

By creating an edible landscape, we're maintaining, establishing or expanding plantings of raspberries, grapes, cherries, apples, black currants, strawberries and a wide selection of herbs (including dill, basil, cilantro, lemon balm, chives). Outdoor spaces are carefully designed to permit quiet, peaceful environments, separate from the operating farm. The wall of grapes added along the front driveway, for example, separates the driveway space (and hammock) under the two maple trees adjacent to the pond. With the addition of the pond as well as evergreens, shrubs, and other plantings, our nature-scaping efforts have led to a wildlife explosion — we even discovered a red fox having a drink from the pond one morning.

USED WITH PERMISSION FROM *THE EARTH USER'S GUIDE TO PERMACULTURE*, BY ROSEMARY MORROW, SIMON & SCHUSTER AUSTRALIA, KANGAROO PRESS, 2000.

TIME

RESOURCES

PEOPLE
SKILLS AND KNOWLEDGE

EARTH
ECOLOGICAL COMPONENTS

BASE PLAN

OBSERVATION
DEDUCTION
ANALYSIS
MAPPING
EXPERIENTIAL
READING PATTERNS

SOILS
WATER
CLIMATE
MICROCLIMATE
PLANTS
ANIMALS

SITE ANALYSIS (INVENTORY PLAN)

PROFICIENCY

IMPROVED BIOLOGICAL RESOURCES

SECTOR ANALYSIS

DESIGN
* IMPOSING PATTERNS
* ZONES AND SECTORS
* MAKING CONNECTIONS

DESIGN
ZONE 0
ZONE I
ZONE II
ZONE III
ZONE IV
ZONE V

GOALS
* SUSTAINABLE LAND USE AT YOUR PLACE
* MEET YOUR OWN NEEDS
* HIGH YIELDS
* LOW MAINTENANCE
* NON-POLLUTING
* DIVERSITY

IMPLEMENTION

The permaculture design process.

SOURCES AND RESOURCES

Rosemary Morrow, *Earth User's Guide to Permaculture,* Simon & Schuster (Australia), Kangaroo Press, 2000.

Bill Mollison and Reny Mia Slay, *Introduction to Permaculture,* Tagari Publications, 1991.

Bill Mollison, *Permaculture: A Designer's Manual,* Tagari Publications, 1988.

Circle of Life

Naked trees, below zero wind chills, icy sidewalks and crusty dry skin. Welcome to winter in Wisconsin. Winter is a tough time of the year to love, but it has been growing on us. It lacks the newness of spring, the warmth of summer, or the fiery colors of fall. But every year, as we grow closer to the seasons, the blessings of winter magnify.

Nature needs the winter to grow dormant, to lay fallow, and restock for future blooms. So do we, as humans, need such a time period. Our soul reflects the landscape, the season surrounding us. The January garden appears to be as alive as a hot dog bun that has been left in the freezer too long: dry, frozen, seemingly lacking any future potential. But underneath the icy hard soil, magic is germinating. The soil may technically be resting and dormant, but scratch the surface and you'll find nutrients being restored with coffee grounds settling in under the mulch. Clip one of the branches in the raspberry patch: the brown dry bark breaks to reveal new green layers ready for spring.

> When we, as humans, realize that we are not the only intelligent life on this planet, it changes us. We feel the connections and realize how our actions affect all life on earth. To watch a fruit tree being transformed — from seeming lifelessness to a bounty of lush pink blossoms, to a vibrant ball of green leaves, then to fruit, and then to dormancy again — is to see the divine in action.
> — Shatoiya and Richard de la Tour, *The Herbalist's Garden*

Even in the dead of winter, the garden is richly alive, regenerating itself for the next growing season. We had lost touch with this essence of being alive during our corporate cubicle stint; surrounded by synthetic walls, recirculated air and processed food products; thousands of feet of concrete separated us from the earth and its natural cycles. Today, each season, including winter, invites us to witness and participate in the circle of life.

Raspberries are one example of how the garden is an active part of our life throughout the seasons. In February or March we eagerly jump into our first official garden duty: pruning the raspberry bushes. We bundle up, clippers in hand, and head into the patch to cut dead branches to the ground. These branches, which were rich and heavy with berries during the previous season, take on a new role as mulch. Being outdoors and actively gardening at this time of year, even as the winter winds blow, is invigorating.

By mid-July, our raspberry patch gifts us with a smattering of fruit, followed by a more bountiful crop in August that continues until our first frost in mid-October. We pick raspberry seeds from our teeth for most of the summer, indulging in fresh berries nearly every day; it's impossible to walk past the patch and not do a little sampling. We make a few batches of raspberry jam and about two gallons of raspberry cordial, and we tray freeze the rest in their juicy natural state. The defrosted berries are perfect for topping a January angel food cake while gazing out the window at the dormant raspberry patch. ·

Winter dormancy is an important part of both the raspberry cycle and our own cycle of living. However, we're often guilty of ignoring the restorative power of dormancy found in winter. The raspberry bush doesn't cling to those last leaves and keep pumping out berries; it gives in and takes a needed rest. It doesn't fight or ignore this process. Maybe our problem is that we seriously think we're above and independent from natural cycles; instead of restorative dormancy, we have to hit burnout, our creative juices and optimism wrung dry, before we'll take a break.

We align with winter and emulate the bare landscape by retreating and hibernating. We use these cold months to rekindle our

RASPBERRY CORDIAL RECIPE

Ingredients
- 2 quarts raspberries
- 2 quarts 190-200 proof whole grain alcohol. Can also use a high proof/cheap vodka - works just as well. One 190 proof bottle is a little more than 1 quart.
- 2 quarts water
- 2 lbs. sugar (about 2½ cups)

Preparation Instructions
- Mix raspberries and alcohol and cover (an old two-quart size pickle jar works well) Let sit two weeks. Raspberries will turn white as alcohol turns red.
- Strain raspberries into a sieve.
- Mix water and sugar. Heat until dissolved.
- Mix water/sugar mixture with raspberry mixture.
- Bottle and age at least six months. Old vodka bottles can be reused and the cordial lasts indefinitely.

creative sides, plan new projects, catch up on loose ends, sleep more, and experiment with new soup recipes. When the fall harvest is in high gear and we're freezing tomato sauce like mad, mulching the garden and running around trying to soak in every last warm ray of sun, we start craving winter. We start the annual winter project list, things we'll get to when we can retreat and focus. One winter John worked with Paul, our contractor, to replace many of our leaky windows with double-pane insulated ones. We watched all three parts of *The Godfather* on video. Lisa experimented with baking authentic sour dough rye bread, worthy of her Estonian and Latvian heritage. John plotted next spring's garden, with books and notes in organized piles. Catch up on social e-mail, make Valentines, linger over conversations sipping cocoa. The bulk of the writing for this book happened under winter's spell. Why? Winter is nature's way of decluttering. Birds have migrated south, insects go into hiding. Even the color scheme is pure and simple: white.

It does take effort on our part to go dormant. The raspberry patch naturally goes dormant, it doesn't fight it or get tempted by other lower priority options. Its natural instinct is to restore and rejuvenate itself, and that is what it does. Dormancy, giving ourselves the space and time to tap into our creativity requires an open receptiveness; the willingness to clear our social schedule, eliminate TV, sit down and start some of those things we've been meaning to do. It took us a while to get in sync with winter, to step back when this season rolls around and tap into the aliveness dormancy brings. Now we crave the long nights and butternut squash soup simmering on the stove. Amazing how, at the time of year when the world appears dead and barren on the outside, the essence of newness is underneath, making preparation for a fruitful raspberry patch next season, continuing the circle of life.

How to

The War on Bugs

"Organic farming" was once called ... "farming." In the post-World War II era, a time of tremendous advancement in technology, came the discovery that petroleum-based nitrates once used in munitions could be used to boost plant growth. Rapid development of herbicides, pesticides and fungicides followed. The shift from organic farming to conventional, chemical-based farming had started, and the silent "war on bugs" had begun.

Presently, over 70,000 synthetic chemicals are now dispersed into the environment on a rather undiscriminating basis, including nearly 700 insecticides, herbicides and fungicides. Thousands of these chemicals are known to mimic the action of hormones in humans and life and are resulting, as so eloquently explained by Rachel Carson in her pivotal book, *Silent Spring*, in declining sperm counts, reproductive failures, high incidence of deformities in frogs, fish, birds, and impaired intellectual and behavioral development in human children. Scientific and medical researchers have found the overuse of antibiotics to be at least partially responsible for the growing occurrence of antibiotic-resistant bacterial infections in humans. Recombinant bovine growth hormone (rBGH) is banned in Europe and Canada, and has been possibly linked to human cancers, sterility, infertility, birth defects and immunological derangements. Despite this, and despite annual milk surpluses, rBGH continues to be widely used in the US.

This silent war continues, with collateral damage ending up on our dinner tables, on the supermarket shelves, and in the woods and watersheds, as industrialized countries around the world continue to support, permit or ignore ecological degradation.

Organic farming systems depend on the development of biological diversity and the maintenance and replenishment of soil fertility, using many of the strategies discussed throughout this book. Organic foods are minimally processed to maintain the integrity of the food without artificial ingredients, preservatives, or irradiation.

Organic livestock production prohibits the use of antibiotics and synthetic hormones in livestock. Feed must be 100 percent organic with only some vitamins allowed, and animals raised for slaughter must be raised organically from birth (by the second day for poultry), and, in sharp contrast to the confined, prison-like cells provided for animals produced at corporate farms, organic livestock must have free-roaming access to the outdoors (or an equivalent area, to be approved by certifiers).

As evidence of the dangers of chemical pesticides and fertilizers continues to mount, the organic food movement has become stronger. Organic foods can be found at natural foods stores and supermarkets, as well as at farmers' markets and through grower-direct marketing such as CSAs (Community Supported Agriculture). Spearheaded by The Chefs Collaborative, many restaurant chefs across the country are now using organic produce because they desire its superior quality and taste, and share the responsibility for the farmers who grow it.

Responsibility for the certifying and monitoring of organic food and fiber producers resides with the USDA. There are several labeling guidelines governing claims made on packaging and the use of the "USDA Organic" seal, including:

- Only 100 percent certified-organic products can be labeled as such.

- Products with 95 percent or more organic ingredients can be called organic on the primary panel of the label.

- Products with 70-95 percent organic ingredients can be described as made with organic ingredients (up to three ingredients can be listed).

◆ Products with less than 70 percent organic content may only use the term organic in the ingredient information panel.

Inn Serendipity, and related enterprises operated from the farm, are not certified organic; the time and cost associated with such certification can be difficult for small scale operations like ours to satisfy, and in our case, are largely unnecessary for us to serve our clientele. So, while no chemical pesticides or fertilizers are used on our farm, certification as an organic farm will not likely be pursued by us anytime soon.

SOURCES AND RESOURCES

Organic Consumer Association
   Website: www.organicconsumers.org
   Website with a variety of resources and activist campaigns for food safety, organic agriculture, fair trade and sustainability.

The National Organic Program
   Website: www.ams.usda.gov/nop
   Information on organic certification.

Chefs Collaborative
   Website: www.chefscollaborative.org
   National food community network promoting sustainable cuisine and the joys of local, seasonal and artisanal cooking.

Slow Food
   Website: www.slowfood.com
   From heirloom vegetables to craft-brewed beers and artisan cheeses, Slow Food is both an organization and a movement dedicated to preserving and celebrating food and drink traditions and the people and land that make it possible.

Eric Schlosser, *Fast Food Nation: The Dark Side of the All-American Meal*, Harper Collins, 2002.

Cynthia Barstow, *The Eco-Foods Guide: What's Good for the Earth is Good for You,* New Society Publishers, 2002.

Rachel Carson, *Silent Spring,* Mariner Books, 2002.

Andrew Kimbrell, *Fatal Harvest: The Tragedy of Industrial Agriculture,* Island Press, 2002.

Michael Ableman, *From the Good Earth: Traditional Farming Methods in a New Age,* Thames and Hudson, 1993.

Free Canning Jars to Good Home

At first glance, canning food seems akin to a late night cable rerun of "Father Knows Best." Quaint and nostalgic, but totally unrealistic for today's modern, allegro world. You plant green bean seeds. Spend summer mulching, weeding and irrigating. Then harvest the beans in late summer, washing and cutting the beans for canning. Sterilize jars, lids, and screw tops. Hot pack beans, process jars, cool jars, place in dark cool corner of basement. That lengthy checklist doesn't sound terribly inviting when shelves of inexpensive bean cans line every supermarket.

Why, then, were the two of us so determined to resurrect this increasingly rare activity when we moved to the farm? We felt compelled to can, to resurrect the art of preserving the harvest, and to be more self-sufficient while gaining personal satisfaction. Perhaps we were drawn to a human instinct to preserve, to "put by" some of the excess of today for the leaner times tomorrow.

The idea of preserving and storing abundant food has been an important part of rural living for generations, and for humankind since early Egyptian days, spanning methods from pickling to pasteurization. It's only been in the last forty years or so that the advances of technology have made home preserving unnecessary, with food and transportation industries creating processed, canned and otherwise preserved foods that are relatively cheap, shelf-stable and "fresh" for years.

Historically, many folks preserved and canned out of necessity, setting aside food supplies for the winter months. For years, Lisa's parents, who lived in a

Chicago suburb, would visit fruit orchards and farms to stock up with pints of strawberries and bushels of apples to turn into jam, sauce and jarred fruit. If you ask any of the retired farmers around us about their canning memories, their eyes will light up as they fondly reminisce about the pear butters, dilly beans and rhubarb marmalade. It wasn't just the taste of the food that was so fondly remembered. The whole process called out: the smell of warm strawberry jam simmering on the stove; listening for the musical plunk as lids seal to the jars; working together as a family; feeling pride and satisfaction in an end result as the motley collection of glass jars gleam on the kitchen counter like a stained glass masterpiece.

Despite living in this high technology world, many retired farmers cling to these memories, even if they are no longer able to garden. The evidence rests in the value placed on canning jars. The canning jars themselves carry little monetary value unless they happen to be rare antiques. We can buy a brand new 12-pack of Mason jars for about fifty cents a jar, and the going garage sale rate is much less.

Saving old canning jars from the recycling center or trash heap is an underground passion of ours. When we were visiting a friend one day, she noticed the assorted collection of canning jars nestled in the back hatch of our car. We sheepishly admitted that these jars were not en route to the recycling center; rather, we had rescued them from there. We're always on the lookout for abandoned canning jars and feel a sense of pride for giving these jars renewed life, housing salsa, garlic pickles or maybe an impromptu bouquet of daisies on a summertime picnic table behind the dairy barn.

When we told our friend of our canning antics she quickly offered her elderly mother's jars. Despite the fact that, for health reasons, her mother would never be able to use the jars again, our friend later confessed to us, a little embarrassed, that it seemed her mother couldn't part with the twelve cases of stacked, dusty Mason jars. But we understood completely. Those jars — even empty — provided her mom with a link to memories of bountiful good food, personal satisfaction and independence; a link to the days when she'd nurtured an extensive garden, canning for her large family. More than just fruits and vegetables had gone into those jars, and she had sealed each one with pride, satisfaction and love for her family.

A similar situation happened to our friend, Becky, also an avid canner of the new generation. Becky was visiting her mother in Stockton, Illinois, a typical small farming community. While flipping through the weekly *Shopping News*, a freebie weekly paper, Becky spotted an interesting miscellaneous category ad: "Free canning jars to a good home," followed by a local phone number. The ad was placed by the daughter of an elderly lady who just passed away, leaving, again, dusty cases of canning jars behind. Becky recounted the story of how she went to this deceased lady's house, and how the daughter had happily loaded her car with the jars. Lisa understood; the daughter probably had warm memories of the pantry shelves stacked with jars as she was growing up. She knew how important the process was to her mother, and knew that her mother would want her jars preserved by continuing in the canning tradition. No money needed to be exchanged; the inherent value was understood and appreciated.

Another reason these elderly folks cling to their canning jars is the special remembrance of a self-created product, a quality lost in today's manufactured and pre-packaged world. While strawberries multiply exponentially in late June, strawberry syrup over pancakes is a decadent, distinctive treat to be savored come January. Canned salsa over eggs adds zest to those dreary gray days of March.

It seems nothing is special anymore, when we can readily have almost anything everyday, as convenient as our local 24-hour supermarket. We indulge in chocolate truffles, imported butter cookies and credit card buying sprees throughout the year, leaving the holiday month of December as just another excuse for overindulgent gluttony, not special treats. A consumer culture tends to destroy self-reliance and commodifies everything. But everything seems to taste sweeter, more flavorful and wholesome when it's our own. There's nothing like eating what we've grown from a garden bed we tended from the early spring to harvest in the autumn.

Canning tomatoes hardly exempts us from the "buy now, buy often," world we live in. However, we can be more selective — connoisseurs of special things, times and experiences — and a bit more self-reliant. We're hardly living the life of rural deprived monks; rather, we've learned to savor the special moments when they happen.

We mix the art of preserving with some modern conveniences; for us, moving to the farm never meant back-tracking to recreate the farmstead of a century ago. Inn Serendipity is not a historic farm replication, plowed by horses, with water retrieved from a hand-cranked well. Instead, the appropriate use of today's technologies make our more sustainable existence more viable — photovoltaic and wind turbine systems meet our energy needs; a chainsaw makes working up logs for the woodstove manageable. Rather than abandon some of the technologies now available, we carefully select those tools that serve our over-arching goals, while still honoring the past, with the traditional methods of quality and craftsmanship that are often lost today. For example, our hand-cranked juicing machine and apple peeler comes from the famous Lehman's non-electric catalog. <www.lehmans.com> No batteries, or electricity, needed.

But even an heirloom process can sometimes use a 21st-century boost. As big-time tomato lovers, we use a lot of tomato sauce throughout the winter months on pizza, over pasta and in chili. As our tomato plants began to bear juicy red ripe fruit, we anticipated cooking up an authentic batch of traditional sauce. And cook up we did. Coming from a long line of hearty Italian cooks, our buddy David sent us his grandmother's tomato sauce recipe. After washing, boiling, peeling and churning the tomatoes through the strainer to get rid of the seeds, we poured the strained puree into a two-gallon pot. We chopped up fresh basil leaves and stirred those into the tomato mixture, along with a dash of salt, pepper and sugar. And then we cooked. And cooked. And cooked for several hours more to simmer off the water to produce a thick sauce. Then we hot packed the sauce in jars and, because of the high acid content of tomatoes, hot processed the jars for 35 minutes. The house smelled wonderful but, after a half day of work and 20 pounds (9 kg) of tomatoes, we ended up with just three quart jars of sauce. Sorry, Dave, but we just didn't have the kind of time or patience that Grandma had. Adding heat to an already steamy July day didn't seem to make sense either.

Enter plan B. We cut up tomatoes, skins and seeds and all, into quarter chunks. Drizzle a couple of tablespoons of olive oil into a baking dish, throw in the chopped tomatoes, add some onion chunks and garlic slices. Bake at 300 for about an hour and a half in the oven, then cool. Drain out as much of the liquid as we can (saving the liquid for a future chili pot) and dump the tomato, onion and garlic mixture in a food processor. Add salt and pepper and a big handful of fresh basil and let the processor chop until it's liquefied. Pour into freezer containers and freeze. Finito! A mega batch of tomato sauce can be prepared this way in an afternoon, and the quicker oven use preparation uses less energy than hours of simmering on the range. The sauce may not be as thick and smooth as Dave's granny's, when the time comes to use it, we sometimes simmer it in a crock pot to thicken; a nice, warm kitchen activity much more appreciated in January than in July.

We still can salsa, which to us tastes better than frozen salsa, along with canning pickles, applesauce and jam. We dehydrate apple slices for trail mix snacks, freeze grape juice and, when strawberries are in peak abundance, brew some wine. Preserving on our own terms, for our own reasons, stocks our pantry and freezer with satisfaction and gratitude.

Basics of Food Preservation

Today's modern Western world may appear to be overflowing with bounty at the supermarket, but it is all dependent on fossil fuel. Take the oil away and the supermarket shelves would be empty. Preserving the harvest is about living more self-reliantly; by preserving and saving the fruits and vegetables we grow, harvested at their peak of ripeness, flavor and nutritional value, we set aside for later, when little else grows in the snow-covered fields.

While there is a wide variety of ways to preserve food, the one thing that unites them all is their relatively low-tech approach. The following are the main methods we use to set aside foods:

- **Cold storage or root cellaring.** Perhaps the easiest form of preserving, cold storage means placing food in a cool, dark place with varying amounts of humidity, depending on the needs of the foods. The temperature needs to be kept between 32 and 40 degrees Fahrenheit (0 to 4 degrees Celcius). We store potatoes, turnips, apples, beets, and carrots in the corner of our basement, while along the north wall of our first floor, we store garlic, onions, pumpkins and winter squash because of the drier conditions.

- **Drying.** Drying, whether by air, sun or oven, is another simple means of storing foods, and helps retain more nutrients than most other preserving options. The goal is to remove the moisture from the foods so that the bacteria, molds and yeast that might cause the food to spoil cannot grow. Almost anything can be dried.

- **Canning.** Canning involves using a boiling water bath to destroy microorganisms and create a vacuum seal around the lid of the jar to prevent any remaining bacteria from reproducing. It requires sturdy canning jars, specially designed canning jar lids, and choosing the method best suited for the acidity level of the food. We use the boiling-water bath method to can strawberries, pears, apple pie filling, applesauce, salsa and pickled cucumbers.

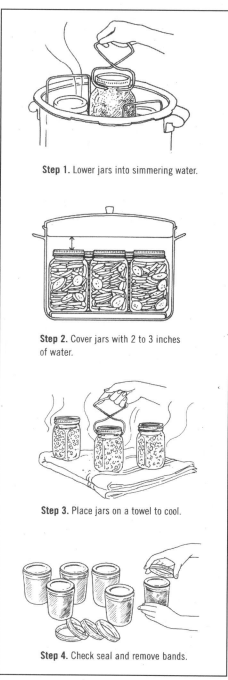

Step 1. Lower jars into simmering water.

Step 2. Cover jars with 2 to 3 inches of water.

Step 3. Place jars on a towel to cool.

Step 4. Check seal and remove bands.

The canning process used for storing tomatoes.

• **Freezing.** The latest entry in the food preservation options is made possible by the development of freezers, among the easiest way to store foods and one which locks in flavors and nutritional value better than many others. Freezers do, however, come at an environmental cost: the energy used to run the freezer, the embodied energy of the freezer itself, and the ozone-depleting freon that is used as a coolant in models built before the mid-1990s. By November of each year, our freezer is packed full with foods that will sustain us until June of the following year. Every year we freeze spinach, tomatoes, Swiss chard, apple slices, grape juice, raspberries, strawberries, black currants, broccoli, green beans, summer squash, sweet peas and rhubarb.

Food preservation is more about recipes and techniques than years of training. It has afforded us time together in the kitchen with time-proven crafts. Storing our harvest has been a communal joy which we try to make as simple and efficient as possible. As a result, most of our food preservation efforts are devoted to freezing, canning and cold storage. Like so many things in our life, preserving foods is balanced with our enjoyment of eating seasonally. Eating with the different fruits and vegetables that ripen throughout the growing season keeps our meals, tastes and attitudes fresh, diverse and creative. Because we eat a mostly meatless diet, we've never needed to preserve meat items.

SOURCES AND RESOURCES

Janet Chadwick, *Busy Person's Guide to Food Preserving*, Storey Books, 1995.

Carol Hupping, *Stocking up: The Third Edition of the Classic Preserving Guide*, Fireside, 1995.

Perennial Magic

Flats of pink petunias, begonias and impatients and pots of geraniums were the extent of our garden flower experience before moving to the farm. Growing up, we each remember our parents who, like clockwork, would buy flats of annuals mid-May, then habitually plant the transplants in rows remarkably similar to what they and their neighbors had done the year before. They'd water and fertilize the plants all summer and enjoy their blossoms until the first frost. Wait until the following spring and repeat.

Our experiences expanded dramatically with the garden that came along with the farm. The garden we "inherited" came stocked with a kaleidoscope of perennial flowers: the golden yarrow, purple irises, the deep reds of bee balm. While we understood the basic concept of a perennial flower — plant it once and it keeps growing back year after year — we didn't anticipate how the perennials would sweep us under their spell, converting us into loyal members of the perennial flower fan club.

When we say we inherited the perennial flower beds, we mean exactly that. Yes, we went through the procedures of purchasing property. But we could tell from the onset that these blooms fell into their own special category beyond legal tender. Now in her 60s, Joy, the former owner of the farm along with her husband Del, lavished tremendous love and care her flower beds. As her children grew up, her responsibilities as a mother lessened, and the size and diversity of her treasured perennial beds expanded. Joy knew her perennials so deeply that the gardens were planned around each flower's specialty and the ecological niche it filled in the perennial bed: early-spring blooming irises balanced the late fall sedum; the towering tiger lilies didn't grow right next to and overpower the lower-growing daisies; shade-tolerant hostas rimmed beds around tree trunks. Del's mother started the largest bed directly east of the farmhouse in the 1940s; her daylilies and peonies still vigorously bloom today.

We knew these gardens would evolve and change when we moved in. We weren't retirees and didn't have as much time for garden maintenance. We committed ourselves to growing organically, eliminating the option of dusting for weed and pest control, and instead of spending hours mowing the lawn, we keep adding new plants, shrubs and trees to the property, turning our land into a more biodiverse farm. The grass now remains mostly as pathways. Those perennial gardens have taken on a wild, still beautiful, native look, under our care. Volunteer plantings, made by birds or other animals, are left to grow on the west side of the farmhouse so that one day, this will resemble a naturalized — and diverse — sanctuary for wildlife and an outdoor classroom for Liam. Still, we have tremendous respect for the garden Joy bequeathed to us. Beyond the farm purchase, we have taken on the responsibility of continuing her garden, adopting her pride and joy.

The perennial flower beds bloom with surprises for us every year. In early April, we clear away the dead growth from the previous year and create a new compost pile. As spring awakens the earth, green shoots appear. By mid-May the first blooms of the season appear as purple irises pop up throughout the garden. The phlox and peonies arrive soon after, followed by day lilies, daisies and delphinium, and the rest of the perennial chorus, peaking in late July and early August with full scale fireworks of color. Through the years, the perennial flower beds have given us more than just prolific bouquets for the dining room table or our bed and breakfast guest rooms; among those roots have grown some life lessons for us to experience, through the magical classroom of nature.

After the first purple-flowered spring lilies bloomed for about a week, they did what seemed to us the unthinkable; they shriveled up and fell off and the plant died back. What?! This felt so wrong, given our petunia "training," where annuals bloomed all summer long. It didn't seem fair that the lilies hung around for such a short time. Why, we had meant to take some photos, give our neighbors a bouquet, and really enjoy them, but now they were gone.

The following day, however, the daisies revealed their petals, crisp and white throughout the garden. We realized that it was our attitude that was wrong. We wanted the garden — and our lives — to be everything all the time. Reconnecting with nature taught us the importance of appreciating the impermanence of things. The lilies, and the fireworks of flowers that successively bloomed throughout the summer, were a reminder to live fully in the moment. Take the time to burrow our noses in the fragrant peony pillows, weave daisy chain wreaths, spice up supper's salad with a sprinkling of lipstick red bee balm petals. The perennials remind us to step back and enjoy; to deeply breathe in the moment before the petals fall and disappear.

The perennials also taught us the importance of giving: the more of ourselves we give away, the more we personally flourish and thrive. Literally speaking, this is also true for perennials. This was a tough concept for us to grasp initially, as we speared our spade into the heart of the hosta plant, dividing it into four sections as if slicing pie. Chopping something up like this seemed the antithesis of helping a healthy plant along, and what would we do with those extra baby hosta plants anyway? We used some of the transplants to expand our own beds, tearing out a little bit more lawn every spring and replacing grass with perennial color and diversity. Not only did the mini hosta plants quickly grow back to their original size, but we found that there are always folks happy to expand their own garden by taking home some of our transplants. We hooked Lisa's mom on perennials, and her suburban flower beds gradually became home to hostas, purple coneflowers and black-eyed susans. We ran special "Perennial Weekends" at the B&B during the month of April, where guests could dig up assorted transplants to take home. Not only were we finding homes for the divided perennials, visitors were finding it fun to dig in our gardens. Plus, it meant less work for us!

By literally giving itself away, the hosta grew stronger. This proved to be another important reminder to us; the more we give of ourselves — be it time, sweaters we no longer wear, or extra green beans — the more whole we become as people.

Raised Beds and Raised Expectations

When folks hear we live on a farm, one of their first questions typically is: "What do you grow?" A fair question, but for a while we stumbled with a reply.

"Oh, we just grow vegetables, fruits, and some herbs for ourselves and for use in our B&B guests' breakfasts," we'd stammer. But this answer didn't sit quite right with us. We knew that our passion for the land goes beyond tending a cucumber patch, yet we never intended to be a family farming operation where we might have perfunctorily replied: "50 dairy cows, 100 acres of soybeans and 200 acres of corn."

A diversity of affairs ebbs and flows through these five and a half acres, from straw bale greenhouse construction to pond digging and summer potlucks. These activities attract a collection of folks who are interested in participating or lending a hand. We now answer the question about what we grow with the reply: "We grow people and ideas."

Stimulate, challenge, inspire, provoke, reflect, and motivate. The farm is as much about growing the mind and harvesting the wind and sunlight, as it is about carrots as crops. We hope our visitors leave invigorated and positively changed. Maybe this means they'll find the creative energy to start a new business or career, consider adding a compost collection bucket under their sink at home, or just that they'll feel rested and restored through the fresh air and nourishment of home-grown food.

As our connection to the land has deepened, we've begun to see the need to promote and encourage entrepreneurship in sustainable agriculture. The average age of farmers today is 56 and rising, and only about 2 percent of American households pursue agricultural vocations today. Since we use only a small fraction of our land, we wondered how we might offer the rest of the acreage to help uncover solutions to this troubling development. We ourselves didn't have much organic farming expertise — we were beginners ourselves — but we did have some experience with business and marketing. We began to form ideas about a sort of educational facility. We could provide resources, room and board, mentoring and ideas on how to run a small business and make a living while stewarding the land.

This idea grew into the Cooperative Enterprise Program, a joint project between Inn Serendipity and the Michael Fields Agricultural Institute (MFAI) of East Troy, Wisconsin. The institute is an educational and research non-profit organization promoting sustainable and biodynamic agriculture. Our joint program is a second-year internship opportunity offered to aspiring farmers who have successfully completed MFAI's first-year organic and biodynamic farming internship. Management interns, as we call them, come to the farm and run their own business, honing skills in planning and managing a farming operation. MFAI provides growing advice and gardening resources and we help from a business perspective, consulting on business aspects from writing a business plan to creating a brochure and logo. One of our personal goals with this venture is to prove through example that it is possible to create a sustainable agricultural business that works with both one's financial needs and with one's ethics. Our strategy is to invest resources in a few talented and dedicated individuals to help them gain the experiences and the tools needed to succeed in their dreams of owning and managing their own farm operations.

The Cooperative Enterprise Program has infused Inn Serendipity with a renewed farming vibrancy, as enthusiastic young people descend upon us for a growing season, dedicated to renewing the land and developing their own entrepreneurial skills. Amy, the first management intern we hosted, completed two growing seasons at Inn Serendipity with her start-up business, Morning Star Garden. During her second season, she expanded her business by taking on two additional partners, Kristen and Dave.

Meeting Amy might be akin to meeting our annual batch of barn kittens: their overwhelming enthusiasm and energy alone can't help but make you smile and feel good. The first time she came to meet us and visit the farm, she was planning to visit for a couple of hours in the afternoon but ended up staying for dinner and spending the night. We didn't have a special supper planned. Rather, we cleaned out the random leftovers that had accumulated in the refrigerator. We must have eaten two bites of ten different things to polish everything off. Tapas!

Management intern Amy, in the field of flowers that was foundation for her startup business, Morning Star Garden.

Morning Star Garden's core business was organic cut flowers, with vegetables added the second year. Crops grew on newly created raised beds, and in rows, with an emphasis on minimal mechanical tillage. Between Amy, Kristen and Dave, they were in charge of the whole operation, from forming a new Limited Liability Corporation (LLC) to paying their own salaries and taxes. Transplants were started in mid-February, and things started blooming in May, with tulips and daffodils and crunchy sweet peas off the vine, followed by a continuous harvest of color throughout the summer.

Morning Star Garden developed a diversified sales base, with the heart of their flower and vegetable business stemming from CSA shares. The trio also attended farmers' markets in Madison and Wilmette, Illinois, and occasionally set up a sales table outside Baumgartner's Cheese Store & Tavern, the nationally-known, local hotspot on Monroe's Historic Downtown Square. "Community service," they called their sales efforts on the Square; there wasn't enough traffic or cash flow to warrant setting up a booth, but connecting with the local community was important to them.

Morning Star Garden and Inn Serendipity turned out to be a tangoing partnership, complimenting, enriching, and at times challenging each other. Pragmatically, with their presence, Morning Star Garden enriched the soil by organically growing a magnificent range of plants, composting, cover cropping, and following an amendment regimen for the soil. They prodded us into using raised beds, making believers out of us, once we'd witnessed the beds' effectiveness and efficiency. Morning Star Garden's organic tactics led to healthy crops, soil and farmers.

Beyond soil quality, Morning Star Garden enriched something more important locally: hope for the future. At first, local folks seemed cautiously curious, politely nodding their heads when Amy, Kristen and Dave zealously described their plans to grow hundreds of different varieties of flowers on a half acre, organically to boot. "That's interesting," they'd say as they gazed over the east field where Morning Star Garden would shortly bloom. One retired local farmer pulled over on County P alongside the field where "the kids" were planting and, after some polite conversation, asked, "So, are you growing any marijuana?" Uh, no.

Amy conducts a garden tour of Morning Star Garden.

There are some situations in life where hard work pays off and is respected, and farming is one of them. Every day, Dave, Kristen and Amy would be out in the field, in the cold and rainy early spring, the scorchingly hot and dry days of July and August, and at the first frosts. Soon folks were stopping by to buy a bag of lettuce from the stand on the Square or to help out weeding for an afternoon on the farm.

John Ivanko

At the end of Amy's first growing season, we threw a harvest party potluck to celebrate. We spread the word among local folks who had come know Amy over the summer; we tried to gather a sense of RSVPs and figured about a dozen folks would come. On that wonderfully warm Sunday afternoon in October, while we brought out just about every plate and chair we owned, and made an additional makeshift serving table from an old door and two saw horses for the homemade food people brought, over 50 people had joined us. They came to celebrate Amy's business and wish her well in her continued venture the following year. We were also celebrating a renewed faith in farming; together, we had re-instilled, in some modest way, the culture of agriculture.

As in any truly mutually supportive relationship, the people, the land and the activities at Inn Serendipity the following year instilled in the Morning Star Garden folks some insight into themselves, business and farming. The summer engulfed the trio in a crash organic MBA, as they lived the realities of running a business. Co-worker interactions and morale, setting prices, and making money with a brand-new business were challenges, complicated by the fact that they were using land that needed restoration. Whatever situation might follow in their farming vocation, they would have the benefit of having gone through business start-up boot camp.

No, their lettuce would never beat out the price of the economy pack at the supermarket. Americans have become so used to cheap, mass-produced food that it became an on-going challenge for Amy, Dave and Kristen to explain and convince people why paying more for locally grown, organically raised food was important. They also had to provide a rationale as to why organic flowers are better; after all, customers didn't eat them.

Morning Star Garden experienced a fundamental lesson new business start-ups often go through: how to successfully run the business while balancing one's health, relationships and sanity. Farming, however, puts additional physical strains on our body that need to be monitored; spring enthusiasm and energy often transforms into August burn-out. Morning Star Garden started over 15,000 transplants from seed, perhaps leading to an over-ambitious garden for three people to manage. Tempers, sore backs and motivation needed to be gently massaged come mid-summer.

After the second season, Amy, Kristen and Dave went their separate ways to pursue various interests, still committed to organic farming. Other interns with different business ideas came to the farm in future years, yet Morning Star Garden

SOURCES AND RESOURCES

Michael Fields Agricultural Institute
Website: www.michaelfieldsaginst.org
The Michael Fields Agricultural Institute
is a non-profit education and research
organization with a mission to enhance
the fertility of the soil, the quality of
food, the health of animals and
the strength of the human spirit by
revitalizing the culture of agriculture.

Appropriate Technology Transfer to Rural
Areas (ATTRA)
Website: http://attra.ncat.org
In addition to a wide variety of resources
for managing farm operations and
marketing agricultural products, ATTRA
provides a listing of internships and
apprenticeships available on farms.

Institute for Agriculture and Trade Policy
Website: www.iatp.org
The Institute promotes resilient family
farms in rural communities and
ecosystems around the world through
research, education, science and
technology, and advocacy.

holds a special place in our hearts as the first to embrace the entrepreneurial spirit of the Cooperative Enterprise Program. They also helped us jump-start our transition back to organic farming here at Inn Serendipity. Their ideas, knowledge, enthusiasm and direction provided the foundations for what we — as suburban transplants —lacked, and what the land desperately needed.

Did the program succeed? Could a business like Morning Star Garden create a livable income and sustainable livelihood? Interns for one or two seasons get a taste of running their own business; but the small-business reality is that markets and sales need to be built over time, with strengthening networks increasing soil fertility, and enhancing operational efficiency. Farming, like any entrepreneurial effort, is fueled by passion and a commitment to innovation. Whether or not the dedicated management interns go on to pursue a livelihood in sustainable agriculture in some form or other will be the final determination as to the effectiveness of the program. We hope that all their organic dreams come true.

CHAPTER 4

Energy, Independence and Interdependence

Renewable Energies

During the warmer months, we typically serve breakfast to B&B guests on the enclosed front porch. When folks come downstairs in the morning and walk onto the porch, the first thing they're often attracted to isn't the freshly brewed coffee or tea. They start playing with a set of kinetic balls on the ledge of the porch window, five metal balls, each hanging by thin strands of plastic from a box-like wooden frame. Pulling one of the outer balls back and releasing, the ball hits the remaining four balls and sends the opposite outermost ball swinging out. Back and forth and back and forth, the balls bouncing outward from the energy transfers between the outermost balls. Eventually they cease, each outward swing decreasing due to gravity (and technically, kinetic energy absorbed by each collision). As we finish up cooking breakfast in the kitchen, we can hear this click-click-click as our guests, mesmerized, watch the silver balls go back and forth.

There's something more going on than killing time before the Eggs Florentine arrives. The idea that energy transfers between people as well, keeping us clicking and moving along, is intriguing. These simple metal balls exemplify a core tenet of how we aim to live every day: positive energy transforming into more positive energy. Food energy converted by our bodies into kinetic energy to allow us to do the things we'd like to do. Solar radiation converted into electricity and heat. Conversations spark inspiration for a new book or enterprise.

Before moving to the farm, we simply thought of energy as the force that makes something do something. Pump gas into the car to make it go. Fill the oil tank to fire the furnace and generate heat. We didn't give much more thought to this whole process until we started learning more about renewable energy, the environmental costs that are associated with fossil fuel energy, and the conversion of energy into work (and how inefficient we were at using it). The idea of focusing on renewable energy gave us a new perspective and responsibility. We could no longer go along with the status quo: When an appliance breaks or when the furnace goes, just buy a new one. While more efficient furnace and appliance models now exist, we realized that we needed a whole new approach to living sustainably through the intelligent use of renewable energy, and a lifestyle that was in balance with it.

Our long-term quest to completely power our home with renewable energy has motivated our ongoing research, relationships, insight and innovation. Our short-term goal — to live in a house not powered by fossil fuels — was accomplished by shifting to an all-electric home and selecting the 100 percent renewable "green energy" option from our local electric utility.

Our local electrical utility is among the growing number of utilities offering green pricing programs whereby we pay a premium for our electricity generated from renewable energy sources such as wind and biogas. Besides being a renewable energy source, capturing methane biogas from agricultural operations helps prevent this greenhouse gas from being released into the atmosphere. Our premium green energy price is based upon the level of renewable energy used, the highest being 100-percent renewable energy. In some parts of the continent, utility customers can directly select an independent renewable energy generator rather than buying from the power provider in their area that may not offer any green energy option.

If we did not live in a place where such a green energy program is offered, we could have purchased green certificates, or "green tags," helping support the generation of renewable energy that is being supplied into the power grid even if our local utility didn't offer it for our use. The US Department of Energy's Green Power Network <www.eere.energy.gov/greenpower/home.shtml>, offers a list of green pricing programs, green power suppliers and green certificate marketing organizations.

As new technologies develop, as funding opportunities arise, and as our own needs evolve, we've realized that running on renewable energy needs to be both an end goal and an on-going, evolving process. Our two cars, gas-powered, are next on the list to explore more sustainable and less polluting alternatives.

We've been surprised on numerous occasions to see the laws of thermodynamics playing out in our lives. The B&B business can drain our physical energy, between changing sheets, baking muffins and spiffying up the house. Yet we've found that the energy we put into the B&B flows back; we get an energy boost from our guests when we're hosting them. We put a lot into taking care of our guests, paying attention to details like hand-picked fresh flowers in their rooms, but we come out of it recharged, and hopefully our B&B guests leave feeling restored as well. Similarly, when baby Liam arrived, our piles of baby books warned that he would take most of our energy, from sleep deprivation and late night feedings to the emotional side of adjusting to our roles as parents. While Liam certainly exhausts our energy at times, he readily transfers back to us renewed inspiration and momentum, many times over. Seeing the world through a baby's curious smile flushes us with hope, particularly when it comes to renewing our commitment to treading more lightly on this Earth that Liam will inherit from us.

We quickly realized that the first step in moving towards renewable energy isn't big projects like installing a solar hot water heating system or wind turbine; rather, it's focusing on conservation and figuring out how to use less energy more wisely. Installing a photovoltaic system is more interesting than caulking the living room windows or pulling down the blinds on the east and west sides of the house to block the intense summer sun. Yet we've realized we need to commit to cutting back our energy use and increasing our energy efficiency before we get caught up in producing more energy, even if it is from renewable sources.

How to

Energy Flows, Conservation and Efficiency

There was a time when a house, and household, was a natural part of the ecosystem in which we live. A house would be made from local materials and would rely on energy produced locally — likely on the property itself. Food would be grown on the premises and water came from a nearby spring or was pumped from the ground using a windmill. Waste wasn't hauled away by garbage trucks to be dumped in a landfill somewhere; rather, waste was recycled, reused or composted.

BIOMIMICRY

Author Janine Benyus's provocative book, *Biomimicry: Innovation Inspired by Nature,* explores how biological laws, processes and designs can be translated into the things and services we use. Her book has helped in explaining, biologically speaking, why our ecological approach and philosophy seemed to make so much sense to us. She calls this quest to learn from nature "biomimicry."

As an example, the solar cells on our PV system, in meeting some of our electricity needs, are modeled after the highly energy-efficient leaf. By focusing on the health of our soil and by growing what grows best locally, we're trying to follow nature's lead. We judge our growing success not by the amount of land we own or crop yields, but how nutritious and tasty our tomatoes are. Our farm has become less dependent on off-farm inputs, with organic waste recycled as composted humus and the wind and sunlight energy available on site transformed to meet our energy needs with minimal impact on the environment. Finally, our many garden lessons tend to spill over into our personal relationships, resulting in a sense of pride for our farm and community, and our role in preserving — if not also restoring — the very fabric which supports us and all life.

Source: *Biomimicry: Innovation Inspired by Nature,* by Janine M. Benyus, William Morrow & Co., 1998.

Our household in its everyday operation uses energy, water, air, and an ever-expanding amount of materials, from the wood used in framing new walls to the wind-up swing we used to rock Liam to sleep when he was young. Our journey toward sustainability involves returning to a lifestyle and household where mindful consumption catapults us forward to living more in balance with a healthy and vibrant ecosystem. Our goal is to waste as little as possible — which, to us, also means not wasting the readily available energy resources of the sun and wind. In essence, we're drawing inspiration from the interconnected natural world; we're working at becoming active participants in the recycling of water, energy, air and materials, rather than being merely agents of throughput, allowing the materials to simply pass through our lives to serve some brief purpose before being tossed out.

Conservation and efficiency — the two most important aspects of our approach to responsible energy use — inspire us through their remarkable simplicity of implementation and through their stunning effectiveness.

Conservation means using less. Efficiency means using the energy we need as carefully and optimally as possible. Some folks have interpreted conservation to mean extreme measures like reading by oil lamps and giving up refrigeration. But we felt that for our approach to living to succeed, it should be one that most of the world's population could embrace. That means indoor plumbing, electricity and even some other kitchen conveniences, like refrigeration.

While our long-term goal of producing a net surplus of electricity remains, we recognized that before making our own energy, we needed to cut back on what we were using, be wiser in what we did use, and more eco-effective in the design of our lifestyle and livelihood. Therefore, from day one we have strived to evaluate our decisions based not only on initial financial costs, but also by the long-term impacts, whether social, ecological or practical. What we also recognized is that what we did could just as easily be accomplished in a suburban ranch house or an urban townhouse, high-rise condo, or brownstone. These approaches can be implemented where the majority of the North American population now lives, with relatively few compromises of comfort. In fact, in places like sustainable Seattle and the Prairie Crossing development outside Chicago, they're already taking place.

Energy Conservation

Before generating electricity ourselves, our first step was to make our home as energy efficient as possible within the limits of our budgets and situation. We did not want to replace something just because it was not an Energy Star appliance, unless it would immediately translate into significant energy savings (as was the case with our refrigerator).

We've realized, too, that our conservation efforts have even broader potential. Given that we run a B&B, work from a home office, and have any number of other work and personal projects on the go, our conservation and efficiency decisions flow seamlessly across our work and personal lives. We are attempting to design, on a small, human scale, a closed loop system — the same way nature operates.

Energy conservation remains the most cost-effective means to become less wasteful and more self-reliant. The following are among the steps we took over the years:

- We've replaced most of our old single pane windows with low emissivity, argon-filled double-pane windows, which have improved the heat retention value of the windows (known as the U-value) and have cut down on air infiltration (reducing heat loss).

- We've added low-flow faucets and showerheads to cut down the amount of flowing water, especially hot water. By using less hot water, we saved the energy needed to heat it.

- We've added a water heater insulation blanket around the old tank and pipe insulation around the copper piping throughout the house, saving on water heat loss.

- We've installed electrical outlet sealers under the outlet plates and put weather-stripping and caulking around doors and windows to help cut down on air infiltration and heat loss.

- We've lowered the temperature on our electric hot water heater to 120-degrees Fahrenheit (49°C). Before that, we had to add cold water to cool the hot water when taking a shower — an incredible waste of energy.

- We turn off lights and appliances when they're not being used. We've also attached outlet strips (power bars) to appliances such as the TV and VCR, which have "ghost loads," a trickle of energy running constantly through appliances, even when they're turned off. Turning off the outlet strip also cuts the ghost load.

- We often turn off the oven for the last few minutes of baking, and we use the smallest pot needed when using the cooking range. In the summer, we try to limit the use of the oven to the cooler evening hours, baking bread at night, for example, to avoid heating up the house and overusing fans.

- We dress for the season, which means sweaters and heavy clothing in winter and t-shirts and shorts in the summer. This helps us avoid the need to "crank" up the heat to stay warm.

Energy Efficiency

What energy we do use, we try to use as efficiently as possible. Based on utility records, we've discovered that we're using about 40 percent less energy as the former owners did, putting us below the state average. The effects of energy conservation and efficiency bring us closer to energy independence and a more favorable economic payback window for generating our own renewable energy. Selecting energy efficient appliances immediately helped reduce the amount of energy we used, which saved us money and reduced our impact on the environment.

In addition to adding a number of new, more efficient appliances, we've also made the following changes:

+ We've added or retrofitted fluorescent lights into existing sockets throughout the house, not only saving energy, but saving maintenance time, since the fluorescent bulbs last eight to ten times longer than incandescent bulbs. About ninety percent of the energy used by an incandescent bulb is given off as heat, not as the light that we actually want; an 11-watt compact fluorescent provides the same amount of light as a 60-watt incandescent bulb.

+ Passive solar design captures the heat of the sun entering our house. Daylighting allows sunlight to naturally light a space or room and reduces the need for electric lighting. We employed daylighting when remodeling our attic and used passive solar design as much as possible in the greenhouse. Our attic remodel involved the addition of a south-facing dormer with low-emissivity (low-E), gas-filled, super-efficient double-pane windows, as well as overhangs over the attic windows to help shade the windows from the hot summer sun. In the greenhouse, extra thermal mass in the form of concrete slab floors, a 250-gallon water tank (946 liters), phase change salt tube, and Kalwall water tubes absorb and store extra heat, which slowly radiates at night. The 250-gallon open water tank doubles as our hot tub. The water for the hot tub is filtered by an ultraviolet light (or "blacklight"), placed next to the transparent filter canister.

+ The pathway to our house is illuminated at night with solar-powered lights. Solar cells convert sunlight into electricity and store it in rechargeable batteries. This way, the need for electrical current from the house and underground wiring were completely avoided.

+ We use rechargeable alkaline batteries for our portable radios, flashlights and camera equipment, and for the nine-volt batteries used in our smoke detectors and wind speed data monitoring equipment for the wind turbine.

+ The small pond west of the house adds to the garden ambiance, supports wildlife, and keeps the home cooler in the summer because the pond water tends to store the cool evening temperatures and absorb the daytime heat.

SOURCES AND RESOURCES

Midwest Renewable Energy Association (MREA)
Website: www.the-mrea.org
Hosting the world's largest renewable energy and sustainable living fair, MREA also features the ReNew the Earth Institute headquarters, which demonstrates how energy independence is viable today with a hybrid system incorporating solar electric, solar thermal, wind and woodstove heat to meet energy needs.

Guy Dauncey and Patrick Mazza, *Stormy Weather: 101 Solutions to Global Climate Change,* New Society Publishers, 2001.

Michael Brower and Warren Leon, *The Consumer's Guide to Effective Environmental Choices: Practical Advice From The Union of Concerned Scientists,* Three Rivers Press, 1999.

Michael Potts, *The New Independent Home: People and Houses that Harvest the Sun, Wind and Water,* Chelsea Green Publishing, 1999.

James Kachadorian, *The Passive Solar House: Using Solar Design to Heat and Cool your Home,* Chelsea Green Publishing, 1997.

The White Buffalo

Luke Skywalker mentored under Obi Wan Kenobi to become a Jedi Knight. King Arthur sought leadership counsel from Merlin. So where do we, two renewable energy newbies, turn for guidance and inspiration? Bob. Super Bob, that is.

We met Bob that first spring when we decided to install a solar hot water heating system for the farmhouse. This solar hot water heating system, or solar thermal system, made sense in our four-season climate to meet the hot water needs of ourselves, visitors and B&B guests. We were a bit cautious about putting it in that first year because of its $4,000 price tag; while we had saved for the farmhouse renovations, we were quickly seeing our bank account dwindle because of the new well, the bathroom additions and various other improvements. However, we knew that the long-term cost savings would result in the system paying for itself within ten to fifteen years. When we learned of the cash rebate offered by our local electric utility based on the square footage of the collectors, which would pay for about a quarter of the installation cost, we decided to go for it.

Solar thermal system for domestic hot water at Inn Serendipity.

Good thing we did, too, since the solar hot water heating system cash rebate program was axed the following year. As a result, we began setting aside and earmarking savings to take advantage of any renewable energy rebates or incentives when they come up, to avoid the risk of missing out.

Once we decided to put in the system, we were left with the bigger question of exactly how to do it. Since this project went beyond our expertise and tool box, we contacted the Midwest Renewable Energy Association (MREA) and Real Goods (since renamed Gaiam Real Goods), both of which told us, "Bob's your man." The actual installation of a solar hot water heating system is mostly plumbing, but it's unlikely that a local plumber will want to do it. Plumbers aren't accustomed to working on a roof — or placing 4-foot by 8-foot (1.2 x 2.4 m) solar collectors at optimal solar gain angles. We needed someone who knew what they were doing and could ensure that the system would continue to run smoothly. So we made arrangements with Bob, a renewable energy contractor and consultant, to design the system and guide its installation.

We didn't know exactly what to expect when Bob pulled into our driveway, hauling behind him a trailer with our three solar collectors. Nearing age 50, he came from a different generation of renewable energy homesteaders who tended to wear their hair long and sport tie-dye clothing. While many of his generation turned mainstream minivan along the way, he and his wife, Marguerite, still exuded an independent, hard-working ethic of self-reliance on their land, growing their own vegetables and generating their own energy. Bob had some strains of gray in his long braided ponytail, but his enthusiasm and passion for living sustainably and close to the land reverberated youthfully.

We gave Bob his Super Bob title when we realized he was one of those people who had been there, done everything, it seemed. Although he's one of the leading experts on solar thermal in the Midwest, Super Bob earned his title for more than renewable energy. He's taught us a range of skills, from how to change a flat tire, fix our leaky faucet, and make the best whole wheat pancakes we've ever tasted.

After working all day on our solar thermal system, Bob would plop down on the kitchen floor and whip out his jar of peanut butter and a chocolate bar and share his stories as he dipped his dinner. Like Obi Wan and Merlin, Super Bob sat cross legged on the floor while we, the students, surrounded him, listening attentively. Super Bob may have been a hippie from another place and time and astutely practiced at rolling his own cigarettes, but a strong kinship bloomed between us (and later with his wife) that bridged generations. At that time, we were very new to farm life and renewable energy, green when it came to living green. Bob was among our first mentors and introduced us to these new ways of thinking, living and being. We have indeed been fortunate to have met up with many people since who have helped and inspired us.

In addition to our relationship with Bob, the whole process of installing the solar hot water heating system was a lesson in teamwork and community building. In addition to Super Bob's expertise, a medley of folks came together to see this project through. The first challenge was how to get the three solar collectors, each weighing over 100 pounds, onto and attached to the roof, over thirty feet up. In a sort of modern twist to the barn-raising community effort, our hog and dairy farm-ing neighbors down the road, Ivan and his son Brett, came by with their tractor to solve our dilemma. Paul, the contractor who was working on our bathrooms at the time, also lent a hand, since neither one of us has an affinity for high places. The guys loaded the collector into the tractor bucket, then Ivan and Brett maneuvered the tractor bucket upwards until it was parallel to the roof. Bob and Paul, naturally at ease on the roof, together lifted the panel out of the bucket and securely attached it to a rack on the steeply pitched roof. As with so many of our other efforts, noth-ing we do is accomplished solo or in a vacuum.

We repeated this process with the other two collectors, after which we gazed at the collectors, toasting our efforts with lemonade and our house bakery spe-cialty, an energy-boosting chewy chocolate and oat cookie bar. Although we'd managed to get the collectors successfully mounted atop our roof with an unob-structed year-round view of the sun, we decided that in the future, our systems would either be ground-mounted or placed atop lower structures. In addition to requiring less in the way of installation acrobatics, this would also make the system much more accessible for occasional maintenance and seasonal tasks such as clear-ing snow off the collectors to increase output.

Over time, we continued to cross paths with Super Bob. While attending the Renewable Energy and Sustainable Living Fair one year, we participated in a fund-raising silent auction, where we purchased our woodstove. Our little Geo Metro couldn't handle the size, much less the weight, of the woodstove, so Bob graciously offered to store it in his garage and deliver it with his truck sometime down the line.

That sometime turned out to be the following year, when Bob and his family were en route to Janesville, Wisconsin to see Miracle, the white buffalo calf. He e-mailed us to say he was going to see the white buffalo, and that he'd stop by on the way to drop off the woodstove. We had no idea what the white buffalo was; once again, Super Bob enlightened us. Not only is a white buffalo scientifically rare, it's a highly sacred symbol to many Native Americans. The appearance of this white buf-falo, the first since 1933, is seen by thousands of people as a symbol of hope for humanity and for greater harmony in our world, particularly to folks like Bob, who revere the sacredness of the Earth. To us, the Super Bobs of the world are our sym-bols of inspiration and renewal, keeping us going on our journey to live closer to, and lighter on, the earth.

Solar Hot Water System Basics

Adapted with permission, in part from the Wisconsin Department of Administration, Division of Energy; and from the fact sheets of Wisconsin Focus on Energy <www.focusonenergy.com>; and in part from materials developed by the Midwest Renewable Energy Association <www.themrea.org>.

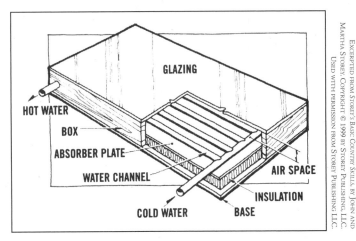

GLAZING

HOT WATER

BOX

ABSORBER PLATE

WATER CHANNEL

AIR SPACE

INSULATION

COLD WATER   BASE

Cut-away of flat plate collector for solar thermal system.

A solar hot water heating system, or solar thermal system, utilizes thermal energy from the sun to heat a transfer fluid, which can then be used in ways ranging from heating domestic hot water for showers to heating air with a liquid-to-air heat exchanger. These systems are considered active closed loop solar thermal systems, since pumps are used to circulate a set amount of heat transfer fluid through a pipe system.

Our solar hot water heating system consists of three 4-by-8-foot (1.2 x 2.4 m) flat-plate solar collectors, heat transfer fluid, a circulating pump, a heat exchanger and a storage tank.

The three collectors are each made up of a flat, insulated weatherproof box containing a dark absorber plate over a grid of tubes covered by tempered glass. We added them to the south-facing roof and pitched at a 45° angle to harness the thermal energy of the sun to heat the transfer fluid, an antifreeze solution (inhibited propylene glycol). The flat-plate collector panels come in various sizes, and the number used is determined by the needs and lifestyle of individual home owners. In our case, three collectors were considered adequate to meet the hot water needs for our family and various guests. The transfer fluid used in our system is inhibited propylene glycol (also called RV antifreeze), a stable, non-toxic antifreeze solution. The alternative antifreeze solution, ethylene glycol, contains highly toxic VOCs, and despite its toxicity, is still readily commercially available.

The transfer fluid is heated by the sun, pumped into the basement tank, and passed through a Quad Rod heat exchanger, where the heat is transferred to the well water stored in a tank. The hot water is stored in an 80-gallon (300 liters) tank connected to our existing 65-gallon (246 liters) electric water heater and tank. By pre-heating our hot water, our conventional electric water heater needs to cycle on far less frequently. Taking seasonal fluctuations and the changing numbers of B&B guests and visitors into account, our system likely meets about 50 to 70 percent of our domestic hot water needs.

The solar thermal system for the greenhouse, designed by our neighbors, Phil and Judy (more on them later in this chapter), collects heat with ten 4-by-10-foot (1.2 x 3 m) collectors, angled about 52 degrees for optimal solar gain in winter. The heat is then transferred into 780 gallons (2,953 liters) of water stored throughout several tanks in the greenhouse. The water acts as a heat storage device; the stored heat is then transferred to the air through a liquid-to-air heat exchanger in a way similar to how an automobile's radiator-cooling system cools the engine, except we are heating the greenhouse.

Solar thermal systems are also commonly used in solar hydronic radiant floor heating systems, where the heated fluid is run through a grid of under-floor tubing to warm a

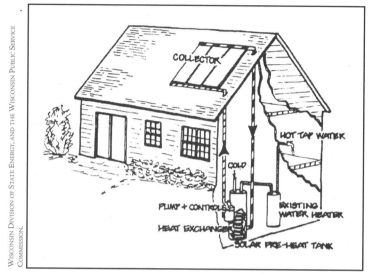

WISCONSIN DIVISION OF STATE ENERGY, AND THE WISCONSIN PUBLIC SERVICE COMMISSION.

Solar thermal system schematic.

Solar thermal system for straw bale greenhouse at Inn Serendipity.

JOHN IVANKO

specially designed floor (usually concrete slab over a sand bed). The thermal mass of the floor stores the heat and slowly releases it during the night. In cold climates, the radiant floor heating systems supplement traditional heating system and can provide 50 to 70 percent of a home's heat. In the summer, the heated fluid is sent to a shunt loop that bypasses the house.

In contrast to the active solar thermal system, a passive solar thermal system uses no pumps to circulate fluid. Since water is among the most effective materials to store heat energy, our greenhouse includes a 250-gallon passive solar tank along with two Kalwall Cylinders filled with water, both of which directly absorb solar energy passing through the insulated south-facing windows. The greenhouse also incorporates a phase change salt tube in which the salt crystals turn to liquid when heated and release heat slowly as they return to a solid. The goal, and experiment, with the strawbale greenhouse is to have a net zero heating cost by utilizing both passive and active solar thermal systems, passive solar design, and the super-insulating qualities of strawbale walls. In traditional greenhouses, with as much as 45 percent of the annual operation costs associated with heating, successfully growing with net zero heating cost means more profit per vegetable or fruit crop sold.

SOURCES AND RESOURCES

US Department of Energy: Energy Efficiency and
    Renewable Energy Portal
    Website: www.eere.energy.gov
    A gateway to hundreds of Internet sites and
    thousands of online documents on energy effi-
    ciency and renewable energy.

Apollo's Blessing

We like to think Apollo, the legendary Greek god of the sun, is smiling down on Inn Serendipity. We're sun worshipers, but not in the traditional lounge on the beach and suntan sort of way (though we don't mind a little bit of that on occasion). The sun plays a starring role in our daily cycles: pragmatically, from a renewable energy perspective through our solar electric panels or solar thermal collectors; and inspirationally, when we take advantage of any opportunity to scatter sunbeams into our days.

We appreciate and look forward to the sun's grand entrance and exit. Sunrises and sunsets are nothing short of a daily dramatic performance. Our farmhouse is fortunately oriented to appreciate both events: the east windows provide viewing spots for the sunrise and the west windows, particularly the enclosed porch off the second floor Music Room bedroom, are ideal for savoring the sunsets. Sunrises in the cold winter months are particularly brilliant, perhaps because the warm pink and red hues make us feel warmed. Sunset watching is a summer tradition, with the warm weather drawing us outside to relish the vivid red and orange display. The best spot for sunset viewing is out a window on the second floor of the dairy barn. This window, once used for loading hay bales, now leads another life as a sunset viewmaster for gazing across miles of farmland into the setting glow.

We also appreciate the sun for its influence on the garden. When we plant the garden transplants shortly after our mid-May frost date, we try to do it on a cloudy day with a gentle afternoon or evening rain in the forecast. This way, the new plants have a chance to settle a bit in the soil and have a good drink of water before taking in the sun's rays the following day.

As important as the sun is to our plants, we're reminded that more is not better. Our first spring we decided to grow some tomato transplants from seed. In early March, we carefully placed the seeds into each plug on the seed tray, covered them with soil, and watered gently and diligently. By mid-March, little green shoots appeared.

> Sunshine knows no boundaries! It's the toll-free, tax-free, energy source that nature distributes over the entire surface of the earth without using towers, poles or high-tension power lines.
> — Solectec

When the first deceiving warm spring afternoon rolled around, our minds danced with spring fever. We took the trays outside to bask in the sunshine. The books indicate that we're supposed to take transplants outside to harden them off before planting them in the garden, but when the plants are much bigger and only for a couple of hours to start. What did we do? Convinced that a bit extra was better when it came to sunshine and tomato transplants, we left them out in the warm spring sun for several hours, only to have shriveled dead seedlings by late afternoon. In the course of our excitement that spring day, we experienced a grave setback — and learned a valuable lesson. Never underestimate the power of the sun.

Despite our shriveled tomato tragedy, however, the more sun we can incorporate into our daily routines, the better our spirits. When renovating the B&B, we took down various curtains in each room so we could more readily paint the walls. The rooms had been a variety of colors and we sought to simplify the ambiance of the home by painting the walls a warm, pastel shade of yellow. Somewhat Shaker-like, the rooms are accented by the patterns of the sun pouring in through the windows, changing with the time of day and the seasons. When the sunbeams come through the window panes, the rooms glow. So much so, that we never bothered to put many of the curtains back on; we didn't want to lose one magical sunbeam. We did eventually add some nondescript blinds to the B&B bedrooms for guests who might wish for a bit of privacy or a little more sleep in the morning.

The sun also provides us with an ongoing reminder to keep things fun and not take ourselves too seriously. When the sun warms up those first early days of spring, it's a reason to celebrate and break out the shorts and have a picnic outside. On those hot July days when the sun graces everything with even-handed warmth, and our indoor motivation to work on the computer grinds to a halt, we strip naked and hide out behind the greenhouse to work on the full body tan. We're sure Apollo would approve.

How to

Photovoltaic (PV) System Basics

Adapted with permission, in part from the Wisconsin Department of Administration, Division of Energy; and from the fact sheets of Wisconsin Focus on Energy <www.focusonenergy.com>; and in part from materials developed by the Midwest Renewable Energy Association <www.themrea.org>.

A photovoltaic, or PV, system generates electricity directly from sunshine without creating any water or air pollution. Operation of a PV system for the first three to six years typically off-sets the energy used in their manufacture, depending on where the panels are located. A PV system is quiet, reliable and relatively easy to install. However, until costs come down on the solar panels, they are more expensive on a per-watt installed cost basis when compared to other renewable energy systems such as wind turbines. Unlike wind turbines, however, PV systems are relatively maintenance-free and could last as long as 50 years.

The PV modules or panels, composed of many individual solar cells, generate electricity when some of the photons from the sunlight are absorbed by the silicon-based semiconductor atoms, freeing the electrons to flow through an external circuit and back into the cell. This flow of electrons provides the electrical current. Solar cells are grouped together into a panel with a specified power, and the panels are then grouped together to form 12, 24, 36, or 48 volt arrays. The number of panels in a PV array varies, based on the desired output of the system and the power of the PV panels.

There are several main components to a PV system: the PV panels, the rack on which the panels are placed, and the inverter which converts the direct current (DC) electricity coming from the panels into alternating current (AC), which is typically used in powering common household appliances.

Installation of the PV system at Inn Serendipity.

There are two basic types of PV modules, each with specific features: crystalline/polycrystalline modules and amorphous silicon modules. Crystalline and polycrystalline silicon modules offer a more time-tested technology, but the modules are fragile and moderately heavy, requiring the PV panels to be mounted into an aluminum frame between a layer of glass and a stiff bottom material. These panels lose efficiency and produce less electricity in hot temperatures and stop producing any electricity if a small portion of the panel is shaded. The newer thin-film amorphous silicon modules, by contrast, resemble shingles and standing-seam roofing panels, and are often called building-integrated photovoltaics (BIPV), or more commonly, solar shingles. These flexible shingles use a stainless steel foil and weatherproof elastomer plastic coating, making them more durable, much lighter and less expensive. Diffuse light, partial shade, and hot temperatures do not greatly diminish energy production when using solar shingles.

JOHN IVANKO

PV arrays can be mounted in various ways, depending on the location and size of the system. Crystalline and polycrystalline silicon modules, because of their properties, are typically mounted on a south facing roof, on a static frame on the ground, or on a tracker that rotates to follow the sun's path across the sky. The goal, of course, is to optimize the maximum solar exposure, which changes depending on the time of year and location. Thin-film amorphous silicon PV cells are installed in a way that resembles a roofing job; the shingles

Solar cell, panel /module and array progression in a solar electric system.

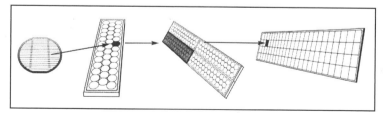

EXCERPTED FROM *STOREY'S BASIC COUNTRY SKILLS*, BY JOHN AND MARTHA STOREY. COPYRIGHT © 1999 BY STOREY PUBLISHING, LLC. USED WITH PERMISSION FROM STOREY PUBLISHING LLC.

ELECTRICITY DEFINITIONS

Watts: A unit of power. Power used by an appliance multiplied by the time it's in use, expressed as watt-hours. For example, running a 100-watt light bulb for 1 hour uses 100 watt-hours. Power is the product of current (amperes, or amps) times voltage (or volts), i.e., 1 watt = 1 amp x 1 volt.

Kilowatt Hours: Often expressed as kWh, this is how most of us buy electricity; 1 kilowatt-hour is 1,000 watt-hours (i.e., 1 kWh = 1,000 Wh).

Alternating Current: Usually expressed as AC, this refers to the electrons vibrating back and forth in the wire. Due to its efficiency at moving electricity over long distances with less line loss, AC is the type of current going into most homes from the power grid and is what most appliances are designed to run on.

Direct Current: Usually expressed as DC, this refers to the electrons moving in one direction which, while effective at providing power, tends to degrade quickly when moved over long distances. DC is the form of current that comes from PV panels or from common batteries, and needs to be converted to AC for use in household appliances.

Frequency: Frequency refers to the number of cycles per second, measured in hertz (Hz). For AC in the US, the standard frequency is 60 Hz.

Inverter: An inverter is used to convert DC to AC. Today's technology can achieve up to 90 percent efficiency (10 percent energy loss).

can be installed directly over plywood. Solar shingles offer many advantages over non-thin-film panels, including, often, a standard 25-year warranty.

There are three basic PV system designs: (1) grid connected without battery backup, (2) grid-connected with battery backup and (3) stand-alone, independent or off-grid system. We selected the grid connected without battery backup system for our 480-watt PV system because our house was already on the grid and Wisconsin is a net-metered state, which allows us to bank excess electricity on the utility grid if we produce a surplus.

To minimize our per-watt installed cost, we attached our four 120-watt Kyocera PV panels onto a Unirac, which we cantilevered off the south-facing wall of our equipment shed. We ran a short DC line through the wall into an Advanced Electronics 1000-watt inverter, then tied it into the nearest breaker box in the equipment shed. We sized our inverter to allow us to expand the system to include additional panels. With respect to our grid intertie with our public utility, a simple contract, certificate of liability insurance in excess of $300,000, equipment specification sheets, and a lockable external AC disconnect (to allow our utility to isolate our system when needed) were necessary for the project.

For a grid-connected system that includes a battery bank to store surplus energy, power service into the home can continue even if electrical service is interrupted on the grid. The stand-alone system is usually a cost-competitive energy option in remote locations where expensive power lines need to be installed to connect to the grid. Banks of batteries, however, increase the cost, complexity and maintenance of the PV system.

The first step in developing a renewable energy system design (after the size of the system is determined based on home energy use), is a site assessment. The three key factors for a viable site for PV are (a) southern exposure with the modules exposed to sun as much as possible, in our case between the peak sun hours of 10 a.m. and 3 p.m., (b) the southern exposure being free from obstructions that might shade the module, and (c) appropriate and sufficient space for the PV system. To address possible obstructions which might shade the panels, a special tool called a pathfinder is often used to evaluate both summer and winter paths of the sun.

INN SERENDIPITY PV SYSTEM

- System: 4 panel, 120-watt Kyocera array on a fixed rack

- System rated at 480 watts (4 x 120 watts)

- Less line loss (5%) and inverter use (10%): 72 watts (.15 x 480 watts)

- Net estimated system output: 408 watts

- Daily system output: 1,469 watt-hours or 1.469 kwh/day (6 average hours x 408 watts x .60 solar gain ratio for Wisconsin)

- Annual output: 536,185 watt-hours/year, or 536 kWh/year

- As an example, during the peak sun exposure in the middle of the day (approximately 10 a.m. to 3 p.m.), the system will produce enough electricity to power four 100-watt incandescent lightbulbs for 1 hour, or the equivalent of sixteen 25-watt compact fluorescent bulbs. The importance of energy conservation becomes obvious, resulting in use of fluorescent bulbs, Energy Star appliances, and other energy-saving strategies.

The installed per-watt cost of PV systems, while decreasing, make the investment in PV worthwhile only if you have a long-term economic payback horizon, have exhausted energy conservation efforts, or are not presently connected to the power grid. Within the renewable energy industry, it's commonly believed that each dollar spent on efficient appliances saves at least three dollars in PV system components.

Social and environmental costs are often more important than economic payback windows when considering conventional energy sources — coal-fired electrical power stations. The decision to add a PV system is about more than the economics of energy, since reducing carbon dioxide, nitrous oxide, and mercury emissions and achieving greater energy self-reliance can be factors. According to the US Department of Energy (DOE); electric power plants are the largest single-source contributor to global warming, and according to the EPA, electricity generation from power plants also cause emissions of sulfur dioxide, the leading component of acid rain; emissions of nitrogen oxides, a key contributor to high ozone levels and smog, acid rain and fine particulate; and are a source of heavy metals (such as mercury), which can contaminate rivers and lakes.

JOHN IVANKO

PV installers who installed the Inn Serendipity system as part of a Midwest Renewable Energy Association workshop.

According to the Wisconsin Focus on Energy, a basic net-metered grid-interconnected system costs about $8 to $15 per installed watt. In some areas, federal or state financial incentives and tax credits can help reduce the installed cost. An increasing number of areas offer net metering, which offers the ability to bank, or store, surplus energy produced on the grid. Producing local electricity reduces the load on the grid and helps support further development of renewable energy sources by encouraging others to adopt their own energy generation systems. In our case, surplus energy generated is credited back to us in the form of a refund check.

For our 480-watt demonstration PV system, the installed cost (including in-kind labor) was about $8,350, less a $3,000 WisconSUN (Wisconsin Energy

Bureau) grant, and a $536 Wisconsin Focus on Energy cash-back grant. This resulted in our PV system having a net $10 per watt installed cost. We hope to generate about 536 kWh per year.

The development of a hybrid renewable energy system using both solar and wind energy generation has enabled us to produce an energy surplus to bank on the grid, and in a limited way, generate income to offset anticipated maintenance costs for the system (mostly for wind turbine maintenance). As it turns out, days with the most sunlight have the least wind, and vice versa.

SOURCES AND RESOURCES

Database of State Incentives for Renewable Energy (DSIRE)
    Website: www.dsireusa.org
    To locate what incentives or renewable energy rebates might be available in our state, we used the DSIRE website.

Steve Strong, *The Solar Electric House: Energy for the Environmentally-Responsive, Energy-Independent Home,* Chelsea Green Publishing, 1994.

Home Power Magazine
    Website: www.homepower.com
    The hands-on journal of homemade power from renewable energy sources.

Interdependence Day

It was an early spring day when Phil and Judy first pulled into our driveway in their white van. They knocked on our door and, with an open smile, said, "We noticed you have panels on your roof. We have those too."

We stared back. Nobody around here that we knew had solar collectors. The three solar collectors we had on the south side of the roof weren't easily visible from the road. We immediately assumed that this couple, probably retired and in their mid-60s, were talking about skylights, which to an untrained eye, the collectors could be mistaken for.

"We mean solar collectors," Phil quickly assured us. "We have six solar collectors that heat all the water we can use. We live down the road. Got so much extra hot water we run it through our toilets. Nice and cozy in the winter," he chuckled with a mischievous youthful grin, his wife Judy joining in with a smile.

Our stares continued, but now for different reasons. Turns out that Phil and Judy, despite their down to earth and humble nature, were experts in the renewable energy field. They ran their own company, Solar Use Now of Wisconsin (SUN for short), doing renewable energy installations and sales in the 1970s when the use of renewable energy during the energy crisis was booming and tax credits readily available under the Carter administration. Here we thought we were our own little island of renewable energy when down the road lived Phil and Judy with their collectors, knowledge and years of experience.

Perhaps not surprisingly, Phil and Judy quickly became an important part of our day-to-day lives. We're reminded time after time that our efforts to become more energy independent would only happen through our interdependence with other people and organizations that guided our journey and mentored us. Since they often passed our place driving into town for various errands, they would stop by, their white van becoming a familiar, welcome, fixture in our driveway. Phil and Judy are among those people whom we affectionately call the onion people: The more we get to know these people, the more layers are unveiled, the more complex and interesting they become. It's grown to be an ongoing joke that whatever it is that we want to learn, Phil and Judy seem to have seasoned expertise to share, and are eager to do so.

For example, one winter we casually commented to them that we thought it would be interesting and fun to tap our handful of maple trees for maple syrup early the following spring. "Oh yeah, we did that," they perfunctorily replied. "Did that" is an understatement. Turns out that Phil and Judy had a 1,000-tap syrup operation going for about seven years on their property. Not only did they have the know-how, they still had some of the equipment and were happy to show us the ropes. Judy even boiled down the sap for us, resulting in a quart of the most special maple syrup we've ever had.

This couple quickly took on the title of Uncle Phil and Aunt Judy in our lives as they became vital mentors on various aspects and topics, including renewable energy. The conversion of the old granary into the strawbale greenhouse would have never happened without Phil and Judy's enthusiasm, support and engineering know-how. The odds and ends of solar equipment from their SUN days took up space in their garage. They were pleased to sell the equipment for pennies to the dollar and, more importantly, offered to help us put it to good use. Phil and Judy, seeming to always work as a team on projects, took charge of installing the ten solar collectors and the entire active solar hot water heating system for the greenhouse. They also, from time to time, helped us with electricity, plumbing and numerous other projects. Their son, Eric, who had helped them build their log home, jumped in on some electric, trenching and carpentry work.

We knew we'd never be able to pay them back monetarily for all they had done for us, and that never seemed an option in their books anyway. Friendship bloomed between us, seasoned with a dose of good humor as we newbies ventured into the world of renewables. Once, not long after we met him, Phil was literally doused when he offered to help us recharge our solar hot water heating system. As he was tinkering in the basement, a pipe fitting came loose and antifreeze (fortunately, the non-toxic kind) gushed out, drenching him. He immediately smiled that elfish grin of his as he said, "Whoops." We shared a laugh and we knew that we'd be forever bonded and indebted to anyone who could smile under a fountain of antifreeze.

Perhaps Phil and Judy are involved with our farm happenings because the years have taught them what we were just beginning to realize: the best form of energy in our lives comes from being interdependent, connected to one another in our community. Over time, Phil and Judy have grown to know the circle of friends who make regular jaunts to the farm so well that our friends, on their own, will head out to our greenhouse to talk shop with Uncle Phil and Aunt Judy. In Phil and Judy's case, perhaps being surrounded by this new and younger generation committed to using renewable energy keeps a vernal spring in their step.

No matter the reason, Phil and Judy are a continual reminder to us of how interdependent we are in achieving our renewable energy goals. We committed ourselves to using renewables without the technical background or unlimited funds to make it happen. Things came about and came together thanks to connections to various people and organizations. Non-profit organizations, like the Midwest Renewable Energy Association (MREA), often provided workshops and technical how-to. Our state and local utility provided rebates and free conservation tools to make things like the solar hot water heating system financially viable. Friends, B&B guests and other folks stopping by stocked us with enthusiasm, pitched in a hand, and offered vocal support to keep going.

Such connections, such interdependence, remind us that we are never truly independent - we are never alone. Nor would we want to be. These social connections are what foster togetherness and positive change long-term. It's the social side of sustainability. Research has time and time again documented that the happiest people are those with strong relationships, friendships and social connections. However, as our modern world lunges forward into seemingly never-ending growth, arms-length relationships, stress and time deficits, such interdependence is increasingly rare.

> What has happened is that most people have given proxies to the corporation to produce and provide all of their food, clothing, and shelter. Moreover, they are rapidly giving proxies to corporations or governments to provide entertainment, education, child care, care of the sick and elderly... that once were carried on informally and inexpensively by individuals or households or communities.
> — Wendell Berry

We see this interdependence and cooperation in the town of Monroe. With its population of about 10,000, Monroe is the closest large community to us. Like many towns in the heartland, it has deep roots and a strong civic pride; town life is still centered around the downtown square.

Today, Monroe's community interdependence is slowly vanishing as the Wal-Marts and fast food franchises west of town siphon dollars and community away from the historic town square. Whether Monroe will succumb to the same troubles as other small towns conquered by big-box stores is still to be seen, but already locally-owned hardware and other retail shops have closed their doors and once family-owned shop employees now join the ranks of the limited opportunity service sector taking orders or stocking shelves.

Similar to how we're reinventing this traditional farmstead with renewable energies and appropriate technology, the Monroe square seems on the verge of rejuvenating itself for a new era. The general store and butcher may be gone, but they are slowly being replaced by new family-operated shops, as Monroe strives to reinvent itself, by serving both the local community and a growing tourism industry. Whenever possible, we try to shop and support the stores on the square, basing our purchase decisions less on price than on investing in renewed community interdependence and supporting the need for a stronger local and self-reliant economy.

Like us, nature is not independent. Rather it's an interconnected and diverse web of ecosystems, species and ecological niches. And just as with the interdependence of nature, we've learned that we are economically, socially and ecologically interdependent and connected to vast financial and trade networks. While we may be inescapably globally linked, we still try to do as much as possible to promote and foster our local economy. The straw bales for the greenhouse were baled and processed by a farmer four miles (about six km) down the road; our hardwood kitchen floor was secured through a sustainable woods cooperative less than an hour's drive away, featuring a value-added product from sustainably managed forests within the bioregion. We're fortunate to have economical access to quality organic Wisconsin cheese and locally made dairy products. This continual interdependence provides both security and motivation. There is comfort in knowing that we are linked to a bigger picture, that we are part of a greater community working towards a shared vision. These connections spark us with motivation as well; having the faith of folks like Uncle Phil and Aunt Judy empower us to keep going, to keep the interdependence flowing as we continue our journey toward living more sustinably.

How to

Winds of Change: Generating Power from a Wind Turbine

Adapted with permission, in part from the Wisconsin Department of Administration, Division of Energy; and from the fact sheets of Wisconsin Focus on Energy <www.focusonenergy.com>; and in part from materials developed by the Midwest Renewable Energy Association <www.themrea.org>.

Not to be confused with the abandoned windmills still dotting the countryside, designed to mechanically pump water from wells or grind grains, a wind turbine generates electricity by utilizing the wind, doing so without creating any water or air pollution or waste.

We have a windy site at Inn Serendipity. There are times when we come inside after working in the gardens with red faces, not from sunburn, but windburn. Sitting high on the ridge where we can see for many miles southwest into Illinois, our farm is well situated for electricity generation with a wind turbine.

While many have seen or read about the large commercial-sized turbines, our wind turbine is a residential-sized system, grid-connected, and rated for electricity generation at 10 kilowatts (kW). Like our PV system, our wind system avoids the bank of batteries needed for energy storage, instead using the grid as storage for excess electricity produced. If we overproduce in any given year, our net metering contract would entitle us to a rebate check from the utility company. In Wisconsin, and in many other states, net metering arrangements are limited to a maximum of 20 kW of combined generating capacity (including wind, PV and hydroelectric). Increasingly, prices for home-sized systems are dropping, and their presence is becoming more readily accepted by utility companies. Still, given the initial investment, energy conservation and efficiency options should be exhausted before an investment in a wind turbine is made.

Wind turbines have five main components:

1. **Turbine (generator):** The electricity generator which is attached to the top of the tower.

2. **Rotor:** The set of rotating aerodynamic blades that turn when air masses move through. The load on the airfoil-shaped blades is captured by the generator to which the blades are attached. The amount of so-called swept area is determined by the rotor diameter; generally, the greater the diameter, the better the generation. Two or three blade rotors are most common. Three blade rotors, while less efficient, spin more smoothly, extending the life of the equipment and allowing the turbine to start up at lower wind speeds.

3. **Tail:** The component which tracks the wind's direction.

The 10 kW Bergey wind turbine at Inn Serendipity, placed on a 120-foot (37 m) guyed lattice tower.

JOHN IVANKO

4. **Governor:** The mechanism which limits the amount of electricity produced, protects the equipment from overproducing and burning up in high winds, and limits the centrifugal forces that might endanger the system.

5. **Tower:** The post upon which the turbine is mounted. It's made from various high-strength materials with three common styles: free-standing, guyed lattice and tilt-up. Towers help the generator avoid ground wind drag (the friction between the earth and moving air masses), and turbulence caused by obstacles on the Earth's surface.

There are several keys to successful wind energy production. First, the site must have consistent wind at an average speed of 8 to 12 miles (13 - 19 km) per hour or higher. A site assessment should be completed using national wind speed data collected by the US

Department of Energy or other appropriate sources. The site should also have enough space to allow a turbine to be placed on a tower with its rotor at least 30 feet (9 m) higher than anything within 500 feet (150 m) of the tower. Typically, a half acre of land would suffice for the actual tower and equipment. The US Federal Aviation Administration (FAA) allows towers to be erected no higher than 200 feet (60 m) without significant and expensive additional requirements. Zoning regulations or proximity to airports can present additional requirements.

Besides the wind itself, there are several variables that determine how much energy can be generated, each having a trade-off in the cost and complexity (and maintenance) of the system. In general, the larger the rotor diameter, the greater the wind swept area and the greater the energy generated. Additionally, the higher the tower, the faster and more regularly flowing the wind, the greater the

Bergey wind generator system mounted on guyed lattice tower with GridTek 10 inverter.

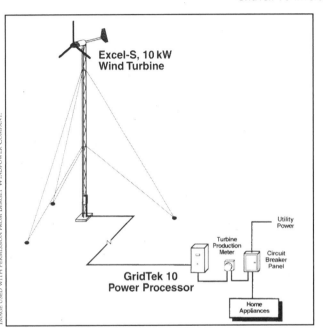

IMAGE USED WITH PERMISSION FROM BERGEY WINDPOWER COMPANY.

WIND TURBINE SYSTEM AT INN SERENDIPITY

- Turbine System: Bergey Excel-S, 10 kW grid connected system without battery bank

- Tower: 120-foot (37 m) guyed lattice tower

- Inverter: GridTek 10 Power Processor

- Rotor Diameter: 23 feet (7 meters)

- Estimated annual output with average wind speed of 13 mph (21 kph): 13,560 kWh

- Installed cost (including labor and in-kind contributions): $39,465

- Actual net out-of-pocket financial cost (after $15,595 state grant and in-kind support): $15,480 energy generated. It's usually cheaper to install a higher tower than install a larger wind generator.

Each wind turbine has different features that provide advantages and drawbacks over its competitors. The key variable for our system, however, will be reliability and on-the-ground system monitoring (i.e., where monitoring the system does not mean climbing a 120-foot (37 m) tower). Our surplus generation sold to the utility company helps offset the service contract we signed with a wind turbine service specialist, since neither of us want to be dangling from the top of a tower to do repairs or maintenance.

Just as with the small PV system, a simple contract, certificate of liability insurance in excess of $300,000, equipment specification sheets, and a lockable external AC disconnect (to allow our utility to isolate our system if necessary) are needed to complete our local electric utility's requirements for a grid intertie system.

SOURCES AND RESOURCES

American Wind Energy Association
Website: www.awea.org
For the latest information related to wind energy generation, regardless of system size.

Windustry
Website: www.windustry.org
From large-scale to small residential wind turbine systems, this non-profit organization offers extensive wind turbine information and the ability to locate systems throughout the US.

Paul Gipe, *Wind Energy Basics: A Guide to Small and Micro Wind Systems,* Chelsea Green Publishing, 1999.

Paul Gipe, *Wind Power for Home and Business: Renewable Energy for the 1990s and Beyond,* Chelsea Green Publishing, 1993.

The Heart and Hearth of Fire

We spend many evenings staring at the black box in the living room. We sit transfixed around it for hours during the cold winter months, entranced by the changing colors. No, we're not talking about a television. We're mesmerized by our woodstove, the warm glow both lulls and stimulates us as we stare through the glass door into the dancing flames inside the burning heart of the stove. When we installed the woodstove, our goal was to heat the house with wood, a renewable resource in our community. It also took us one big leap away from fossil fuel dependency, since our home originally used fuel oil and an electric heat pump. Because wood is readily available, often for free, the woodstove also significantly reduced our heating costs in the winter. We didn't realize that we were putting in more than a heat source; we were creating the hearth — and the heart — of our home, a sensory focal point for our daily life, particularly during those icy Wisconsin winters.

EPA-certified airtight Lopi Endeavor woodstove at Inn Serendipity.

The installation of the woodstove was beyond our technical expertise and tool box capabilities so, once again, we called on our open-minded contractor, Paul. He had never installed a woodstove before, but by this time he was used to — and perhaps perpetually amused by — our projects. He was willing to regress to step one: read the installation manual that came with the woodstove and the literature about the rest of the system: the stove pipe, chimney, roof mounts, and clearance requirements. This project reminded us again why, despite our desire for greater self-reliance, we needed Paul's expertise. Rather than frustrating and possibly endangering ourselves, we blended his professional expertise with our limited skills as basic do-it-yourselfers. This guided independence, as we call it, allows us to get far more done in a far better fashion and in less time than if we try to go at it alone.

Our woodstove project demonstrates the blending of the traditional and the high tech. On one level, we were going back to the way houses were heated a hundred years ago: through a woodstove or fireplace centrally located in the house. Yet on the high tech-note, we installed an EPA-certified, non-catalytic converter, air-tight woodstove that's among the most efficient large stoves on the market.

Paul took out the wall between the kitchen and our combo dining-living room. Putting the woodstove there would let the heat radiate throughout the first floor and up the stairs to the second floor bedrooms and office. The kitchen and the din-ing-living room were merged into one L-shaped great room, with the woodstove a central feature. The woodstove weighs over four hundred pounds, and for weight and fire safety reasons sits on a 4-foot by 5-foot (1.2 x 1.5 m) tile section Paul laid with tiles made out of recycled auto windshield glass (left over from the upstairs bathroom projects).

From its first inaugural burn, the woodstove quickly became an important, intimate core of our household rhythm during the cold months. We rearranged the living room furniture for the winter season with the chair and couch directly facing the fire; when anyone walks into the house in the winter they are immedi-ately drawn to stand in front of the stove and stare at the flame behind the glass door. When we first brought Liam home from the hospital during a chilly late October spell, John made sure the fire was stoked up to welcome him with a cozy warmth.

Before winter sets in, we need to make sure we're stocked with wood. This is always a bit of a guess since we don't know exactly how cold the upcoming winter will be, but we learned the hard way that this is one of those situations where more is better — the first season ended with us down to our last pieces of wood in early April, when a cozy fire makes the damp coolness of early spring bearable.

We typically stock up on wood mid-summer. From time to time, we'll borrow a neighbor's pick-up truck in exchange for twenty dollars and a sampler pack of Lisa's latest brewing efforts, and head to the local lumber mill. For fifteen bucks a pick-up load, we sort through the mill's leftover piles and pick out the most weath-ered and sun-dried pieces of oak and hickory of the right dimensions to fit in the woodstove. Sometimes the piles are free for the removal. With four truckloads in an afternoon, we're set with wood for the season. Other years, Uncle Phil and Aunt Judy have invited us into their 30-acre stand of woods, where we cut, split and store next season's heating fuel.

Kindling comes from a local cabinetry shop in town. The owner of the shop — who might actually be mistaken as the twin brother to Gepetto of Pinocchio fame — lives true to his frugal and practical Swiss heritage. Not wanting to waste anything, he cuts all his scrapwood into foot-long pieces about an inch wide and stacks them neatly in the back of his shop, waiting for someone like us to come and freely take some for kindling.

Once we're into the woodstove heating season, the stove becomes a part of our household, dependent on us to keep it going. John is the resident Sparky, drawing back to his Boy Scout days of fire starting. Lisa was rather new to fire starting and tending when we started heating with the woodstove; her experience limited to her turning on the gas starter of her parents' family room fireplace on Christmas Eve. But after practice and effort, she can now get a hot burn going. Typically, John stokes the fire with a load of wood when he goes to bed in the late evening. At 5:00 a.m. when Lisa wakes up, she'll spread the ashes to reveal the glowing hot coals underneath. Moving the coals to the front and adding a little more kindling, followed by a few larger pieces of hardwood, the firebox returns to a hot blaze. A fan on the floor in the kitchen helps circulate the air through the rest of the house.

> Just possibly, in this age of nuclear fires, it is time to regain some control over an element central to our lives, and to restore some of the attentiveness and respect for fire that even our remote ancestors knew.
> — David Lyle, *The Book of Masonry Stoves*

Once a day one of us heads outside to the machine shed to bring in four 5-gallon (19-liter) buckets of wood. We've learned to always have enough wood in the house to take the fire through the night and into the next morning — throwing a coat and boots over pajamas and heading outside for wood on a cold January night or early morning is hardly pleasant. About once a week we let the fire die down and we shovel out the ash buildup. When the ashes are completely cool, we dump them in the chicken coop for the chickens to roll around in, since the ashes are a natural deterrent to parasites.

Sure, the woodstove routine is more complex and time-consuming than switching on the furnace and waiting a couple of seconds before hot air starts blowing in. Yet the fire provides more than heat. Sitting around the fire seems to naturally build conversation, community, and peace, whether it's just the two of us or a group of friends. The fire provides a safe haven for us to express ourselves while gazing into accepting flames. The fire seems to ignite conversations while warming our bodies.

Campfires also provide us with similar experiences. Prior to our arrival at the farm, fires were functional: scrap items were burned in the fire pit, instead of being dragged to the township dump. Overnight, we changed the fire pit into a social campfire spot, using tree stumps or old benches as seats. We constantly collect scrap wood pieces for the campfire all year long, including the branches from the annual apple tree pruning. We throw our Christmas tree in the fire pit after the holidays and by the time of our first campfire of the season around the vernal equinox, we ceremoniously light the tree. The tree's dry pine needles quickly ignite like a fourth of July sparkler.

During the spring and summer campfire circles, much like around the wood-stove, folks open up as they stare at the flames. We'll often have campfires when hosting B&B guests, assembling a basket of s'more supplies for all. Most of our B&B guests come up in pairs, be it married couples, dating pairs, siblings or friends. They are people who already know each other pretty well, yet it's amazing how many new relationship revelations take place around the campfire. We once hosted a professional couple in their late 20s, Sharon and Pradeep. Both were doctors, shared an Indian family background, and had been married for a couple of years. We exchanged our introductory pleasantries and took them on a customary tour of the farm when they first arrived, but conversation really crackled around the campfire.

Somehow the discussion around flames and under the stars that night got on the topic of the supernatural: did we individually believe in ghosts and UFOs? As we went around the circle with each of us sharing our perspective on the topic, it grew clear that Pradeep was quite fascinated by this topic and had put a lot of thought to the matter. He seemed convinced that there was indeed something else out there in a positive sort of way. At the same time, we noticed his wife Sharon grew clearly spooked by the whole supernatural topic, feeling that even if there was something else out there, it wasn't friendly. She didn't want anything to do with it.

As the flames flickered and the conversation continued, it became more of a two-way dialogue between Sharon and Pradeep, with the two of us as quiet bystanders and fire tenders. Sharon and Pradeep were in a close relationship with history and time behind them; they felt they knew each other intimately yet this was clearly a topic that had never come up until they were sitting around the campfire. This wasn't at all a tense exchange between the two of them, but rather one of open discovery as they learned things about each other that simply had never come up until they were brought out by fire. A spark of serendipity.

Heating with a Woodstove

Adapted in part, with permission, from materials developed by the Midwest Renewable Energy Association <www.themrea.org>.

We don't mind getting snowed in, even without power. We'd survive quite comfortably. If we lose power for a long duration, we could move frozen foods from our freezer to the front porch and refrigerated foods that can't be quickly eaten could be placed in the coolest corner of the basement. With our woodstove aglow, we can snuggle self-sufficiently around the stove, able to prepare our meals on top of the stove and drink melted snow.

A woodstove is a system much like other renewable energy systems. It's composed of the stove, stovepipe, chimney, floor protection, building code and manufacturer

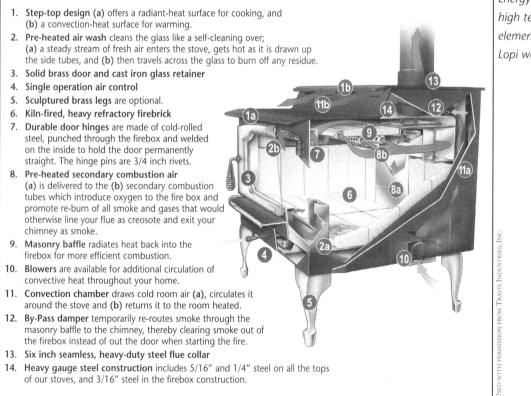

Energy efficient high tech design elements of a Lopi woodstove.

1. **Step-top design (a)** offers a radiant-heat surface for cooking, and **(b)** a convection-heat surface for warming.
2. **Pre-heated air wash** cleans the glass like a self-cleaning over; **(a)** a steady stream of fresh air enters the stove, gets hot as it is drawn up the side tubes, and **(b)** then travels across the glass to burn off any residue.
3. **Solid brass door and cast iron glass retainer**
4. **Single operation air control**
5. **Sculptured brass legs** are optional.
6. **Kiln-fired, heavy refractory firebrick**
7. **Durable door hinges** are made of cold-rolled steel, punched through the firebox and welded on the inside to hold the door permanently straight. The hinge pins are 3/4 inch rivets.
8. **Pre-heated secondary combustion air** **(a)** is delivered to the **(b)** secondary combustion tubes which introduce oxygen to the fire box and promote re-burn of all smoke and gases that would otherwise line your flue as creosote and exit your chimney as smoke.
9. **Masonry baffle** radiates heat back into the firebox for more efficient combustion.
10. **Blowers** are available for additional circulation of convective heat throughout your home.
11. **Convection chamber** draws cold room air **(a)**, circulates it around the stove and **(b)** returns it to the room heated.
12. **By-Pass damper** temporarily re-routes smoke through the masonry baffle to the chimney, thereby clearing smoke out of the firebox instead of out the door when starting the fire.
13. **Six inch seamless, heavy-duty steel flue collar**
14. **Heavy gauge steel construction** includes 5/16" and 1/4" steel on all the tops of our stoves, and 3/16" steel in the firebox construction.

clearances from combustionable material, wood for combustion and other components depending on the size, location, and type of stove. Where wood is readily available, a woodstove can be a sustainable and appropriate technology to meet heating needs. Choosing an EPA-certified airtight stove will result in minimal impact on the environment, too. According to the Midwest Renewable Energy Association, the cycle of burning of wood and regrowth of trees produces no net increase in carbon dioxide to the atmosphere. We make sure our tree planting efforts replace the equivalent number of trees that we end up burning.

By using an efficient high-tech Lopi Endeavor non-catalytic woodstove, our winter heating bill has plummeted, conversations around the hearth have mushroomed, our reliance on fuel oil has largely disappeared, and our environmental impacts have lessened. Burning readily available and renewable hardwoods - oak, elm and hickory - we are often warmed twice, once with the physical cutting, splitting, and stacking of the wood and then again, when the pieces are burned in the stove. We make sure that we get the stove roaring hot and use dry, seasoned, hardwoods. Letting the wood sit for a full summer season drops the moisture content in the wood down as much as 20 percent, improving efficiency. Some of our wood sits in the northern room of our garage which, during the summer, tends to get quite hot when the sun strikes the western wall of the building in the afternoon. The rest of the supply is placed on the west wall of the equipment shed to dry.

The EPA has found the Lopi Endeavor stove to be the cleanest burning large stove ever tested, in part because of the design, the use of fire brick (which helps the firebox burn at higher temperatures) and the baffles which insure that the gases are burned in the combustion chamber. The five-sided convection combustion chamber, or firebox, circulates oxygen around the stove and pushes the warm air back into the room.

Our chimney is checked or cleaned once a year, which is more for our peace of mind than anything else, since burning effectively and efficiently produces little smoke, which reduces creosote buildup in the chimney. The reality of living in an old farmhouse, even with our numerous energy conservation efforts to reduce air infiltration, is that we still find fresh air drafting in around the older windows, sashes or floor boards. This allows us to balance energy efficiency with a healthy home; the air exchange insures that our stove always has plenty of oxygen for consumption in the fire.

In contrast to the inefficient traditional fireplace, which does little to heat a room, and the older pot-bellied woodstoves, which are often dangerous, the new woodstove models have up to 75 percent fewer emissions, according to the EPA. An open fireplace sends up to 80 percent of the fire's heat up the chimney and significantly contributes to air pollution, since incomplete combustion of gases occurs. The key to burning wood efficiently is to burn all the gases that the wood releases. These gases are not only dangerous if left unburned, but contain over 50 percent of the available energy. The gases burn only at temperatures in excess of 1,100 degrees Fahrenheit (593°C), which can rarely be achieved other than through modern airtight woodstoves.

Other types of stoves we considered include the catalytic, pellet and masonry stoves, each with cost, design and heating considerations. Catalytic stoves are most similar to our non-catalytic stove with the key exception that it features a catalytic converter which helps burn gases before they escape through the chimney. Smoke from the fire chamber passes through a ceramic honeycomb coated with platinum or palladium which chemically interacts with smoke particulates, resulting in a more complete combustion at half the temperature of the firebox. Pellet stoves, stoves that burn pellets made of sawdust or corn, provide another option for biomass heat and tend to burn even cleaner than current woodstove models but require electricity in their operation. A masonry stove — also known as cook-stove-oven-fireplace — resembles a fireplace, and is a sophisticated system with an immense thermal mass of brick (or stone) and mortar to store the heat generated from burning a short-lived but intense fire.

As fossil fuels become more expensive and extract an ever greater toll on the environment, airtight and EPA - certified stoves can provide cost and energy efficient alternatives for heating, especially in cold climates.

SOURCES AND RESOURCES

Stephen Bushway, *The New Woodburner's Handbook: A Guide to Safe, Healthy & Efficient Woodburning*, Storey Books, 1992.

David Lyle, *The Book of Masonry Stoves: Rediscovering an Old Way of Warming*, Chelsea Green Publishing, 1998.

Precious Water

"At least you guys don't have to worry about wasting water. You have a well." We hear comments like this every so often from visitors with metered city water.

True, by having our own well we are not paying for water in annual dollars and cents; we don't receive a water bill with payment due at the end of the month. Yet we're still compelled to give an extra handle twist to stop the drippy faucet, pour the old water from the daisy vase on the house plants instead of down the drain, and only run full loads of laundry. We conserve water because we know there isn't an infinite supply within the aquifer from which our well draws water. Whether the aquifer goes dry next week, in our lifetime or in a hundred years, we share in the responsibility right now of managing its use.

Such an attitude is a new perspective for us: the concept of conserving something that is commonly viewed as free. Living closer to the land, we're reminded on a daily basis that all our actions have consequences. Just because something is abundant and free today, like the water gushing out of our garden hose, doesn't mean we shouldn't value its presence.

Old time farmers realize this concept. Between growing up during the Great Depression and world wars, things were simply not wasted, no matter what their price tag may be. We first learned this lesson when our neighbor, Joyce, was in the local hospital for a couple of days for some surgery. Knowing she probably was not in the mood for hospital visitors but wanting to let her know we were thinking of her, we created an arrangement of flowers from the garden. We put the flowers in a rinsed out old pickle canning jar and put the water-filled jar in a box stuffed with newspaper, so that Joyce's husband, Burnette, could easily bring the flowers to the hospital.

A week later, once Joyce was home, Burnette dropped off a sweet thank you note, along with the dried out pickle jar in the newspaper-stuffed box. We used this throwaway jar because we had intended for Joyce and Burnette to do exactly that: throw it away once the flowers died and not be concerned with returning something to us. But return it they did, reminding us that all things do have value. We're now accustomed to the Returning Society around here; in fact, we're active participants. Any throw-away container we use to give someone some muffins, raspberries or extra soup, is usually returned, often refilled with another home-baked goody.

Perhaps one of the reasons we value water so much stems from the ordeal of putting in a new well when we moved in. Having moved in during November, the new well couldn't be installed until the ground thawed the following May. So we used our water — high in nitrates and bacteria — for showering and cleaning and we dragged recycled plastic gallon milk jugs to a public spring in the nearby town of Winslow, Illinois, filling them with water for drinking and food preparation. This was before the B&B opened, so it was the two of us for the winter, yet we were continuously filling up and dragging those water jugs. We grew to be painfully aware of using every last drop. That pre-well winter quickly caused us to realize, and appreciate, the amount of water we use on a daily basis. When safe water started flowing from the tap, we drank an official toast to the new well with a silent promise to continue treating our water source as if we had hand-delivered every gallon.

In addition to the well, we're reminded of our connection to water every time the open skies darken with rain clouds. Rain in the city was an inconvenience to us, a reason to run faster to the car or bus before getting wet and complain about forgetting our umbrella again. On the farm, thunderstorms are now anticipated entertainment and celebrated arrivals for our sometimes desperately dry gardens and growing fields. Summer storms are particularly poignant as the winds pick up and gray clouds roll in. John is the resident storm trooper, proclaiming with increasing accuracy when the storms are going to be a "woo-woo." Lisa now knows not to panic if she can't find him when the storms are pounding; he's out under the roof of our shed "cantina," protected from the rain but with a clear view of the lightning and thunder show.

We learned the hard way how powerful such a rainstorm can be. Electrical outages are not unusual. When the power comes back on, it has a tendency to surge and fry electronics, so now we're extremely careful to unplug the office outlets with our higher value items like the computers. These storms don't typically last very long, but they are both magnificent and intense. When it's all over and the sun breaks through, we run around outside like leprechauns, searching for a glimpse of that magical rainbow.

While the woodstove provides snuggling opportunities and the warm sun gives us reason to strip down to the buff, water engages our playful side and compels us to have some fun. Water balloon skirmishes are the norm when friends visit in the summer. The kids love to see the adults running around like kids, hiding behind the corners of the barns and outbuildings preparing for attacks. Sometimes, when the weather is particularly hot and steamy and we all need to cool off, water balloons will give way to buckets of ice cold water from the garden hose, mischievously dumped on unsuspecting heads (and watering the parched grass underfoot).

From the rains above to our well down below, water is an important life force that keeps everything going. While water may not come with a price tag, we realize every day its intrinsic value — and our responsibility for using each drop. We make sure those water balloons are accurately aimed before throwing.

Water Conservation

Abour 70 percent of our bodies are made of it, and only 3 percent of the planet's surface has it in fresh, drinkable form. Yet it is being wasted, used up — or polluted — at a rate far beyond its ability to restore and replenish itself. Water. Without it, every living thing will perish. There are now many who feel that wars will be fought over this natural resource, especially given that two thirds (and growing) of the planet's inhabitants do not have access to safe drinking water.

We're blessed, now, with our own well that goes deep enough to reach an aquifer containing fresh water that's free from agricultural nitrate contamination and other possible poisons. Given our commitment to drink safe water, we also feel the responsibility to use it carefully and conscientiously. Like the air, it doesn't belong to us; it's a part of the commons we want to help conserve, if not also restore.

Therefore, our approach to water is no different from our approach to energy — or to our livelihood. We've undertaken several strategies to help preserve and conserve our water, described below:

- Throughout the house, water conservation measures have been employed, including low-flow shower heads, faucet aerators, an efficient dishwasher, low-flow toilets and, when guests aren't present, the toilet bowl measure: if it's brown, flush it down; if it's yellow, let it mellow (within reason). Cumulatively, we save thousands of gallons of water a year by not flushing every time we add a pint or less of pee. According to the EPA, faucet aerators reduce water flows by 50 percent, and using the dishwasher when it's full uses less hot water on average than hand-washing in the sink (as long as we break the habit of pre-washing in the sink first). Gone, too, from our daily routine is our want for a wake-up shower; cleansing showers are now taken every other day unless we're doing something like cleaning the chicken coop or weeding on a hot summer day.

- In the gardens, we've tried to rely on mostly native plants and heavy mulch during the heat of the summer to minimize the need for irrigation. For the food crop beds, highly effective drip irrigation and selective hand-watering are used. To water plants, we've also created a simple water catchment system using the south roof of the farmhouse, funneling the rainwater down the gutter and through a pipe that spills into a small pond on the west side of the house. We then can use five-gallon buckets or sprinkler pails to transfer water to needy plants.

- By gardening organically and keeping poisonous and toxic chemicals away from the farm, we're helping the aquifer to naturally cleanse and restore itself from years of chemical pesticide and fertilizer use.

- We have an old septic system, and we're exploring options for its replacement when the time comes. Constructed wetlands are specially designed ecosystems that biologically treat waste, made famous by Jonathan Todd at Ocean Arks International <www.oceanarks.org>. Todd has created systems that are cleaning up rivers, lakes and treating wastewater in projects around the world, mostly in cities, at industrial facilities, or for entire communities. If these systems become more widely accepted by sewer and waste treatment departments, we may build one, rather than replacing ours with another conventional system. In the meantime, we get our septic tank pumped every year or two and add bacteria to keep it functioning properly.

- When our current toilets need to be replaced, we'll add the new air-assisted flushing toilets which use a little more than half a gallon of water per flush. Until we can get state regulations changed for bed & breakfasts, composting toilets will have to wait.

- The cabin property features both a pond and regularly flowing stream, and we approach both with an interest toward enhancing water quality and biological health. Discussed in more detail in Chapter Seven, a riparian buffer was added to protect the stream, prevent soil erosion and enhance wildlife habitat.

Sources and Resources

Michael Ogden and Craig S. Campbell, *Constructed Wetlands in Sustainable Landscapes,* John Wiley & Sons, 1999.

Personal Energy

If you ask how the labyrinth came about, we'll quickly reply: It was Lisa's idea. Or shall we say, she came up with the idea first. On one of those dark and cold January days, she became entranced by a magazine article on garden labyrinths, shades of vibrant green popping off the page. She clipped the article for John's reading pile.

Then, a few weeks later, we enjoyed our first labyrinth walk at Grace Cathedral in San Francisco. By then, we were both hooked in by a simple — yet compelling — idea for the farm: A place to which we and our guests could escape and take time out to relax, to ponder life, to be. Unlike a maze, a labyrinth is a symmetrical pathway, often beautifully landscaped and designed, created to help us slow down, look within and seek balance in our life. John ended up installing the labyrinth that following May, from mapping out the design to lining the finished paths with

The garden labyrinth at Inn Serendipity.

JOHN IVANKO

woodchips, with the help of some friends. Such a creative flow, bouncing ideas back and forth between the two of us, is one important way we keep our personal energy renewed and creatively active.

Often overlooked and undervalued when talking about renewable energy, the concept of personal energy is at the core of everything we do. We would never have been able to undertake all the conservation and renewable energy efforts we have if our own internal energy and motivation wasn't high. Physically, we need energy to do things like restock the wood in the wintertime and haul the wet laundry out to dry on the clothesline by the dairy barn. Even though we're not the ones installing the PV panels, such systems still require mental energy on our part to conceive and manage. In cases where there is some opportunity for state or federal grant funding for such renewable energy systems, we devote our energy to proposal writing and grant applications; without such support, many of our ideas would still be pipe dreams.

Personal energy is infinitely renewable, yet it seems like it's an endangered commodity today. We've discovered that keeping our personal energy recharged does take maintenance and commitment — but the benefits are worth it. When our personal energy is recharged, the world feels like an open book and we're engaged in authentic living and active learning. Everyday experiences hold infinite possibilities; things that may have drained us in the past now invigorate us. We may spend a couple of frigid hours outside clearing the half foot of snow off the driveway, warm up and dry off around the woodstove, and then flow into creative mode and finish off an essay on the computer. The key has been to learn and identify the ways we can best rekindle our personal energy — what experiences and situations help keep us in creative flow?

> The labyrinth symbolizes the cyclic journey that each of us must take daily, seasonally, in life, and in death and rebirth.
> — Alex Champion,
> *Earth Mazes*

Sacred space — places that have spiritual connections — does a lot for our personal energy. Walking the labyrinth provides such an experience as a moving meditation. One approach we've used with walking the labyrinth is to silently ask a question while walking to the middle. This may be dealing with a creative block on a writing piece, apprehension over an upcoming workshop presentation, or it may simply be, after a busy week, How can I rekindle my personal energy? As we walk the labyrinth towards the center, we seem to be symbolically walking to the center of ourselves, and perhaps gaining an answer to our question. Despite the fact that the actual path of the labyrinth is always the same, each walking experience is different. One time the sunflowers surrounding the labyrinth may be in full bloom, another time a dusting of snow between the woodchipped walking path adds a different feel, a different perspective.

Our idea of sacred space extends beyond the labyrinth and to the land. We've discovered that interacting with the land keeps us connected to our selves, our energies. We see the renewal effect every spring when we have our annual planting weekend. Typically, the second weekend in May, we close the B&B and invite friends up to share in the planting of the garden, gathering a household of folks who drive in from the city with a handful of kids and a few dogs. We try to have things well organized for a day of gardening on Saturday as we divide and conquer the yearly to-dos: We plant the tomato transplants, direct seed the zucchini, and add more mulch to the potatoes. We'll cook up a hearty dinner Saturday night and usually top off the day with a relaxing campfire under the starry sky.

This planting weekend may at first glance seem like an odd equation: people drive here on their own time and gas, willingly labor for free in someone else's garden, and all they get is an all-you-can eat spaghetti dinner at the end of the day. As

THE POWERS OF A LABYRINTH

Dating back to as early as 2,500 to 2,000 BC, the labyrinth has been a spiritual, reflective and meditative manifestation of human creation. Unlike a maze, a complex puzzle with branch points and dead ends, the magical labyrinth is a one-directional pathway which typically reflects a balanced symmetry and pattern which is not meant to confuse or trick the walker.

There are two popular labyrinth designs: the ancient Cretan labyrinth and the circuit labyrinth, based on the number of times the path loops around the center. Entry to our seven-circuit Inn Serendipity Labyrinth is made from the west side, taking us to the center without any choices to be made; once there, we retrace our steps to exit.

Labyrinths have been used in many of the Gothic cathedrals of Europe, for fertility rituals by pre-Christian agrarian societies, and as magical talismans by Swedish fishing communities. The Hopi nation consider their four-circuit labyrinth design a symbol for Mother Earth. The Celts used labyrinths in their art. Among the best known and most visited labyrinths are found at the Chartres Cathedral near Paris, and at Grace Cathedral, atop Knob Hill in San Francisco. The labyrinth also resembles the mandalas of Buddhism and the practice of walking in Zen meditation, both of which calm and proffer opportunity for awareness.

Adapted in part, with permission from *Earth Mazes*, by Alex Champion (self-published 1990). <www.earthsymbols.com>

most of the planting weekend entourage are urban dwellers, garden work uses muscles that they may not have been in touch with for a while. Massages around the evening campfire are common.

After the strong response the first year, we realized there was something deeper going on than spring fever. By connecting to the land even for a weekend, by literally feeling the soil on their hands, these folks seemed to feel renewed, inspired — just as we do. We were collectively part of something greater; we were preparing the garden for the upcoming season, caring for the land and as a result, for ourselves. That wasn't any old spaghetti that our friends were eating; the tomato sauce was made from the tomato plants, spinach, onions and squash that many of the same people helped plant the year before. These connections to the garden, gifted us all with renewed energy.

We've also realized the importance of renewing our personal energy through ongoing creative self-expression. Sometimes this creativity has evolved into its own annual ritual: Lisa collects a basket of pinecones each fall and places them throughout the house as decoration. We put out 5 gallon (19-liter) buckets of red, yellow and blue dye for tie-dye art during our Fourth of July Reunion festivities.

On New Year's Eve, John often makes candles using scrap wax pieces from old candles we've saved. He melts the wax down slowly in an old crock pot, and we use milk and ice cream containers for molds. Sometimes we'll have some folks over to share in the fun. One year we added a new twist by putting ice cubes in the molds prior to pouring in the wax; the ice melted up against the hot wax, leaving bubble-like holes that added an interesting effect to the candle. On New Year's Day morning, we tear open the mold to reveal our set of new candles for the year. Our candle ritual has grown beyond arts and crafts for us. Something about starting the year with new candles, made up of last year's reused odds and ends, gives us a renewed sense of hope — and illumination — for the new year.

Our personal energy needs nurturing. The labyrinth serves as a constant reminder of this need for renewal, since this has not been a project that we could do and forget about. Ongoing efforts are required to keep the labyrinth weeded; invasive quack grass took over the clover we planted the first year and every season we work to overtake the grasses with a heavy planting of creeping thyme and other perennials. A fence around the labyrinth now keeps the chickens out. We learned the hard way that chickens love to scratch for bugs under the woodchips, kicking up the chips and rearranging the labyrinth path in the process. We need to tend to our personal energy on an ongoing basis as well, tapping into new ways of renewing our drive and enthusiasm. That renewal can come from engaging conversation with friends around the dinner table, going for a solitary walk in the woods, going to bed early or meditatively walking the labyrinth. These experiences fuel our personal energy, keeping us going, and keeping us focused on the big picture.

> Our hope does not come from convincing ourselves the good news is winning out over the bad. Hope comes from a place deep within...It is a stance, not a calculation. We find hope because we have to. We find hope because our planet needs us to. We find hope because we are alive.
>
> — Frances Moore Lappé and Anna Lappé, *Hope's Edge*

How to

Walking and Designing a Labyrinth

Drawn into the ancient world of labyrinths, we were awestruck by both the beauty of the labyrinth and its message: know thyself. Perhaps the most important use of the labyrinth today is its power to help us slow down, look within and seek balance in our life. Time is not of the essence. The purpose of walking the labyrinth is not to quickly get to the center — we'll get there soon enough. Rather, the goal is to center ourselves and consciously dwell in the present. By walking the pathways, the magical properties of the labyrinth quiet the mind and soul, easing away the hustle and bustle of day-to-day living.

According to Veriditas: The World-Wide Labyrinth Project, there are three stages of the labyrinth walk: (1) purgation, a releasing, a letting go of the details in our life, quieting and emptying the mind; (2) illumination, the arrival to the center and an unlimited time for meditation, prayer and thought; and (3) union, the process by which we join the healing forces at work in the world, connect with nature, God, the higher power. For us, when we connect this way, we feel empowered to continue along our journey of right livelihood and sustainable living.

The labyrinth at Inn Serendipity is circular in design, with a diameter of about 50 feet (15 m). A wall of radiant sunflowers, their flower heads following the arc of the sun during the day, encircles three-quarters of the labyrinth. Oriented like a compass, with the entry point on the west side, each loop radiates inward until the walker reaches the center. The two-foot wide woodchip pathways are marked by white clover, with fragrant perennial creeping thyme groundcover and other flowers slowly being established.

SOURCES AND RESOURCES

Veriditas: The World-Wide Labyrinth Project
   Website: www.veriditas.net
   Reintroducing the labyrinth in its many forms as a spiritual tool, Veriditas features extensive information on labyrinths and its website includes the Labyrinth Locator for over 600 labyrinths, including the Inn Serendipity Labyrinth.

Alex Champion, *Earth Mazes,* self-published, 1990.

Lauren Artress, *Walking A Sacred Path: Rediscovering the Labyrinth as a Spiritual Tool,* Riverhead Books, 1996.

Melissa Gayle West, *Exploring the Labyrinth,* Broadway Books, 2000.

CHAPTER 5

Creating and Caring For Community

Feeding Community

We knew something was cooking when one thousand toasted pirages were consumed within the first twenty minutes of our wedding reception. A new community germinated then, and continues to grow through the sharing of food.

We married in November of 1996, not long after closing the deal on the farm. John finished his master's thesis at Penn State and we moved our collected belongings from various apartments and parental basements. It was a chaotic but cumulatively inspiring couple of weeks. Our wedding ceremony and reception evolved into a blend of ethnic traditions, personal expression and a dash of good humor. We hoped the diverse group of people attending would have a good time at the wedding; what we didn't anticipate was that a deeper connection to our green dreams would be made among our closest circle of friends.

Back to the pirages, a traditional Latvian and Estonian food originating from Lisa's ethnic roots. Pirages are made from a sour cream-based yeast dough wrapped around a sautéed onion-bacon filling and served warm as an appetizer or snack. The overabundance of wedding pirages were the wonderful result of Lisa's mom deliciously channeling her pre-wedding mother-of-the-bride anxieties into baking.

The pirages were quickly devoured, as well as the twenty gallons of homemade lager, the fish dinner, and fourteen different desserts baked by Lisa's mom. Around midnight as the dance floor buzzed and the dessert table emptied, someone asked: "So when are we going to do this again?"

We perfunctorily replied, "Why don't you come to the farm next Fourth of July weekend?" At the time, we were fixated on social fun and farm-fresh meals, but we later realized that something bigger was brewing. Folks were hungry, but not just for food. We were all craving a slice of community, a connection to a shared table where we could discover ourselves, connect with friends, and immerse ourselves in outdoor fun. At the time, we didn't realize the nourishment we were creating.

The following Fourth of July weekend our Reunion, now annual, took place. We chose the name Reunion on intuition that first year, sensing that it would be a gathering of kindred souls, even if many had never met. The Reunion name sticks to this day, as does the tradition. While many of the original wedding crowd still make a yearly July pilgrimage, new friends have joined this evolving, eclectic fellowship. Every year, between twenty and forty people arrive, to sleep in all corners of the house and camp under the stars.

Active participation is the underlying theme of the weekend. Many folks teach or share something for which they have a passion. We've had mini-workshops on topics from envelope-making to organized discussions on relationships in the 90s. Some help out with projects around the farm, including building a garden trellis, constructing solar collectors, and digging a pond. Some people contribute through cooking a special meal. For several years, Marshall, a writer from northern Indiana with Amish family roots, has fried turkeys with an outdoor fryer bubbling with five gallons (19 liters) of peanut oil. Someone else pumps out Belgian waffles the morning of the Fourth of July, served with strawberries, blueberries and whipped cream.

> The trick is to grow up without getting old.
> — Frank Lloyd Wright

With such a crowd, sleeping space on beds is at a premium, reserved for families with little bambinos. Showers are rationed. A port-a-potty was used for years, until a Sun Mar Excel composting toilet was added. The weather has run the gamut from blistering heat to torrential downpours. And yet, every year, folks from as far away as California and Virginia fly or drive to the Reunion. Why do they put up with these inconveniences when the local motel is available?

There is more going on than fun and games. We were all, in our own way, yearning to reconnect, to feel a true part of a community, and to be accepted for who we are. We're breaking routines, enjoying companionship, breathing fresh air all day, and developing ourselves instead of depleting our bank accounts.

On one level, the Reunion weekend exudes a dose of goofy fun. Hours are spent flying kites and engaging in water balloon skirmishes. Bobby, a frequent guest, is a small-town Virginia lawyer by day and by night and on weekends, performs magic, making cards disappear. Stoic grown-ups smile and kids scream in glee. At the Reunion, Bobby's talents extend to balloon hats, created in time to wear to Monroe's Fourth of July fireworks. Bobby floors us with his creativity in balloon hats, nary a design repeating itself. He's created the Titanic, the Statue of Liberty, a basket of fruit and mice in search of Wisconsin cheese — all in the form of balloon hats.

Open mic night in the barn during a July 4th Reunion at Inn Serendipity.

Community provides us with a safety net, an island of acceptance where we can let our guards down, relax and be ourselves. A popular Reunion event is the open mic night, an ad hoc talent show held in the second floor of the dairy barn. Bobby perfectly fits the role of emcee and creates a supportive performing environment that resonates under the mortis-and-tenon barn. People are empowered to get up on stage. They dust off guitars that have been sitting in the attic and sing songs they haven't sung since

their lead in the high school play. Favorite poems are shared, as well as an original song that chronicles the weekend's events.

This safety zone is also evident in families with babies. At first, we couldn't understand why people would come to the Reunion with newborns. Yet families with the youngest children seem to be the first to enthusiastically RSVP. One year we realized what was happening while watching new parents Toni and Rick, a somewhat typical dual-income suburban family from Michigan, relaxed and chatting under the willow tree. Where was their six-month old son, Brendan? Toni and Rick are devoted and protective parents, so the scene seemed odd until we saw Brendan, giggling as he bounced from lap to lap by a group of folks sitting on the opposite side of the yard. It does takes a village to raise a child. Parents don't have to worry about where their kids are or what they are doing because they know that the community keeps watch.

Sharing is another important community element manifested in the Reunion weekend. The folks coming in for the weekend are intensely busy people: fast-tracked jobs, volunteer activities, a chaotic social schedule, workouts at the gym. They're understandably tired. One would think that a couple of days off over a holiday weekend would prompt a vegetative couch potato state, prone to long naps and disconnecting from the world. But that's not the case.

By escaping their harried lifestyle and replacing it with a heavy dose of community and camaraderie, an inner energy source is rekindled. Engaged, provocative and deep conversations are the norm, covering life passions, potential change, dreams and goals, the fate of the planet, and reviews of upcoming summer movies. Kara, a high school teacher from Kansas, wants to do a quilting demonstration. Dave, a big Italian teddy bear kind of guy from Pittsburgh, taught how to make his family's authentic Italian homemade pasta — from scratch. Marshall and his wife Bethany led a Sunday morning interfaith discussion on the meaning of grace in our lives. The farm sets the stage for making this happen. Something about being in the country, among wandering butterflies, attention-starved barn cats, and the star-studded night sky, brings out the best in us, lets our souls shine.

Communal experiences and inspiring moments are also a core element of community. At the Reunion, food is the catalyst that sparks this fusion. Lisa's critical responsibility every morning is to get the army-sized coffee maker plugged in and percolating. Morning conversations start as soon as the java brews, lingering over hearty breakfasts of build-your-own burritos or raspberry cream cheese French toast casserole. At every meal, we start talking about and anticipating the next one: authentic Wisconsin brats on the grill, midnight apple crisp, bountiful salad bowls fluffy with fresh salad greens from the garden, a sundae bar after the Fourth of July fireworks with homemade hot fudge sauce. People pitch in and help chop cabbage, wash lettuce, and load the dishwasher. These meals provide nourishment, spark conversations, and inspire change.

We communicate the Reunion specifics to our friends through a website, trying to welcome a diversity of faiths, ethnicities, political views and sexual orientations. We can think of no better gift than sharing our farm with an evolving group of eclectic soulmates on this journey called life, at least for one weekend in July.

Join the Anti-consumer Community

Participants in the Reunion pitch in to make the event fun and enjoyable, but without the waste. We use reusable dishes, silverware, and plastic stadium cups left over from our university days, maximize car space together when catching the fireworks in town or the drive-in double feature, and taste our way through many of the flavors of locally-produced foods and beverages, with names like havarti, Swiss and Gruyere cheeses, and Berghoff brands of craft-brewed beers from the Joseph Huber Brewing Company, the second-oldest brewery in the nation. We eat through a bounty from our gardens — no plastic wrap or supermarket runs needed — as well as those of Kara, who arrives with coolers of her freshly harvested Kansas produce. While the group's spirit over the Fourth of July holiday reflects the nation's holiday mood, by keeping money local and waste to a minimum we are perhaps celebrating the true patriot spirit: Conserving our country's resources, supporting local commerce and caring for rural community.

The non-profit organization, Center for a New American Dream, has devised the Turn The Tide project, composed of nine personal actions to protect the environment. These actions have guided many of our group's efforts during the Reunion, and can be readily adapted for use by individuals or organizations. Handy calculators tally and track individual and collective impacts of the actions taken. The nine steps are:

1. **Skip a car trip each week.** Replace a weekly 20 mile car trip by telecommuting, biking or combining errands, and we reduce our annual emissions of the greenhouse gas carbon dioxide by nearly a thousand pounds.

2. **Replace one beef meal each week.** Meat production is extremely resource-intensive – livestock currently consumes 70 percent of America's grain production. For every 1,000 of us who take this action, we save over 70,000 pounds of grain, 70,000 pounds of topsoil and 40 million gallons of water per year.

3. **Shift your shrimp consumption.** Today, nearly 70 percent of the world's fisheries are fully fished or overfished, and about 60 billion pounds of fish, sharks, and seabirds die each year as "bycatch" – animals caught accidentally as a result

of wasteful fishing techniques. For every 1,000 of us who stop eating shrimp, we can save over 12,000 pounds of sea life per year.

4. **Declare independence from junk mail.** We started by using the Center for a New American Dream's online form to get ourself off junkmail lists. For every 1,000 of us who succeed in cutting our personal bulk mail in half, we will save 170 trees, nearly 46,000 pounds of carbon dioxide, and 70,000 gallons of water each year.

5. **Replace four standard light bulbs with energy-efficient compact fluorescent lights (CFLs).** Replace four standard bulbs with low-mercury CFLs, and we reduce our electricity bills by more than $100 over the lives of those bulbs. More importantly, we prevented the emission of five thousand pounds of carbon dioxide.

6. **Move the thermostat 3° F (16°C).** Heating and cooling represents the biggest chunk of our home energy consumption. Just by turning the thermostat down three degrees in the winter and up three degrees in the summer, we can prevent the emission of nearly 1,100 pounds of carbon dioxide annually, per household.

7. **Eliminate lawn and garden pesticides.** Americans directly apply 70 million pounds of pesticides to home lawns and gardens each year and, in so doing, kill birds and other wildlife and pollute our precious water resources. By refusing to use pesticides, our three-person household keeps 45 ounces of poisons out of our watershed, a quantity which seems small, but which is capable of contaminating millions of gallons of water.

8. **Install an efficient showerhead and low flow faucet aerators.** Available water supply is diminishing rapidly as human populations swell and inefficiently drain precious aquifers. For every 1,000 of us who install faucet aerators and high-efficiency showerheads, we save nearly 8 million gallons of water and prevent over 450,000 pounds of carbon dioxide emissions each year.

9. **Inspire two friends.** There's an easy way to triple the positive impact we make with these nine actions — convince two friends to join in our effort. Just pass a copy of this list to receptive friends, direct them to <www.newdream.org/turnthetide/>.

SOURCES AND RESOURCES

Center for the New American Dream
   Website: www.newdream.org
   The Center for a New American Dream helps Americans change the way they
   consume to improve the quality of life, protect the environment, and promote
   social justice. A copy of the *More Fun, Less Stuff Starter Kit* comes with a basic
   membership.

Unappreciated Rhubarb

Unless you grew up with rhubarb, you probably haven't been properly introduced. There's someone reading this who is already cringing at the word rhubarb, recalling sour nightmares of the time when they bit into a fresh rhubarb stalk; that unexpected, bitter tartness of rhubarb still lingering in their mouth. From then on, they've declined offers of rhubarb pie or anything else containing that demonic fruit.

We all share dour food experiences, particularly when we expectantly bite into something new, anticipating one cast of flavors and textures only to get another. We bite into a chunk of tofu because we hear it's supposed to be good for us and become overwhelmed by its rubbery, slimy texture. It's supposed to be seasoned and cooked. We pop a handful of gooseberries into our mouth, expecting the same juicy, luscious taste common among other summer berries, only to have a tart rhubarb flashback. Foods like oysters, sushi and olives can also traumatize virginal palates, particularly when the unknowing connoisseur eats one without context or proper accompaniment.

It's easy to chuckle over such poignant food encounters, but we find ourselves often transferring the rhubarb reaction to other areas of our lives. We have a bad experience with someone or something, and we write off any future potential immediately. Sometimes gas-guzzling SUVs really are needed by those who drive them. Some health insurance companies really do put the quality of care over their bottom line. These rhubarb reactions sometimes happen so naturally and without question that we don't see what we're doing. We don't realize what we are writing off, and can end up losing the opportunity to influence or change the way things are.

Sometimes we need to whip up a little extra effort to taste the goodness in our lives. Judge less and embrace and listen more. Often, one of two things can make a meaningful difference in dealing with the proverbial rhubarbs in our lives: adding an extra ingredient or offering some hand-holding support.

A dash of an extra ingredient can turn a situation upside down. Our herb garden is right out the back door, primarily devoted to basil to indulge our love affair with pesto. We prepare savory pesto, blending the fresh basil, olive oil, walnuts, garlic, parmesan cheese, and a dash of salt in the food processor. The taste is a delight, but our first pesto batch turned ugly green when it was exposed to air. After a couple experiments, we discovered a splash of lemon juice preserves the basil in its natural color. A dash of an extra ingredient, in this case lemon juice, made all the difference.

The second element that can turn around a rhubarb moment is some hand-holding support. What we sometimes need is someone with experience to introduce us to a new design or approach. We have a natural tendency to surround ourselves with people similar to ourselves, people who mirror our life stages and perspectives, thereby validating our existence. If everyone around us operates the same way and wears the same thing, we must be okay.

Falling victim to this peer group echo while living in Chicago, we surrounded ourselves with twenty-something clones. We had been to London, hung out at Wrigley Field, and sipped wine together at art gallery openings. While moving to a rural community didn't increase social diversity from an ethnic or racial perspective, we developed several deep bonds with some local senior citizens who have guided us to new insights and experiences. Retiring from active living, they're not. They are busier and more involved in our community than they were when they worked full time. John and Mary are among those.

We met Mary and John when we began looking for a farm in Green County. While we had been in the area for weekend getaways, we didn't know anyone personally. Through a group called Servas, an international peace organization that promoted cross-cultural understanding through homestays when traveling, we decided to explore Green County the same way. The philosophy behind Servas is that if we each opened our doors to another, shared a meal together as friends, we'd be closer to world peace. We met many fascinating Servas folks while traveling abroad and thought perhaps there was a Servas member in the Green County area we could contact. Sure enough, one listing existed for Green County. We contacted them to see if we might arrange a visit. Could we meet with them and ask questions about the area? We received a postcard back, welcoming us for a visit that led to friendship, deepening with time.

We think John and Mary are somewhere in their 70s. It's hard to guess the age of people when their energy level is as vibrant as the crocuses that pop up outside our kitchen window every April. Both remain practicing doctors, sometimes leading Sierra Club trips in their spare time. Serving as Peace Corps volunteers in Afghanistan during the 1960s — with their kids in tow — they later returned to Monroe and designed and built their energy-efficient passive solar home with a backyard garden that feeds them throughout the year. If you ask folks in town about Mary and John, adjectives like eccentric and odd might surface — in a respectful sort of way. Folks see them riding around on their bicycles in all kinds of weather. They're often circulating a petition, serving on different community boards, planning new international adventures, or reading books and publications by the pound.

People like John and Mary who promenade into our lives expand our lives and hand-hold us through new experiences, assuming we remain receptive and open. Mary and John taught us how to grow soybeans, can pears and carbonate grape juice. They help jump-start our garden with pepper and eggplants transplants. They introduced us to the realtor who helped us find our farm, were our first customers when we started selling eggs, and took us to our first nude beach in Wisconsin - by canoe. We would have missed out on these experiences, and the friendship we have with them, had we not kept our hearts and minds open during those first encounters.

Meeting John for the first time can be a bit like biting raw rhubarb. His sharp wit and puns causes our minds to spin off into space. We nod politely, often struggling to understand what he's said, let alone comprehend the punch line. Such an initial encounter can curdle a relationship, but something about John fascinated us. We kept returning to ring their doorbell, welcomed inside for a glass of homemade sherry and whatever was simmering on the stove. We observed how Mary's sweet demeanor cooked down John's tart witticisms, and together they blended into a quirky, balanced, partnership.

Rhubarb is a hearty plant, readily transplanted from another's garden. Rhubarb is among our first garden harvests, reminding us that a little sugar — or a little friendly support — goes a long way.

Searching for Underrated Treasures

In the transition from an urban world to green acres, we've encountered a range of underrated treasures. We're talking about things that aren't fully appreciated in our culture, yet are overflowing with potential. In several cases, it took us a while to warm up to these treasures. We carried assumptive baggage: we tried beets, heavily pickled, and didn't like them. We shut our minds and hearts after one experience. Then we learned we could eat them boiled and mashed with butter, or formed like a burger and baked. We avoided rain by hurridly running inside to avoid getting wet. Now we relish thunderstorms and often run outside as the last drops fall, trying to discover a rainbow with Liam.

We are learning to be more open-minded, to give things and people a chance before jumping to any conclusions. Here are some of our favorite underrated treasures:

- **Swiss chard.** Before we ever tasted swiss chard, we condemned its appearance, looking like a cross between overgrown, tough spinach and bolted lettuce. Therefore, it couldn't taste good, we thought. Swiss chard is the underrated second cousin of spinach: its larger leaves make it easier and quicker to clean and eat. While all chard doesn't taste the same, the varieties we grow, and grow easily, have a distinct sweet flavor and readily blanch to be preserved in the freezer, increasing our enjoyment of healthy dark leafy greens in February. The rainbow varieties of swiss chard with their palette of brightly colored stems are so vibrant we've thought about sneaking them into flower arrangements on the table.

- **Youth hostels.** While in our mid-thirties and statistically outside the typical backpacker budget traveler population, you'll often find us staying at a youth hostel during our travels. The word youth is a bit of a misnomer, since most youth hostels are open to all ages and are among the best travel values around. Today's hostellers are just as likely to be in their thirties and bring their family by car; people of all ages use hostels as a gateway to cultural exploration and the appreciation of nature. For an average of $15 per person per night, we can surround ourselves with stimulating conversation with other travelers, curl up in a clean bed, use the kitchen to make our meals, and stay in some unique places, including closed army barracks, lighthouses and historic buildings. Hostelling International currently provides over 35 million overnight stays a year through 4,200 hostels in more than 60 countries.

• **Handwritten notes.** For the price of a first class stamp, we can send handwritten on a piece of paper to someone anywhere in the US. Add a bit more change and it can fly anywhere in the world. In our world of e-mails and voicemails and other forms of techno-communication, sometimes pen and paper has the ability to evoke emotion, appreciation and lasting sentiment far more than cable wires. While we use e-mail — it's our primary form of informational communication both on a business and personal level — there is something personal about a handwritten note expressing thanks, support, celebration, sadness, or some other communication. We've learned not to obsess over a perfect card or words, but to get our thoughts on paper, stick on the stamp, and get it in the mail. We thrive on creatively recycling various materials into cards, like clipping used stamps from received mail (especially international stamps) to create our own cards.

• **Sub-compact cars.** We heard Amory Lovins with the Rocky Mountain Institute talk about a product that is so poorly designed that it's only 1 percent efficient at accomplishing what it was designed to do: move a person or objects from one place to another. That invention, known as the internal combustion engine, is not only wasting resources, it's polluting the air, water and soil, and is among the most significant contributors to the greenhouse effect. For every gallon of gasoline burned, about twenty pounds of carbon dioxide is released into the atmosphere.

When it came to meeting our transportation needs, we wanted to select something that was as fuel efficient as possible within our budgetary means: a Geo Metro. We call it our go-cart. When we do end up leaving the farm to drop off mail, attend meetings or take care of a few errands — usually several times a week — we use one of the more fuel efficient cars on the market. When we need a pick-up truck for a heavy load, we'll rent or borrow one from our neighbors. Once we're back in the cities or traveling overseas, however, we return to our old ways, riding the trains, subways and buses. During the years living in downtown Chicago, we never owned a vehicle; we were not alone.

It's easy to rail about some vehicles as gas-guzzlers. But in so doing, we miss the opportunity to praise sub-compact cars or hybrid vehicles. Fuel technology and automotive efficiency has blessed these little cars, giving them pretty good mileage and reliable use, though there's plenty of room for improvement. We're probably among the few farmers who drive used Geo Metros with pride, cutting down on the pollution we add to the atmosphere and reducing our car ownership costs. Every time we make the choice to avoid buying a vehicle larger than we need, we support a market for more fuel-efficient smaller cars.

+ **Crafting and handiwork.** Despite being able to buy just about anything any-where — or maybe because of this — crafting and handiwork, creating

SOURCES AND RESOURCES

Environmental Defense
Website: www.environmentaldefense.org
Environmental Defense is dedicated to pro-tecting the environmental rights of all peo-ple, including future generations. Among these rights are clean air and water, healthy and nourishing food, and a flourishing ecosystem. They offer a research tool to help determine how fuel efficient your vehicle is and how much carbon dioxide, among other things, your driving will emit in a year.

Hostelling International
Website: www.hiayh.org
This network fostering meaningful, afford-able travel accommodations both in the US and throughout the world offering hostels in over 60 countries.

Rocky Mountain Institute
Website: www.rmi.org
From sustainable development resources to easy-to-understand tools for greater resource efficiency and restoration, this innovative non-profit helps organizations and individuals achieve greater security and prosperity in a life-sustaining economy.

Paul Hawken, Amory Lovins and L. Hunter Lovins, *Natural Capitalism: Creating the Next Industrial Revolution*, Bay Back Books, 2000.

Katie Alvord, *Divorce Your Car! Ending the Love Affair with the Automobile*, New Society Publishers, 2000.

Jane Holtz Kay, *Asphalt Nation: How the Automobile Took Over America and How We can Take it Back*, University of California Press, 1998.

CREATING AND CARING FOR COMMUNITY   161

something personal with our hands, feels good. We're always looking for opportunities to craft treasures out of throwaways, rescuing items destined for the trash and giving them a new life. A well-received tradition of ours is to make scrapbooks out of wedding cards for newly married friends. What can be done with that pile of greeting cards post-wedding? We cut out various pictures, words and phrases and glue them to the outside cover of a plain scrapbook or photo album with white glue, then seal the cards with a couple layers of decoupage glaze. Lisa first experimented with this idea when we didn't know what to do with our wedding cards post-event, and now it has become our specialty, using the same idea for baby scrapbook gifts as well.

That Interesting Couple on County P

If you hear someone around these parts refer to that "interesting couple on County P," that would be us. Guess we've earned that reputation. A solar hot water heating system sits on our roof. We're continually tearing out our lawn and replacing it with native plants, trees, shrubs and perennials. We built some strange pagan thing called a labyrinth. We constructed a greenhouse using straw bales. We grow organically, are married but have different last names, and host a curious lot of people passing through the farm, from songwriters to peace activists.

We wear interesting as a badge of honor. When someone calls us interesting, it's sort of a polite way of saying I have no idea what you're doing or why you're doing it, but I'm curious. Tell me more, show me how the wind turbine system works, and let me taste the Estonian pickled pumpkin. Interesting isn't slamming the door in someone's face. It's leaving the door open a crack, offering an opportunity to try, listen, understand, respect and positively grow from the experience. Interesting is approachable, a potential bridge to something new, and an opportunity for us to grow as a result. And it's met by a reciprocal response from us: marshmallow-pear jello, watercress early spring salads, and using Coca-Cola to loosen bolts on the lawnmower — how interesting.

We're on a secret quest to introduce our local friends to new foods when we host various potlucks and gatherings throughout the year. Some entries turn out better than others. The first year John made hummus, which, when we placed it in the land of the familiar by describing it as garlic-flavored mashed potatoes, went over well.

The Swedish glogg, a warmed port wine with brandy and spices, was an easy winner. One retired farmer friend barely made it out of his chair after three glasses. One of the biggest hits was a surprise: arroz con leche, a warm milk drink we discovered when traveling in Guatemala, made from milk, honey, cinnamon and rice. The street vendors would sell it at night, making it a perfect nightcap. We thought this topped the interesting taste chart, something we crossed borders to discover. When we put it out in the crock pot at a holiday gathering, the retired farmers started drinking it up as if they were little boys who had just come in from the cold. Turns out, many of them had something just like it when they were young. A couple of guys asked for raisins and some of them ate it with a spoon. Interesting. Here we thought we were expanding tastebuds. In the end, we were the ones expanding.

That interesting label, that bridge to new experiences, applies to our relationships with people as well. We don't see a whole lot of folks walking down the streets where we live. But a couple of years ago we kept seeing this lanky tall guy walking through town. That's interesting, we thought. In small towns today, you're a bit unusual if you walk while the rest of us sit behind the steering wheel at traffic lights. This guy was walking, wearing a beret (not exactly a common Wisconsin fashion item). We nicknamed him Pierre. We thought he looked interesting. Walking.

Eventually we met Chris, a.k.a. Pierre, when we crossed paths at the gym. Indeed, he is gloriously interesting and has probably been written off as a little too odd by many people in his lifetime. Chris was born and raised in Monroe, but had returned to help his elderly parents. In between, he traveled the world several times over, often by foot. He ran a restaurant in Israel, a bookstore in New York City, makes an Indian curry that could tingle the deadest of taste buds and has such an extensive music collection that the Smithsonian has expressed their desire to acquire it. And that's the short, interesting, list. Chris has evolved into a soul mate, a kindred, mysterious worldly spirit that ended up in this little corner of the world. We have learned much from him and relish his company, conversation and cooking, not to mention the evenings shared with him at the local drive-in theater, which he managed for a couple summers.

The challenge is to actively seek out the interesting. On one level, this isn't too hard in our increasingly homogenized world. Interesting stands out like a dandelion in the middle of a putting green. Interesting encounters, experiences and friendships take our journey in potentially new and unforeseen directions. We strive to keep a place open on our table of life for something interesting to serendipitously arrive.

Thinking Outside of the Box

Whether we live in the heart of the urban jungle, along a winding road in the sub-urbs, or end up living in the middle of a cornfield, encouraging diversity and foster-ing new perspectives is an essential element of leading a passionate and engaged life. Here are some of the ideas we thrive on:

+ **Foster friendships of different ages.** In Chicago, we almost completely sur-rounded ourselves with folks that mirrored ourselves through age, occupa-tion, interests, and movie choices. Now we have connected with a deeper and wider range of age groups, particularly generations older than us. There are many retirees who have evolved into adopted family. We have much to learn from their years of experience, and we like to think that we blow a youthful gust of energy their way, too.

+ **Host potlucks.** A "Club of the Leather Aprons," or "Junto" for short. These were the names Ben Franklin gave to the 1727 gathering of colleagues and friends. They discussed current events and heady topics in an informal, but enterprising, round-table format, with lots of food and drink for all. Inspired by Ben, we intermittently host our own Junto among our circle of local friends, with everyone bringing a dish to share over a potluck meal. From debating the word "consumer" to discussing organics and creativity, our group has also demonstrated a penchant for cooking gourmet and gar-den-fresh food with an ethnic flair. The leftovers, when there are any, aren't bad either. Bob, a lanky surgical assistant at the local clinic, brings a few loaves of his hearty breads, earning him the honorary title of "Baker Bob." John, a cherubic man who ran the town flower shop for many years and has quite the culinary flair, specializes in grilled meats with lip-licking flavorful basting sauces.

+ **Travel to open the heart, mind and spirit.** No matter what type of situa-tion or community we live in, getting out of that context and into another stimulates the mind and soul. Travel, whether it's a day-long field trip or a month-long international pilgrimage, gives us enough of a dose of newness that we come home changed, revitalized, and inspired.

- **Keep a diverse reading list.** We are selective on how we spend our reading budget, particularly when it comes to magazines or newsletters. By no means complete, since we often read many other publications at the library or at friends' houses, we have a few favorites that bring an eclectic range of opinions and information to our attention, including:

  - *Utne Reader.* A collection of articles from alternative presses around the country, organized into thematic issues like love, peace, or a sustainable economy. <www.utne.com>

  - *E/The Environmental Magazine.* Among the most practical sources of information for more environmentally responsible and educated living around. <www.emagazine.com>

  - *In Business.* One of the best resources for information on innovative new companies with products or services which protect, restore, or preserve the planet. <www.inbusiness.org>

  - *Natural Home.* Offers well-researched information we need to practice earth-inspired living. <www.naturalhome.com>

  - *Mother Earth News.* The guide to living wisely on Earth, addressing food, shelter, renewable energy, and many other ways to live lovingly and lightly on the planet. <www.motherearthnews.com>

  - *Yes! A Journal of Positive Futures.* Both inspiring and informative with positive information that helps us make changes in our daily life. (www.yesmagazine.com)

- **Turn Off the Stimuli.** The corollary to horizon-broadening travel is pulling the plug on the TV and on mainstream media. From hundreds of cable TV stations to contrived shopping malls, from pop-up ads on the Internet to billboard bloated-highways, we live in an era of sensory overload. It's no wonder we can recite the ingredients of a Big Mac but can't identify all the trees out our windows. Sometimes the quickest route to feeding innovation (and perhaps achieving peace of mind), is turning off the noise in whatever guise it might take, whether it's turning off the television or skipping the pre-movie commercials at the theatre.

The peace and quiet does wonders, allowing our mind and emotions to wander.

Cappuccino and Community

Our neighbor, Anna, telephoned one evening. "Hey Lisa, I have something to ask you," Anna said, anxiously.

Immediately thinking something was wrong, Lisa quickly answered, "Sure, anything."

"Have you ever had one of those cappuccino things?" Anna asked.

It's moments like these when we feel like we're on some catwalk between urban and rural worlds. Have we had cappuccino? We've had cappuccino from Florence, Italy to Little Italy in Boston and a slew of coffeehouses in between. During our transition between the office cubicle and the farm's barns, John worked as a barista at a Starbucks in downtown Chicago. He could pull a shot of espresso with the best of them.

On another, more deeper level, when Anna called asking the cappuccino question, we felt like we were finally at home, accepted into a community. Anna's question reflected her interest in a new experience, just like the time we toured her farm to learn about raising pigs and cows. We trusted that she'd not make a mockery of our ignorance about how farms operate. She trusted that we'd not make her feel self-conscious about never having had a cappuccino. That we could be trusted meant more to us than she may have ever realized.

But then Anna knew from the start how to garner our eternal loyalty: through food and drink. Anna and her husband, Ivan, are family-size traditional dairy and hog farmers. They live on County P about a half a mile east. We first met Anna on one of those bleak early winter days where gray skies foreshadow a long, bitterly cold winter ahead. We heard the doorbell ring and there stood Anna, balancing a fresh pie in each hand.

She unpretentiously announced, "I happened to make some extra pies. Would you like some?" Would we like some? Is the sky blue? Did the Titanic sink? Perhaps she could see the twinkle in our souls as we gratefully nodded in appreciation. The pies were hot out of the oven, one rhubarb and the other blueberry. All of a sudden, the house grew warmer.

Flash forward fourteen months later to the cappuccino question. Anna and Ivan, along with one of their sons, Brett, and his girlfriend, came over one night for coffee class. John explained the differences between a latte, espresso and mocha, and the importance of quality Arabica beans. Variations of coffee drinks were taste-tested by Anna, while Ivan and Brett concluded that they preferred Lisa's home-made beer. We shared our beverages of choice, while also sharing conversations about travel and their experiences growing up in the area.

Part of our reason for moving was to find such community, to discover our neighbors, to share experiences, to grow roots, to become more whole. Community, like the human spirit and the vibrant energy of the land, takes us in and renews us. It embraces our connection to place. Community is a precious gift when it suddenly appears, sometimes bearing warm pies, on our doorstep.

Despite Chicago's high population density, we felt terribly disconnected and alone at times when we lived there. We rarely met the neighbors in the apartments adjacent to ours, much less felt the urge to share pie with them. The feeling was apparently reciprocal. We're not sure if it was us, or the pace of the city that caused us to feel this way. So we moved to the country with the hopes of finding a connection, a sense of belonging to something deeper than an address and mortgage. And we did.

We realized that community isn't really a noun, it's a verb. It's not something that quaintly descends upon us because we live in an area with more cows than people. Moving to the country from the an urban setting means more than filling out a change of address form at the post office. We have voluntarily joined a different culture, engaged in a conversion of sorts. In our American society of homogenized suburbia or increasingly gentrified urban enclaves, we forget to realize and appreciate that being surrounded by privacy fences and gates is not the only way to live. It's up to us to meet the other side with openness and understanding.

Building barriers came easy in Chicago; that's how we survived. No eye contact with the homeless. Avoid conversations on the bus by keeping our nose in the newspaper. One day we read about a young woman, living in the building across the street from Lisa's apartment, who had been followed home on the bus and into her apartment, and then brutally murdered. A random act of violence in a community where no one knows each other's name. Our anonymity was our choice while living in the city — so caught up in our careers and routines that we never embraced community.

We needed a fresh start on a farm, away from the city life. We needed a compelling reason to break these barriers and our defensive attitude, to skip the caller ID, drop the double lock security system, and leave our car unlocked. Some city folks do move to the country with an attitude of isolation, fear and distrust, however. Fencing quickly goes up, followed by no trespassing signs. Laverne at the post office doesn't recognize them by name, and they quickly grow disillusioned with their preconceived expectations and blissful perception of country life.

We can't construct privacy fencing barriers and expect a neighbor to climb over with fresh baked goods. Community isn't a cable channel we can turn on and off at will. It's a relationship, a commitment, built upon trust, respect, sharing and caring. Admittedly, we've learned to agree to disagree with our neighbors on a good many topics. But these issues have not interfered with us being neighborly or involved in the community in different ways, developing trust with those around us.

Buying a home is a leap of faith on the buyer's part. It's a financial commitment as well as an emotional, time-consuming project. What we didn't realize at the time while putting an offer and arranging house inspections, was that this was an even bigger deal for Del and Joy, the couple who sold us the farm. They were not selling a building for profit, they were sharing history — and a piece of their community.

Since purchasing the farm, we've been warmly adopted by Del and Joy. Joy gives us garden lessons, not once laughing at our lack of weed identification skills. Del helps us understand how the water softener system works and keeps our lawn mower blades sharp. While Joy and Del realized we would be bringing change to their farm, something in their hearts told them the first time they met us that things would work out fine. What we're describing goes beyond a sale price and title deed. It's about having trust. Their trust went beyond the legal parameters of a house sale, guiding us to where we are today. In a way, they gave us seeds to grow our life journey: faith in people, trust in community, and a hope that we can continue the love and memories passing through the doors of our, and their, farm. Years later, when folks still refer to our farm as Del and Joy's farmstead, we feel connected and honored.

Supporting the Local Economy

Ecological communities offer insights as to how we might approach our local community. When we take time to examine our energy flows, the cycling of matter and materials, the interconnection of food webs, the movement from chemical-based mono-culture to organic polyculture, and other factors on our farm, we better understand how life manages to sustain itself — often, despite unwise human decisions.

Communities that exist within ecological perspectives, tend to thrive as well, providing healthy, safe and viable livelihoods for their members. Country and small-town living thrives on shared experience and cooperation. Whether it's to support the Monroe Balloon Rally, silent auction fundraiser for the arts center, or our area's biannual celebration of cheese and Swiss heritage, we're amazed by our community's commitment to working together.

In an ecosystem, numerous self-preserving mechanisms are in place to keep a system in balance. Healthy communities are much the same. The citizens must be active, engaged and empowered for the community to be vibrant. We are active participants in our community's continued prosperity, development and future. People wave, offer greetings, or smile because they know us as residents in the community. The library staff, Sue at the post office, and even the mayor recognizes us, and we them. Our local involvement has grown slowly while we learn more about the values, needs and interests of those who have lived here all their lives. We devote time to get to know people and discover the heritage that makes the community what it is today. What cheese factory has the best Swiss cheese? What tree is the golden eagle nesting in, down the road? Where is the abandoned railroad bed with the best wild berry patch? We're learning. We recognize, too, that a stong community goes hand-in-hand with a strong and diversified local economy.

The following are among several approaches we've taken locally:

• **Keep our dollars in the community.** Whenever possible, we try to keep our spending within our community. By patronizing local and family-owned businesses — even if it may cost a bit more — we form relationships with shop owners, people learn about what we're doing, and community grows.

Money is a tool, has value, and can send a clear message. In an effort to encourage local purchasing power, some communities have developed a local currency. As much as 30 percent of the revenue from sales at chain stores and big box stores leaves the community. As these retailers move in, smaller mom-and-pop stores close down, unable to compete with deep discount pricing and tax benefits extended to big retailers by local governments.

- **Buy and use locally-made products or services.** The corollary of keeping our dollars local is to seek out goods that are produced as close to our home base as possible. A locally-based economy greatly decreases the need for shipping, which in turn reduces both economic and environmental costs. It builds pride in local products and services, and can greatly reduce North American support of unfair trade.

- **Borrow a cup of sugar.** Community is built around relationships. Often, the most important ones are the simple ones that meet day to day needs: a missing cup of sugar, an extra wheelbarrow or longer ladder that's needed for a day, an extra tablecloth for a potluck supper. Whenever we needed that cup of sugar, our first response was, at one time, to drive into town to pick it up. We weren't used to having neighbors that (a) we knew and (b) we could call on in these situations. We wasted time and energy heading into town while overlooking a chance to build community connections. As time passed, we overcame this streak of misplaced independence, and we now enjoy helping neighbors and friends in much the same way.

- **Share the excess.** We are blessed with bounty in many different forms. Too many zucchinis, holiday cookies, duplicate photos, packing boxes, and scrap wood. As we continue to build community relationships, we develop a deeper connection to our neighbors and their needs, and how we could help fulfill them. We bake extra and drop off cinnamon rolls or tell a visiting writer about a great new greenhouse our neighbors devised using an old hog shed, hoping to spark interest in an article about their new business. It did.

+ **Barter and exchange more.** When we started having success raising chickens for farm-fresh eggs, we realized we finally had something valuable to barter. Appreciated, especially by old-time farmer neighbors who could remember the days when fresh eggs were the norm, our free-range eggs added up to a lot of goodwill. Familiar with living in the cashless economy of credit cards and writing marketing plans, we struggled with providing services or products needed locally. This slowly changed. Our multicolored eggs are now an Inn Serendipity currency, exchanged for help in changing spark plugs on our car and for our wonderfully talented wood-working neighbor, Burnette, who artistically crafted fallen trees from his woodlot into the Inn Serendipity sign and a chair for Liam. Money is not the only currency around. Sometimes currency comes in the form of gratitude, utility, compassion and smiles.

SOURCES AND RESOURCES

Institute for Local Self Reliance's New Rules Project
 Website: www.newrules.org
 Offering resources on ways to rebuild local economies, invigorate democracy, strengthen the sense of community and plan for the next generation, the New Rules Project addresses agriculture, electricity, environment, equity, finance, governance, retail, sports, information, and taxation sectors.

Mark Roseland, *Toward Sustainable Communities: Resources for Citizens and Their Governments,* New Society Publishers, 1998.

Michael Schuman, *Going Local: Creating Self-Reliant Communities in a Global Age,* Free Press, 1998.

Stacy Mitchell, *The Home Town Advantage: How to Defend Your Main Street Against Chain Stores and Why it Matters,* Institute for Local Self Reliance, 2000.

A House of Straw

The three little pigs had it wrong. The pig that built the house of straw has the house with the most potential. It just needed a little cement, clay and community to hold things together.

Our vision for the strawbale greenhouse evolved over time. Of the two barns on the farm, the granary had been a distant cousin to the dairy barn. The granary wasn't as grand a building and it had outlived its present day usefulness. It was also in much worse condition. Every winter we'd lose more barn siding or roof shingles, flying off like Frisbees during windy days. The granary needed a new lease on life.

We did have a simpler option for the granary than rebuilding it — burning it down, an increasingly common last rite for old wooden barns across the country. Expensive to maintain, these historic barns often provide a last service as training for the local volunteer fire department.

Our goals have been to restore nature, preserve historic structures, and to renew farm life. Giving new life to traditional agricultural buildings is consistent with this strategy. The granary proved to be an ideal opportunity; but what we failed to anticipate was how building a house of straw serendipitously builds community, and is yet another refrain of the energy theme: positive energy attracts and further stimulates positive energy. Our visions stimulate other ideas, and community is expanded in the process.

Corn crib and granary in need of repair.

JOHN IVANKO

Our vision is to cultivate Wisconsin-grown bananas or papayas in the greenhouse, furthering our food independence while also offering niche agricultural crops for sale. We also have tropical visions of soaking in the greenhouse hot tub on icy January days.

The straw bale greenhouse is oriented south, with east and west-facing walls containing insulated glass glazing. The remainder of the structure is in-filled with straw bale and covered with 2 inches (5 cm) of cement-based stucco on the exterior

Granary-greenhouse

and a locally procured clay-based stucco on the inside. Our vision is for the 1,200-square-foot (111 m²) greenhouse to serve as a demonstration project for family farmers looking to survive in an increasingly challenging agricultural economic climate. Unless small farmers can find new or alternative markets for cultivated or value-added crops, the current trend will continue with lost livelihood, farmlands, and agricultural traditions. By demonstrating the feasibility of retrofitting an existing agricultural outbuilding into an energy-efficient, sustainably-designed greenhouse, we could expand into new specialty crop markets by growing and selling year-round, or meeting food needs on the farm.

JOHN IVANKO

The bulk of the greenhouse project took place during so-called Strawbale September. By the time straw bales were being stacked, the original granary walls had been stripped, revealing the foundation, timber framing and roof - ready for the straw bale infill, chicken-wire lath, stitching and stuccoing.

Straw Bale September brought a constant stream of curious, inspiring, and memorable people who willingly stacked bales, sewed walls together and plastered. All the straw balers who came that September gave a bit of themselves to bring our dream into reality. Matt, Joe and Karl were the three "straw bale boys," the backbone of the straw bale aspects of the project. Matt's company, Native Earth Construction, provided the technical expertise and experience we lacked. Karl, a devoted bicycle repair person and jack of most trades from northern Wisconsin, seemed to most enjoy the work when he was up thirty feet or more. "Captain" Joe was the straw bale rookie, aspiring to a career in green building.

Uncle Phil and Aunt Judy stepped in to contribute their renewable energy technical expertise designing the solar hot water heating system for the greenhouse. They also lent their camper to house the straw bale boys. Two MREA straw bale workshops during weekends in September brought in another twenty pairs of helping hands, along with friends from all over the continent. John's mom kept the cookie jar full, and evenings were filled with good food and conversations around the dinner table and the campfire. As community blossomed and the canvas of straw unfolded, so did our ties to friends, family and neighbors.

As the two of us look back on that month of September, we realize that much more than a building was created. Things came together and connected in ways we never dreamed possible. Friends in town gave us a call and said they had a stockpile of old windows stored in their barn they were happy to get rid of if we could use them. A local contractor called to see if we could use a couple of storm doors he was ripping out that would have otherwise been destined for the landfill. Judy and Phil brought over orange pudding flavored ice cream from the local creamery one night for everyone, which hit the spot in more ways than one.

Strawbale September was also particularly poignant because it happened during the September 11th terrorist attack on the US. While many Americans were glued to the TV, watching the tragedy over and over, those of us working on the project were joined together to partake in the work at hand, restoring the structure while perhaps reflecting on our purpose on Earth. After urgent calls to a few family members, our work commenced in earnest, the straw bales, stacking, stitching and framing seeming to center us, even in the midst of tragic events.

DESIGN CONSIDERATIONS FOR THE INN SERENDIPITY GREENHOUSE

The following items were considered in the design of the greenhouse:

- Climatic appropriateness.
- Minimization of the embodied energy — the energy needed to grow, harvest, extract, manufacture or otherwise produce a product — represented in the project.
- Bio-regionalism and local sourcing of building materials.
- Aesthetics, efficiency and eco-effectiveness.
- The enhancement of biodiversity.
- Cost (strawbale is not typically cheaper than more conventional approaches).
- Consideration of William McDonough's Hannover Principles.
- Replicability and feasibility.
- Consideration of the impacts on the Seventh Generation.

How to

Building with Straw Bale

A two-string straw bale.

While interest in and construction with straw bales has skyrocked recently, the straw bale construction movement started taking shape in the early 1900s, when compressed straw bale technology began to develop.

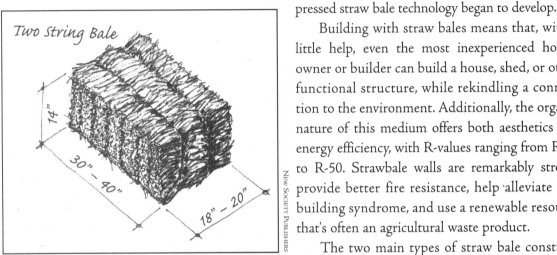

Two String Bale

14"

30" – 40"

18" – 20"

NEW SOCIETY PUBLISHERS

Building with straw bales means that, with a little help, even the most inexperienced homeowner or builder can build a house, shed, or other functional structure, while rekindling a connection to the environment. Additionally, the organic nature of this medium offers both aesthetics and energy efficiency, with R-values ranging from R-35 to R-50. Strawbale walls are remarkably strong, provide better fire resistance, help alleviate sick building syndrome, and use a renewable resource that's often an agricultural waste product.

The two main types of straw bale construction are post and beam infill and load bearing. With post and beam infill construction, straw bales are inserted between supporting studs and other framing which supports the roof. Load bearing construction, more often challenged by zoning and commercial codes, means that the roof and windows are supported by the straw bale walls.

There are many creative ways to build useful and practical buildings with straw bale, and no two structures seem to be the same since so much is based on local knowledge, materials, needs and economy. Most straw bale buildings involve a com-

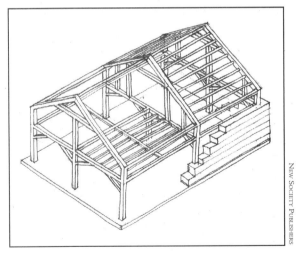

NEW SOCIETY PUBLISHERS

Straw bale infilled between timber framing.

munity of helpers attracted to the materials, camaraderie and sense of accomplishment achieved after a day of stacking bales or plastering. It's a modern day revival of the barn raising.

There are six main steps in straw bale construction:

1. **Pouring the foundation, framing, and adding the roof.** Although probably the most skill-intensive part of the whole process, these aspects need not be particularly complex. For load bearing construction, only the foundation needs to be done at this stage.

2. **Stacking bales.** With an enthusiastic crowd, it's amazing how fast a wall or building can go up. Additional detail work needs to be completed prior to the stacking of bales in places where moisture might possibly enter the wall, for example where the straw bales come in contact with the foundation.

3. **Adding lath.** Lath, which in strawbale construction often means chicken wire netting, is added to interior and exterior walls to allow plaster to adhere more readily.

4. **Stitching.** Stitching involves using polytwine to stitch up the walls, thus compressing the loose straw and connecting the lath (and other elements) together.

5. **Plastering.** Often the most messy, fulfilling, and fun, plaster is usually applied in three layers of varying thickness to cover the bales and create a

Straw bales stacked as organic infill for greenhouse walls at Inn Serendipity.

Scratch coat application over straw bales.

smooth wall surface. The first thick coat is called the "scratch coat." This coat is usually scored, or scratched, to allow the second coat (the "brown" coat) to adhere. The brown coat smoothes out the surface and fills in any major depressions. The final "finish coat" goes on very thin, can be colored, and is often followed by a sponging technique to create texture. Specific recipes for each tend to depend on the purpose, structure and climate.

6. **Finishing the carpentry work.** Adding windows, doors, and vents and, in the case of load bearing construction, the roof, makes up this final stage.

JOHN IVANKO

Scratch coat application over straw bales, next to a dried finish coat.

SOURCES AND RESOURCES

International Strawbale Registry
    Website:
    http://sbregistry.greenbuilder.com
    A database of buildings constructed
    using straw bale.

Dan Chiras, Cedar Rose Guelberth and
    Deanne Bednar, *The Natural Plaster
    Book: Earth, Lime and Gypsum Plasters
    for Natural Homes,* New Society
    Publishers, 2003.

Bruce King, *Buildings of Earth and Straw,*
    Chelsea Green Publishing, 1997.

Athena Steen, Bill Steen and David
    Bainbrindge, *The Straw Bale House,*
    Chelsea Green Publishing, 1994.

*The Last Straw: The Journal of Strawbale
    and Natural Building*
    Website: www.thelaststraw.org

CHAPTER 6

Loving Our Livelihood

Right Livelihood

The ladybugs and Japanese beetles that invade our house in the late fall and buzz around inside all winter provide a lot of free entertainment, landing upside down on the kitchen counter or crawling across and tickling the back of our necks. A ladybug will often crawl across the edge of the printer in our home office. When reaching a corner, the ladybug stops, seemingly overwhelmed by all the directional choices — it could go left or right; it could cross diagonally or head down the side of the printer. We can't help but stop what we're working on and watch this ladybug ritual which always seems to end the same way: unable to just choose one option, the ladybug stops crawling and flies away to another vantage point entirely.

> It is never too late to be what you might have been.
>
> — George Eliott

We can empathize with that little bug. When we grew restless and gloomy in our corporate jobs, we sensed the need for change but felt so overwhelmed by our daily grind that we didn't know which way to turn. Early morning and late evening commutes in the dark and long days in the cubicle left us wondering what the weather was like outside. We itched for fresh new directions and flooded ourselves with various career options. We thought: maybe the problem was the "selling stuff" aspect of advertising. Maybe if we did marketing for a non-profit organization, that would be more fulfilling than launching a new video game system, or promoting another cheesy card-giving occasion. Maybe we should start our own consulting business. Maybe pursue writing and photography more or head back to grad school. We imagined the possibilities: to be outdoors more, active in a portfolio of things we care about, and around diverse people who bring out the best in us. It brought a smile to our faces.

Like the ladybug on our computer, we paused at an impasse of one-way career paths set forth for us at the ad agency. Career paths were what college career counselors and professors prepared us for, and our parents reinforced. Have a nice, succinct, well-paid answer to the question: What do you do? But, like the ladybug, we realized we felt uncomfortable choosing just one option. No singular career path felt right. We are, after all, multidimensional, complex beings with differing talents, interests and gifts. So, like the ladybug, we flew the career path coop. Rather than getting hung up on finding the right next job, we focused on creating the environment we wanted to be in, crafting a livelihood from that place.

> In turbulent times people get serious about finding meaning. If life could end tomorrow, you won't be content pushing papers around a cubicle.
> — Daniel Pink, *Free Agent Nation*

Right livelihood is an evolving concept. Elements come and go, some are income generating while others reap other rewards. Right livelihood is made up inclusively of all the things we do in any given day: selling photos, planting sweet peas, sharing s'mores with B&B guests around the campfire, nursing Liam. As an artist utilizes different media, moving from brush and watercolors to clay, we too create our livelihood from a variety of elements and interests. In this sense, we're artists of life.

Our satisfaction with our livelihood stems from the opportunity to work together on an intimate, daily basis. This wasn't some deep profound discussion we had when we first met and started our relationship journey. We didn't have a preconceived idea of what our partnership would eventually be. But once our visions merged with a goal of living closer to the land, things positively clicked and evolved into a

RIGHT LIVELIHOOD

Right livelihood is about working for your passions without destroying the planet. Originating in ancient Buddhist teachings, right livelihood means work that is also ethical. According to the Right Livelihood Award Foundation <www.rightlivelihood.se>, it "reflects a belief that each person should follow an occupation consistent with the principles of honest living, treating with respect other people and the natural world. It means being responsible for the consequences of one's actions, living lightly on the earth and taking no more than a fair share of its resources." Annually, the Foundation bestows honors to individuals who share a "vision of an indivisible humanity, a commitment to careful stewardship of our small planet and an ethic of justice and sustainability."

livelihood partnership, a love connected and vested by much more than a legal marital document. Our projects blend and merge, our daily schedules are plotted together, and our challenges debated in the hallway, or with knees touching under the dining room table at lunch.

The concept of right livelihood provoked us to think more expansively on how we do what it is we do. Rather than get hung up on what we do, we've evolved to focus more on the how we do it, what elements and qualities need to be present for us to achieve our right livelihood. For us, self-employed independence, flexibility, creative stimulation, ecological stewardship and balancing a diverse portfolio of projects are key factors, with the farmstead serving as headquarters. For other people we know, a trilevel house in a suburban neighborhood or townhouse in the city forms the backdrop for their own diversity of livelihood activities, interspersed with block parties and public transportation to connect them to clients.

Traditional farmsteads were founded on entrepreneurial principles; farmers determined what to plant, how much seed was needed, when to harvest, how much income resulted from their activity, and how to steward the land while caring for their families. Likewise, we need to have control over our daily lives, something that was lacking in the corporate world where we'd have to repeatedly cancel commitments to friends, families, or with ourselves because of clients' needs. Self-employment offers an opportunity to be in charge, controlling our own time and schedule, enabling flexibility that helps us ensure that we walk our sustainability talk as best we can.

In our right livelihood, rural living and self-employment are key components, but right livelihood can blossom from a variety of living and working situations. Our friend Jim lives in a house at the end of a cul-de-sac in a suburban community north of Chicago, and enjoys his job as the manager of a construction crew. We met him when he came to the B&B as a guest through a gift certificate we donated to a non-profit fundraiser. We cross paths during events like Earth Month Chicago (he bikes into the city for the day). Quick with humorous stories of coworkers, Jim is re-creating a sustainable haven among the conventional surroundings of aluminum sided and two-car garage homes. Backing up to a forest preserve, his home sports a photovoltaic system to generate his own electricity. Passionately active with the Chicago Botanic Gardens, he often offers space in his home to interns working at the Gardens. Jim celebrates life while doing his part in making the world a better place.

Having multiple income sources gives us the ability to choose how we spend our time. If it isn't fun, why do it? This is only possible when we don't have all our eggs in one basket. Case in point was our relationship with the North American Bluebird Society, an international non-profit organization dedicated to conservation of cavity-nesting birds. We job-shared the executive director position for four years, dedicating ourselves to helping this twenty-plus year-old organization get back on stable financial ground by fundraising, computerizing its operations, expanding its outreach and guiding the organization to better achieve its stated research mission. It was a great situation for several years, enabling us to work together and from home, offering an outlet for our conservation passions, connecting us to enthusiastic and dedicated bluebirders and providing more steady compensation. After about four years, the board of directors shifted focus, both in personality and strategic direction. Programs we worked hard to help create were headed for the cutting block. The changes happened when demands of a baby Liam beckoned. It wasn't fun anymore, so we parted ways after analyzing our income pie chart and coming up with a new livelihood plan. We re-committed ourselves to frugality, took a leap of faith, and landed just fine.

Self-employed right livelihood is not, however, all happiness and bliss. Not being defined by one job title and working from home takes continuous effort to help people understand what it is that we do and how we spend our time. For our parents, it might be a lot easier to simply tell their friends that their daughter, the accountant, is doing fine at her job and just received a pay raise and promotion. At times, our parents may not see the direct connection to the things we do and the projects we work on. They enjoy and appreciate our flexible schedules, however, and we spend a total of five or six weeks together each year. That we — and they — can experience and be a nurturing part of Liam growing up is part of why we made the changes we did. Flexibility and control with self-employment can do wonders for family relationships.

Another opportunity that self-employed livelihood affords is the ability to at least try to keep things in balance. Every so often one of us calls a planning meeting, where the two of us talk beyond the daily to-do lists and touch base on the big picture projects. Where do we want to be spending our time? Is a current project taking up more time than it is worth, either intrinsically or financially? We're guilty of taking on too much, and it has been a continual challenge for us to cut back on things that suck up too much of our time. Our diversity of projects is balanced with our own physical health: eating right, exercising, and getting enough sleep. When our system starts to shut down, our equilibrium falls out of balance. Without good health, the rest won't matter.

Life may have appeared simpler when we could just whip out the corporate business card with a compact two word job title. But if a pink slip arrived or if our boss kept dumping new projects on our desk, we realized how vulnerable and powerless we were. Today we carry several business cards in our wallet reflecting the different projects and businesses we have going on. Like the ladybug on the office printer, why limit ourselves to one direction when we can truly fly?

How to

Work For Our Passion and Follow Our Bliss

It's in retirement, say many, where we get to do the things we want to do. Sell stuff, build things, or answer calls until the day arrives when we have enough money or assets to retire, then go out and do the things we've always wanted to do. What makes the two of us happy isn't a gold watch, lots of money or a prestigious corner office and fancy title, but rather living a passionate life, filled with an energizing diversity of experiences, people, tastes, and business activities.

The following are strategies that we've used along our ever-evolving journey toward right livelihood, creating a lifestyle that reflects more balanced and nature-centered values and a work-style that contributes to a living economy, rather than a life-destroying one.

> Very few of us are pure homo economicus; we do certain things for the joy of it even though they're economically inefficient.
>
> — Bill McKibben

• **Practicing life-long learning.** We're learning from old traditions as well as incorporating new technologies, utilizing the best of both worlds. For us, being knowledge workers means that, in an era where information quickly grows obsolete, we constantly seek out new experiences and explore fresh ideas. In some cases, as with preserving and growing our food, we draw from the rich heritage and experience of now-retired farmers to carry forward these valuable skill sets. We try to connect the worlds of words, ideas and technologies with a more soul-satisfying livelihood. Knowledge is the glue to hold it together.

Being knowledge workers, we find joy and greater self-reliance by continuing along our path of life-long learning. Upgrades in computer software require upgrades in knowledge. The Internet changes. Life evolves. Wind turbines and heirloom tomatoes both require careful study and consideration. Books, the Internet, conferences, a network of colleagues and friends, active mentors and travel help keep us learning, growing, and curious.

Much of our learning comes from doing. Helping to build a straw bale greenhouse on our farm has been empowering, allowing us to reclaim the thrill of seeing a project, in part, being built with our own hands. Experimenting with vegetable crops and varietals and finding which grow best and which are the most prolific — and tasty — allow us to grow ever more connected to the land while continuing to grow our intimate knowledge of it.

- **Keeping an idea journal.** Ideas are everywhere and anywhere. Seeds for a new business, book or approach to living can be collected when we're open and observant. The idea journal, whether it's a scrap of paper that's always in John's pocket or the notebook that Lisa uses, is a place to note these observations, ideas and inspirations quickly on paper before the moment passes. When we review these notes, patterns emerge that can guide us to right livelihood.

- **Embracing failure.** Thinking back — either to our university days or to our corporate existence — we see that too often we stuck to the tried-and-true path, the seemingly safe and secure. Going to college was what you did after high school. In school we learned to follow directions and regurgitate the right answer. At the advertising agency, we told the client what the client wanted to hear first, then added our own spin.

As conservation entrepreneurs, we're trying different ways to enhance and restore nature. This is particularly challenging in a culture that generally devalues the environment, creativity and humanity; a culture that sees labor as a factor of production, and humans as mere consumers. We find ourselves embracing failure as a means to learning, innovating and growing. There are no perfect answers. Passions change, interests blur, and knowledge reveals previously inconceivable possibilities.

Living will always be a journey of discovery and of pressing up against possible failures, with success to prevail — or a failure which results in us learning something new along the way. We've learned that an hour of weeding in June saves three hours in August. All the effort we put into our B&B newsletter to guests does more than just lead to B&B or cabin reservations; it builds community, perhaps plants idea seeds of a different way of living, and reminds folks of their connections to nature and community.

+ **Traveling for knowledge and understanding.** Travel can build our understanding of how connected we are to the Earth and to its inhabitants. Travel is pivotal in opening our eyes and increasing our appreciation of how other cultures have frugality and simplicity as part of their everyday routine. Providing stimulation, exposure and immersion into cultural and ecological diversity, and meaningful direct connections to the global commons, travel is the best non-accredited, non-academic educational program we've ever participated in. Compared to what college costs these days, it's a better deal. The key to travel, however, is being open, compassionate and engaged; traveling in taxi cabs and staying in luxury hotels while in Cairo will do little to accomplish a greater worldview. We strive, wherever possible, to travel as ecotourists, discussed later in this chapter.

+ **Allowing for serendipity and small-sizing our business.** Structure, daily routine and scheduling often lead to stability and security; it's the most efficient means to get everything done. Yet the daily grind, commute, errands, and obligations tend to steer us away from our calling, our passions and our purpose. Unprogramming our lives creates the space — mentally, spiritually and physically — for serendipity to seep in and help the transformation process happen. Many of our experiences and accomplishments are the result of some unpredictable turn of events. The comings and goings create a buzz of ideas and energy, helping us craft a new lifestyle and workstyle based on living with, rather than against, nature. Inn Serendipity's artists-in-residence come and go, visitors drop by and often lend a hand, and companies and non-profit organizations searching for ways to incorporate more sustainable approaches to building or working visit our website for ideas. On a human scale, small is beautiful and manageable.

+ **Reinvesting green in the green economy.** We're not big-time investors, but what we are able to invest, we do so in as socially responsible a way as we can. We invest in companies that have a track record of environmental and social responsibility, invest in for-profit cooperatives, and sometimes hold shares of companies we'd like to change or influence. We review GreenMoney Journal <www.greenmoney.com> and use the book *Investing with Your Values: Making Money and Making a Difference*, by Hal Brill, Jack A. Brill, and Cliff Feigenbaum Bloomberg Press, 1999, as a reference guide.

Given the diversity of our interests and entrepreneurial activities, we try to constantly evaluate our endeavors with an eye toward achieving financial stability, personal balance, creative expression and ecological restoration. We are the sole stockholders in what we own, which is a small subchapter S corporation, so there is no quarterly profit or growth targets that we must reach for other shareholders. To avoid having to return to the big corporate scene, we reduce expenses and strive to make wise business decisions that also consider ecological and social impacts. We have shifted from a time-based, profit-driven career to a nature and relationship-centered livelihood where time is no longer about money. Rather than the goods of life, we choose to experience the good life.

More than a decade after leaving fast-track ad agency careers, our combined income is significantly less than what one of us had individually earned at the agency. Yet our quality of life is significantly greater, as if we retired in our mid-30s. We didn't retire, however, we just reoriented our pursuits to life-sustaining and meaningful activities, activities that satisfied our souls and allowed us to meet the financial obligations of mortgages, property taxes, and other needs. We didn't skirt the law by working under the

BIONEERS

Mind-blowing and soulful — that's how we describe the Bioneers Conference, an annual conference in San Rafael, California held by, and for, bioneers: "biological pioneers." According to conference co-producers Kenny Ausubel and Nina Simons, "Bioneers are an improbable collection of visionary innovators working with nature to heal nature and our relationship as human beings with the natural world." The conference offered practical solutions for our most pressing environmental and cultural crises, and left our hearts, minds, and souls spinning with new ideas. Plenty of information, including how to order the radio series Bioneers: Revolution from the Heart of Nature, is available on their website. <www.bioneers.org>

counter for cash, or lie on our tax returns. Instead, we took advantage of an entre-preneur-friendly tax system and sidestepped the popular dream of retiring as mil-lionaires or owning more stuff than we could use.

Our journey reaffirms that these changes can be accomplished, incrementally. The pace depends, of course, on our situation, property, responsibilities, and will-ingness to follow our bliss and trust our intuition. There doesn't need to be Monday morning blues or TGIFs. We don't have to separate our personal ethics from our at-work ethics.

Our approach to right livelihood involves two key elements: maintaining a highly diversified income-producing portfolio of work and a new definition of wealth.

Diversified Income-producing Portfolio of Work

Our highly diversified income-produc-ing portfolio is in stark contrast to our singular advertising executive jobs with one boss, one paycheck, one cubicle. In addition to helping advertise socially and environmentally questionable products, our work at the agency generated little personal satisfaction (which might have been why the agency offered free therapy services to its employees at the time). Today, our work and projects follow the seasons and changes in the marketplace of ideas and our passions. For each, the corresponding percentage of income is noted, though it changes from year to year.

(a) **Inn Serendipity Woods cabin rental (32%):** We manage cabin rental contracts, web site marketing, and guest relations while also main-taining the cabin and property.

Diversified income pie chart.

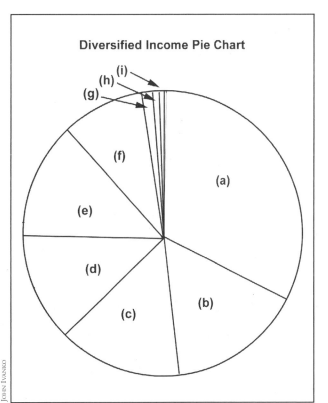

JOHN IVANKO

(b) **Inn Serendipity Bed & Breakfast (17%):** We manage all facets of this two bedroom bed & breakfast, sharing cleaning, breakfast preparations and hosting guests.

(c) **Consulting (13%):** Because of our varied backgrounds and educational experiences, we've consulted on projects ranging from database management to public relations, as well as advertising and marketing endeavors for our local chamber of commerce.

(d) **Special projects (11%):** Sometimes one-time opportunities offer the ability to generate our electricity or work on specially funded projects. This is the most serendipitous aspect of our income.

EQUILIBRIUM ECONOMICS

Equilibrium economics can be described as operating a business in such a way as to provide the necessary financial returns to meet obligations, without destroying the planet or exploiting people. Rather than needing to grow revenues from one year to the next, an equilibrium is established in which enough revenues are generated to cover expenses and pay wages, taxes and other obligations. In this sense, commerce serves to provide jobs, and income, to people in a way that doesn't degrade the environment or people. This economy is characterized by enterprises that are small and human-scaled, locally-based, and eco-efficient.

(e) **Authoring books (11%):** Much more involved than writing for magazines or newspapers, authoring books provides an avenue to address in a comprehensive and artistic way those issues closest to our hearts. Income varies greatly from nothing in one year, to several thousand dollars in another.

(f) **Freelance writing and photography (10%):** Among our passions is the need to express in words or photographs how we interpret the world. John's photography and writing clients are varied and international, with a focus on tourism, environmental issues and sustainable development.

(g) **Workshop facilitation and speaking (4%):** Conferences and fairs allow us to share our perspectives while learning about the many inspiring ways others have embarked on similar journeys. From the upper Midwest Organic Farming Conference to the Penn State Green Design Conference, our presentations or workshops hopefully jumpstart others into action and reinvigorate our commitment.

(h) **Sales of agricultural products (1%):** We sell free-range chicken eggs, surplus flowers, vegetables, fruits and herbs grown on the farm, and eventually, unique niche agricultural crops grown in the strawbale greenhouse.

(i) **Cottage retail store (1%):** We sell our books, photography prints and hand-made mugs to B&B guests.

Adopting a Different Measure of Wealth

We measure our wealth in friends, the health of our land, our community and ourselves, our creative and spiritual development, our intellectual growth and know-how, and peace. We no longer use income or the things we buy with money as a way to keep score in life. Our abundance of wealth comes in non-monetary forms: the power of greater self-reliance; the leisure that comes from living life off the clock; the security that comes with the knowledge of being able to meet more of our needs; the companionship and community that comes from shared meals with visitors and guests; the love of all life that comes when the sun sets over distant cornfields.

The way we've chosen to operate our business departs from capitalism's model of infinite growth and the conversion of capital into wealth. Our human-scaled, localized model seeks to provide enough income to allow us to live the good life without all the goods. In equilibrium economics, our income target is based on local taxes (that in turn support community services) and other financial obligations we need to meet. Our business is designed to prosper and contribute to a living and restorative economy. It is our continuing goal that our life not diminish the possibilities for future life.

SOURCES AND RESOURCES

The New Road Map Foundation
>   Website: www.newroadmap.org
>   The New Road Map Foundation promotes financial integrity and financial independence as a route to health and social revitalization based on *Your Money or Your Life*, by Joe Dominguez and Vicki Robin.

Renewing the Countryside, Inc.
>   Website: www.renewingthecountryside.org
>   Through innovative books, calendars, websites and other resources, Renewing the Countryside showcases individuals, businesses and organizations that are "renewing the countryside" through innovative, diverse enterprises and initiatives that combine economic, environmental and community benefits. It offers great inspiration and resources for business diversification and lifestyle integration.

Jack V. Matson, *Innovate or Die: A Personal Perspective on the Art of Innovation*, Paradigm Press Ltd., 1996.

Bob Willard, *The Sustainability Advantage: Seven Business Case Benefits of a Triple Bottom Line*, New Society Publishers, 2002.

Laurence Boldt, *Zen and the Art of Making a Living: A Practical Guide to Creative Career Design*, Penguin USA, 1999.

Julia Cameron and Mark Bryan, *The Artists Way: A Spiritual Path to Higher Creativity*, J.P. Tarcher, 2002.

Richard Nelson Bolles, *What Color is Your Parachute? A Practical Manual for Job-hunters and Career Changers*, Ten Speed Press, 2003.

Juliet B. Schor, *The Overworked American: The Unexpected Decline of Leisure*, Basic Books, 1993.

Juliet B. Schor, *The Overspent American: Upscaling, Downshifting, and the New Consumer*, Harper Collins, 1999.

Anita Roddick, *Body and Soul: Profits with Principles: The Amazing Success story of Anita Roddick and The Body Shop*, Crown Publishers, 1994.

The Bed & Breakfast Lifestyle

"Quaint setting, Grandma's quilts, relax and step back into yesterday, delicious gourmet breakfast, historic home, close to shopping and restaurants." Flip through an accomodation directory and these words repeat, over and over again, describing bed & breakfasts. This is why it's unlikely that you'll find Inn Serendipity described that way in such listings. Instead, our listing might read: "Funky farmhouse powered by renewable energy, eclectic alternative library, hearty seasonal vegetarian breakfasts fresh from the organic garden, philosophical debates over coffee and around the campfire, line-dried organic cotton linens, llamas, ladybugs and chickens with attitude." That's a more accurate description, uniquely our own.

There is a veritable buffet of learning options for folks interested in starting a B&B, from weekend workshops at community colleges to books and web resources. We even spotted a B&B cruise for several thousand dollars, offering participants the chance to cruise the Caribbean while learning how to run a B&B. Topics range from how many towels to purchase per guest, an introduction to marketing, and a B&B site assessment. We didn't do any of these.

We always wanted to run a B&B as part of our portfolio of farm-based endeavors, but we have a different approach to business. Don't tell us the laundry lists of how things are supposed to be done; fat binders of rules and guidelines crush creativity and inhibit innovation. We're not disparaging serious research; an understanding of the specific business is key to starting an enterprise that will last and be sustainable. But taking class after seminar after workshop can impede the determination to just do it. While the ideal property may come on the market, don't underestimate what creativity might bring when settling on a less-than-perfect place.

We've seen this issue come up among our B&B guests and visitors. Folks comment about how they would love to run a B&B someday, asking us questions about how we decided on our location, how we do our marketing, and what kind of preliminary research we did. They are often a bit surprised when we turn the tables and ask them a few questions: What are you most passionate about? What is that topic that you can talk about for hours and feel as if only minutes have passed? Our approach has been to identify what we're passionate about, and then create our B&B around those interests. Not only will our energy and enthusiasm multiply, but we attract the kinds of people and energy to our business that feed our passion and promote a deep sense of satisfaction. This approach extends to any type of business, but we feel it is particularly salient in this industry, as a B&B can be a perfect canvas for personal expression.

Yet we meet folks who go into innkeeping and feel compelled to fit an expected mold. For example, we attended an organic farming conference and stayed at a B&B in a small town along the Mississippi River. We often stay at B&Bs while traveling; we learn a lot from other innkeepers, while supporting the local economy. This particular B&B was in a meticulously restored Victorian house filled with antiques, polished silver and heavy print wallpaper. It was a beautiful home and reflected the Victorian era, right down to serving a complimentary tea in the afternoon. As we sipped Earl Grey tea out of delicate bone china cups and snacked on dainty lemon butter cookies, we chatted and shared stories with our amiable hostess, Kathleen. She was married to a career military officer and had lived all over the world. Her husband had taken early retirement, and they'd settled down in a place where she could live her dream of running a B&B.

Warm, friendly and open, Kathleen exuded all the characteristics of an ideal innkeeper and we felt comfortable in her company. However, as our conversation continued, something felt out of place. She animatedly talked about living abroad, particularly Italy, where her husband was stationed for several years. Kathleen had a strong artistic side, relishing the galleries and creative energy of Italy as well as the food and people. She could tell we shared her international interests and she took out a couple of boxes from the closet and unwrapped a few pieces of carefully packed Italian stoneware. Hand-painted in bright colors, bold brush strokes ran across the platters, plates and espresso cups.

Yet the dishes sat unused in a box. As we looked around at the delicate tea cups in our hands as we sat on heavy dark velvet chairs in the parlor, something didn't connect. While we enjoyed talking to Kathleen about her passion for Italy, her surroundings were a far cry from the bold, colorful ceramic dishware. We gently approached the topic with her. "The complimentary English tea is a really nice touch, but have you ever thought about doing an Italian version and using your lovely dishes to serve espresso and biscotti?" we suggested. Kathleen smiled hopefully. "You mean I can do that?" she asked, not realizing that she had already done the sometimes hard work of discovering her passion.

Why not? We launched into a zealous pep talk about how this is her business, her B&B and her home. Don't keep your passions packed in a box — share them, and yourself. Express who you are, your history and interests. Kathleen had felt a necessity to re-create the norm of what a B&B in an old Victorian house *should* be.

We don't know the ending to this story, whether the espresso cups ever made it onto the table. Yet this experience was particularly poignant for us. It's a story we often share with our B&B guests who ask us about running a B&B. Discover who you are and your passions — admittedly not always an easy thing to do — and build your business around that.

Inn Serendipity is our testimony to this philosophy. It's an ongoing, eclectic, evolving B&B, reflecting our interests, values and abilities – and the interests of many others who pass through our doors. One important motivation for starting the B&B was to create our sense of community, based on the people attracted to the Inn. We realized that by moving to the country, we would no longer have the diversity of people, cultures and perspectives that we had while living in Chicago. It was relationship-focused more than meeting the business bottom line. We yearned for interesting, diverse people who enjoyed debating global economics, sharing travel stories, discussing current events, and debating political elections.

Equally important, we strive to create a small business that would have a net zero environmental cost over time. Realizing it would take several decades, we set a realistic timetable for ourselves. We aspired to operate the business in a way that didn't destroy the Earth but instead, helped restore it. Intentionally keeping our operations small and human-scaled, we used our business to explore ways in which sustainability and profitability could go hand-in-hand. Recycling, composting, generating electricity and growing much of our food have all helped in our journey toward sustainability; it also made great financial sense, and our organically-grown foods were appreciated by our guests.

Creating a business that reflects our passions has worked, though Lisa's parents still ask us who in their right mind would want to pay to spend a weekend in our funky farmhouse. From the renewable energy systems to home-grown organic breakfasts, the people coming as B&B guests are often interested in or searching for authentic experiences that engage, relax and inspire. More often than not, our guests share their ideas and experiences over morning coffee. By the time they leave, we have pages of notes from our discussions: books to read, videos to borrow, places to go, recipes to try. This aspect of the B&B business creates a diverse, engaging community that we would not have had otherwise.

Our B&B guests feel like old friends. From rabbis to rock climbers, from war protesters to Internet consultants, our guests have enriched us with their company. And we do our best to provide the relaxing space, peace, and food for them to take a break from the hustle and bustle of life.

We're a small B&B with two rooms and intend to stay that way, in direct contrast to the old business maxim, "more is better." We've learned that paying for advertising in mainstream media isn't the most efficient way to attract the guests we desire and enjoy, and who most enjoy what we have to offer. Instead, we use our marketing funds selectively, working with various like-minded non-profit groups or companies with similar values. We may, for example, pay for an ad in a food cooperative newsletter, or donate a gift certificate for a night's stay to a fundraiser for a Montessori school. Such marketing efforts not only connect us directly with people who would most likely enjoy staying at Inn Serendipity, but it also lets us to use advertising dollars to support causes and organizations that resonate with us.

Our long-term goal with Inn Serendipity isn't a plan of national franchises or multi-room expansions. Bigger is not better. Rather than one end-goal, we have three ongoing goals for the B&B. First, that we attract enough guests —and business income — to make it a viable part of our income. Second, that we continue to reduce our impact wherever possible, whether social or environmental. Whether we're growing our food or buying organic, fairly-traded items from a food cooperative, our impact is at least as important as the amount of money left in the bank account. And third, that we continually work to build our relationships with both our immediate community and with the global society. When we buy a product or service, we strive to consider the social and environmental costs as much as possible, whether or not these costs are actually reflected in its sales price.

Our long-range personal goal is to be the oldest living innkeepers. Opening the Inn's doors when we were both 30, we have years to go but we're off to a solid start, since the average tenure of innkeepers in the United States is only four years. Why so low? Innkeeper burnout, where too much work and over-committed innkeepers take the fun out of the vocation. By keeping our operations small, keeping things green, and keeping the good humor flowing, we hope months add up to a lifetime of B&B livelihood.

A Short Course on Starting a B&B

According to the Professional Association of Innkeepers International, there are over 28,000 B&Bs, inns, guesthouses and similar accommodations in the US, serving over 50 million guests and generating about $5.5 billion in local tourism-related expenditures annually. The majority of B&Bs and inns are located in rural or small resort villages. Many occupy restored historic buildings or reused abandoned structures like lighthouses, warehouses or schoolhouses.

As with sustainable agriculture, running an environmentally and socially responsible B&B helps restore community vitality, preserve historic architecture, and reinvigorate a local economy. In sharp contrast to the extractive industries of mining, logging, and agro-industrial agriculture, operating an eco-B&B could be among the many types of service businesses that support the rebirth of rural and Main Street America, encourage a more sustainable suburbia, and foster urban renewal — assuming city and zoning offices are willing to be more flexible and responsive to changing times.

In addition to social and ecological issues, we also considered the following points when we first started the B&B:

- **Guests prefer private bathrooms.** Shared bathrooms, while the norm in European B&Bs, tend to limit American B&B guests, who prefer more privacy. Before we purchased the farmhouse, we evaluated a closet and a half bath on the second floor for a later renovation into full bathrooms for two guestrooms.

- **Location is key.** Of course a good location is critical. But what is a good location? In the case of B&Bs, we found that the large majority were located in restored homes in highly scenic areas, usually small towns with historic downtowns or main streets. Additionally, they tend to be within a three-hour drive of some major metropolitan center. Both Inn Seredipity and Inn Serendipity Woods fit these criteria.

  Opening as a bed & breakfast is usually straightforward, with a few relatively simple health requirements. Most regions require B&Bs to be inspected on a regular basis (usually annually). In our case, proper refrigeration (with thermometers), smoke detectors in rooms and on all floors, fire extinguishers (checked annually) on each floor, and a clean and safe home are all that is required. Many states or regions have B&B associations that help promote B&B travel with listings of B&Bs. Depending on the association you join, an inspection might also be involved. Our membership in state organizations has been spotty over the years, due to both cost and differences in values. In towns, suburbs and larger cities, zoning approval may be necessary, and can be complicated.

• **A knack for hospitality.** Obviously, a love for entertaining and hosting people is required for running a B&B. It's amazing how many curious prospective B&B owners we meet who confess that they like to sleep in, don't like people snooping around their house, or get nervous around people they don't know. For us, running a B&B has always been about sharing experiences and our home with others, whether they're on a weekend getaway or visiting because they want to learn more about making a garden labyrinth in their own backyard.

• **Treat the B&B (and our other enterprises) as a business, and keep good records.** We're conscious of the fact that Inn Serendipity is a business and as such, the IRS has requirements that must be met, including operating at a profit. Earning a livelihood off renting two guestrooms is practically impossible unless we lived in a major tourism center and were booked every night. Our addition of the cabin rental, however, provided the means to derive enough revenue to support salaries and even contract with local part-time help so that we didn't have to drive to the cabin every time we had new arrivals.

Like any other business, meticulous book-keeping is a must. Keeping the tax people happy means keeping receipts and records. Perhaps our most painstaking task, keeping detailed and current records of our business expenses and financial transactions has meant numerous hours using the computer accounting program, Quicken, and endless folders and envelopes serving as depositories for the receipts, bills and paid invoices.

SOURCES AND RESOURCES

Co-op America's Business Network (CABN)
> Website: www.coopamerica.org
> The Co-op America Business Network, now over 2,000 businesses and growing, provides tools and resources to expand our market, and reduce the cost of doing business - responsibly.

Green Hotel Association
> Website: www.greenhotels.com
> The Green Hotel Association encourages, promotes and supports the greening of the lodging industry and offers a directory of approved lodging establishments.

Home Sweet Office

We've never actually seen a ghost, but our place is haunted. We're connected to kindred working-at-home spirits of past farming generations. On the surface we may appear different from previous generations, with our Internet connections and home computers. But past generations of family farms exemplified home enterprise, managing and merging their business and personal lives under one roof.

While we brought a new generation of ideas, technology and skills, our goals are similar to those of generations past: the desire to be farm-based and self-sufficient, to integrate our family into the operations and spend the majority of our working hours on the farm. We proportionally spend more time in the second floor home office working with the computer than we do outside in the field. We carry a cordless phone in a fanny pack when we're weeding the asparagus bed if we need to catch an important call. FedEx picks up packages placed at the back door. Still, the land supports our headquarters and base of business, and we share the same views of the sunrise and sunset as original farmers did over a century ago.

Several key elements make our home office in today's times viable. One key aspect is affordable, accessible technology and services. We couldn't manage our chosen livelihood without computers, Internet access, multiple phone lines, a fax machine and special delivery services like FedEx and UPS.

As soon as we moved in, we called the phone company to install a second line for our fax machine and Internet connection. Fortunately, the phone installer knocked on our door to introduce himself before putting the line in. He assumed that we wanted it in the barn, he just didn't know which one. After all, we lived on a farm. The second line, instead, was added to the second floor.

E-mail plays a couple of roles in our home office. First, it allows us to be efficient. We confirm and organize the majority of our B&B reservations through e-mail contact. Second, it helps meet our commitment to minimize our environmental impacts. Less paper, no stamps, and fewer fossil-fueled trips to the post office.

Reliable delivery services also make our home office work, and FedEx drivers have become a part of our home office community. One of our favorite FedEx drivers, Buzz, had us on his delivery route for several years. Funny how he always seemed to serendipitously make his delivery stop at our place as muffins or cookies were coming out of the oven. When the winter snows fell, we'd wait for our FedEx "plow" to arrive. We rarely get heavy snowfalls, most are under six inches, but even that is too much for our lightweight Geo Metro to handle and too little to justify paying our neighbors to plow us out. So we'd sometimes wait for Buzz to make his stop, his weighted FedEx truck creating tracks in the snow. Once he realized our system, he'd be sure to run the truck up and down the driveway a couple of times. While Buzz has since been transferred to the main FedEx distribution center, he still writes us little notes on our packages, staying connected.

Finally, what really keeps our rural home office running is the strong working partnership between the two of us. Farmstead families have historically worked together, sharing different responsibilities and roles. Every morning we hook up for a daily mini-meeting. Coffee cups in hand and Liam in lap, we go over our work schedule for the day: John is going to edit the book chapter that morning; Lisa is going to can salsa in the kitchen while keeping an eye on Liam; meet with the director of the local chamber in town at noon to go over the marketing plan we helped draft; Liam naps in his sling at the library; we both work out at the YMCA; Lisa and Liam do a post office run; reconvene at home to weed the garden for a focused hour in the cool evening air. After that, it's a casual supper of salad greens and homemade bread on the front porch; after dinner, John returns e-mails, Lisa throws in a load of laundry and sings Liam to sleep.

While each day may be different in topics and schedule, how we work through things depends on how well we work with each other. Such a partnership goes beyond stereotypical romantic relationships and marriage parameters; we're co-managers of a shared livelihood. Working together on a daily basis has strengthened and enriched us as a couple in ways we never expected. We've learned that physical intimacy can develop beyond the bedroom; that being physically together for the majority of our waking hours has connected us more deeply. We are intertwined like the grape vine that winds it way along the fence.

Taking our partnership to such a close working relationship does have its share of challenges. We don't have a boss looking over us or a human resources department instilling employee morale. We've learned to do both ourselves, so when one of us is off for any reason - physically or mentally - our home office routine is under stress. We're each other's best critic and cheerleader, and we've learned to read each other's faces, sense the onset of burnout or stress, and send that person directly to the hammock for a nap or outside for some therapeutic weeding.

How to

Home Office Economics

While no two situations or businesses are alike, we recognize that there are several aspects of running a business from home that should be considered. Our home office includes our computer equipment, boxes of John's 35,000 plus slide photographs, and lots of file cabinets. The room has a splendid view north into corn and alfalfa fields, facing into our birch tree and County Road P (easy to notice the mail delivery or an approaching FedEx truck). A large world map hangs on the east wall. Our office is mission control and looks like it.

In no particular order, we found the following aspects to be the among the more important variables in managing our home office and business:

- **Insurance (home, car and health).** In our litigious society, where lawsuits sprout as quickly as weeds, we realized that having liability coverage protecting us from an unforeseen accident was unavoidable. With our two properties, and with the addition of renewable energy systems on site, an umbrella policy was the most prudent choice. As for health insurance, we have settled on state-sponsored coverage, which bases its premium on household income <www.insurekidsnow.gov>. This plan has so far provided us with quality care for the family, and at an affordable rate.

- **Paying ourselves rent.** Being in business usually involves a payroll. In our case, it also means paying ourselves rent for the percentage of our house used for the B&B and for the home office. For the cabin, since it's rented out to recreational guests, we'd established what's called a triple net lease, where, in addition to the rent, the property taxes and utility costs are paid for from business receipts. Rent charged is set at an amount which exceeds the annually accruing principal and interest payments.

- **Local banks and virtual banks.** Small town banks have a lot of advantages, including tellers who greet us by name as we walk in the door, an inexpensive deposit box, and a nice calendar and cookies at holiday time. What our local bank doesn't have, however, is a free business account that earns interest. So we blend our local bank account with the new virtual banks, credit unions and brokerage money management accounts with features local banks cannot offer. We view money as a tool to support our endeavors, not as something to gamble with on the stock market.

- **Business expenses.** Business expenses are just that, expenses related to the operation of the business, whether organic ingredients for our B&B breakfasts (that we can't grow ourselves) or the business miles we put on our car when we need to zip up to clean the cabin. We've learned to ask for receipts habitually, since the IRS requires documentation.

SOURCES AND RESOURCES

American Small Business Association
  Website: www.asbaonline.org
  This association provides a variety of resources, including newsletters, tip sheets, forums, chats, information on how to operate your home-based business efficiently and effectively, and the latest information on federal legislation that could affect your business.

Daniel Pink, *Free Agent Nation: The Future of Working for Yourself*, Warner Books, 2002.

Lifestyle and Workstyle: Blending Work and Leisure

Our farm is more than a few acres, a farmhouse and half a dozen outbuildings. It's the living canvas on which we paint our livelihood; the elements of our lives blend together like colors on a palette. John is on the phone taking a call from an editor interested in his photos while downloading e-mail containing a B&B reservation. Lisa sticks mailing labels on our B&B newsletter while Liam plays on the floor with Lego.

What is work and what is leisure? Are we ever off the clock? Just as the yellow and blue blend on the palette to create green, traditional notions of work and leisure blend together in our lives, resulting in a fused livelihood of creative energy.

Traditional boundaries between work and leisure are meaningless to us. We don't start and stop work at certain times; weekends and weekdays merge. We have no Monday blues or TGIF build-ups. In general, we probably spend more time and creative energy working on projects than we did during our stint at the ad agency. This is our workstyle, our approach to defining how we function best and fall into that state of flow where we are so absorbed in what we're doing that we're oblivious to time passing. Drafting an article, facilitating a workshop discussion, reading to Liam — even picking strawberries; they're all different aspects of how we achieve our workstyle.

The way we blend work and leisure is, admittedly, not for everyone. Some B&Bs have a clear distinction of guest space versus innkeeper space; some even go so far as to have a separate suite for the innkeepers' living quarters. Aside from our home office and our bedrooms, everything is common space. Nap on the living room couch, take the art supplies outside and sketch the willow tree, play Monopoly on the front porch. We're comfortable with things this way. We thrive on knowing that B&B guests feel as relaxed and at home here as we do.

Tom and Diana live in the nearby artists' community of Mineral Point and have crafted their own workstyle. Their livelihood journey has taken several turns since their years as high school sweethearts, including stints as organic farmers, training for the professional golf circuit, as caretakers for the Unitarian Church in Madison, and as potters exhibiting at craft fairs across the country.

They eventually settled down into their pottery business, with their studio and their family of four all nestled in the 5,000-square-feet (465 m^2) 1850 structure formerly known as the Mineral Spring Brewery. They create a dizzying array of bowls, mugs, pitchers, tumblers and vases, and they also own a gallery in Mineral Point. Much like ours, their short commute is to the downstairs studio.

"We're in a partnership together," Diana says, "and we can't imagine any one way of living in this creative place we call home." They've restored much of the historical building and transformed an old keg room into an indoor basketball court.

"Is what we do work or leisure? It is all a part of life. I don't see much difference between creating in the pottery studio, washing dishes, playing a game of golf. It is all our life," adds Tom.

After spending time with Tom and Diana, it's clear that following your bliss can happen wherever you plant roots, even in an old brewery.

One result of our blending of work and leisure is that we've lost the need to vacation in the traditional sense. We love a summer afternoon on the beach curling our toes in the sand, but we've found that one afternoon on the banks of the Wisconsin River is enough leisure and relaxation. When we're in creative flow, when we're balancing our multiple projects, we don't want to check-out of things. Engaged living, whether it might be called work by some and leisure by others offers fulfillment, satisfying any need to escape.

Ecotravel, or ecotourism, helps conserve fragile ecosystems, support endangered species and habitats, preserve indigenous cultures and develop sustainable local economies. By looking at travel alternatives and making informed choices, you can minimize your impact and positively contribute to the conservation of natural environments, local economies and cultures.
— Megan Eppler Wood,
The International Ecotourism Society

That's not to say we don't travel. We relish the opportunity to go mobile and experience cultural diversity, explore exotic ethnic restaurants and wander the pages of books in funky bookstores. While our roots run deep, we realize we need to keep those home experiences balanced with continually exploring the world hands-on. This type of travel, however, is different than what we typically call a vacation. Instead of checking-out, travel for us is a means to check-in with the world around us. We need to creatively stimulate our minds, introducing ideas and perspectives to refresh our quest for right livelihood.

Sometimes this type of travel is just a "field trip" to Madison, to run some errand we couldn't accomplish more locally. These errands combine with a stop at the bookstore, a walk down State Street near the University of Wisconsin campus, and a browse through whatever shop looks interesting. We might leave for Madison in the morning and get back after dark; a full day of creative stimulation in a completely different world from our rural experience.

We also savor international sojourns. We scrabble together frequent flier miles left over from previous days of more footloose travel, and look for airline bargains, staying with friends and at youth hostels to enrich our experiences (and cut back on lodging expenses). We hit the local grocery store for sandwich supplies and yogurt to stretch our food budget when traveling. These types of trips are the ultimate in the work and leisure combo since we'll often add additional travel time around an existing business trip to explore the area, take photos, research potential new story ideas, and taste the local food flavors. We have, however, brought a new perspective on travel to our rural community where the traditional notion still prevails that whenever you leave the farm you are on holiday.

> As promising as ecotourism is as a tool for environmental conservation, and cultural enabling, travelers - even the most well-meaning - have an undeniable impact on the places they visit. The key is to insure the impact is minimal and better than the alternatives [i.e., mining, oil exploration, logging]. In some instances, the impact actually improves the environment visited.
>
> — Richard Bangs in Foreword of
> *The Least Imperfect Path*

Travel offers us the opportunity to visit other farms and businesses, returning with new ideas and perspectives. One winter we cashed in some frequent flier points and journeyed to St. Martin, a French-Dutch island in the Caribbean. There we visited Loterie Farm, a creative eco-farm project undertaken amidst the growing industrial-scale tourism development occurring on the island. Loterie Farm, at the base of Paradise Peak, is a tropical forest conservation site located on an old sugar plantation. Part of the richness of our experience was, of course, the climate contrast. Going from our farm of rock-hard frozen ground to a place where lettuce and tomatoes were in season and mangos hung from the trees inspired us for the labor of the spring planting ahead. We also took home several ideas from BJ, the owner-conservationist of Loterie Farm, including the idea of creating an interpretive nature hike through the woods surrounding our cabin property. The mere existence of Loterie Farm as an ecotourism destination on an island otherwise destined for the bigger-is-better, mass tourism market reinforced our belief in the possibility of more sustainable, experience-based tourism. As visitors trickle in to Loterie Farm from cruise ships and packaged tours, the dividends generated go toward preserving this bit of paradise.

For us, the blending of work and leisure has caused some unique situations, particularly when it comes to maintaining a balance between business and friendships. We always wanted our home to be a place where our friends would feel welcome. Yet we are still running a B&B business that we rely on for income. We couldn't financially justify turning away paying B&B guests if friends wanted to visit.

After opening the B&B, we experimented with a plan to handle the business and friend blend that has generally worked. Friends are welcome anytime, and they can choose to come as a "paying" or "working" (non-paying) guest. Paying guests come as regular B&B guests with all the service and attention this entails. This option works well for those friends who can readily afford it and would be staying at other B&Bs anyway. By paying, they feel free to come and go as they please, sleep in, not worry about doing dishes and can otherwise enjoy themselves, regardless of what we might be doing. We're happy to go in full B&B service mode for a friend, and this way, no business revenues are lost either. Other friends, typically for financial reasons, choose to come as working guests, in which case we ask that they help us out with whatever the project of the day is. This may be a greenhouse building project, giving us a hand weeding, or keeping an eye on Liam while we meet a manuscript deadline. Sometimes friends stay for a longer time, a week or more, when they are between jobs or at other times of transition. We happily call these working guests our artists in residence; the farm has the opportunity to reciprocally benefit from their creativity, and we're all enriched by the experience.

One thing that is different between this living canvas of our livelihood and a completed fine art painting is that our work is never finished. Our livelihood will never be something we hang on the wall and look at contentedly. As a living canvas, we're always evolving, growing as people and refining our passions. This continuum approach works in that it keeps life fresh, enhancing our palette with the blended shades of work and leisure.

How to

Traveling as an Ecotourist

We've joined the ranks of other footloose farmers recognizing the immense amount of knowledge, goodwill, and understanding that can come through travel. We've avoided owning any livestock (other than the chickens) or pets that might tie us down. When we do travel, we spend little of our time "vacating" on vacation. Rather, we find ourselves recreating through recreation and the exploration of new cultures and perspectives. Much of our travel is, in fact, income-generating or central to the success of our workstyle.

Tourism is the world's largest industry. Ecotourism, a small but growing segment of tourism, offers the same opportunities as our decisions about day-to-day living, livelihood and lifestyle: we can make choices that make a difference. Although ecotourism attempts to recognize the incredibly complex interactions among the environment, culture, economy and travel, it often defies clear definition. Ultimately, the responsibility for the impact of our travel rests not with a label, but with ourselves.

On the road, we're activists — mindfully selecting locally run accommodations, avoiding chains or fast food restaurants, and picking up garbage left on trails by other users. On the rare occasion that we select an organized ecotour, we always ask about the trip fee and how it's being spent. Besides responsibly sourced food and lodging, the fees should also help defray the cost of fieldwork, support local education or health programs, or leave economic dividends with the host community. At different times, we've participated in Earthwatch expeditions and Oceanic Society expeditions, helping in scientific research while learning about the ecology of the destination and the threats it faces.

> With every true friendship we build more firmly the foundations on which the peace of the whole world rests. Thought by thought and act by act, with every breath we build more firmly the kingdom of non-violence that is the true home of the spirit of humanity.
>
> — Mohandas K. Gandhi

LEAVING ONLY FOOTPRINTS

- Choose destinations that are not over-crowded or over-developed, or visit those that are during off-seasons.
- Select responsible tour operators and guides who are aware of environmental and cultural impacts and who contribute financially to conservation and preservation efforts.
- Seek out responsible, environmentally and culturally sensitive, locally owned accommodations and businesses.
- Follow all advisories, rules and regulations regarding protected areas, water sources and wildlife habitats.
- Subscribe to the doctrine: Take nothing but pictures and leave nothing but footprints.
- Never touch, chase or harass animals or marine life.
- Learn about your destination's culture and natural history before you get there.
- Stay on trails, pack out your trash and utilize renewable resources whenever possible.

Adapted from *Your Travel Choice Makes a Difference*, by The International Ecotourism Society.

Searching for adventure, the authentic, the exotic and the new, we try to blend in as best we can to the places we travel. Included in our approach to travel is our involvement with Servas, a membership-based international organization which fosters relationships between travelers and hosts in over 100 countries. We regularly stay in hostels and B&Bs, especially those that seem to share our values. As with our guests' travel to our Inn and our own travel excursions, we off-set our carbon dioxide emissions by supporting Trees for the Future reforestation programs.

SOURCES AND RESOURCES

The International Ecotourism Society
Website: www.ecotourism.org
One of the best places to start traveling intentionally. Their website provides links to operators and information to consider before you go on any trip.

Earthwatch and Oceanic Society Expeditions
Website: www.eathwatch.org
Website: www.oceanic-society.org
Two of the more popular research-based ecotours, where participants help offset research costs and help in hands-on involvement in the projects undertaken.

Conservation International
Website: www.ecotour.org
Conservation International joins many other non-profit conservation organizations in using the power of ecotourism to help protect, preserve and restore threatened areas around the world.

Trees for the Future
Website: www.treesftf.org
Offers a variety of programs to off-set carbon dioxide emissions resulting from travel on airplanes, cars, or other vehicles.

United States SERVAS
Website: www.usservas.org
Servas is an international network of hosts and travelers building peace by providing opportunities for personal contact between people of diverse cultures and backgrounds through mutually arranged individual visits. These encounters help form the building blocks of peace in the spirit of mutual service and respect.

Blending Baby and Business

A couple of years before Liam was born, we were guests on a Wisconsin Public Radio program, "Conversations with Jean Feraca." The topic of this show was our move from the city to the country, running multiple businesses from the farm, living closer to the land, and raising chickens. Conversation was lively, with listener call-ins ranging in topics from asking us how we kept foxes away from our chickens to permaculture design. Then someone called in and asked: "The two of you living on the farm sounds wonderful. I was just wondering, do you plan on having kids and what are your thoughts on raising them in the country?"

Dead silence is not a good thing when you're on the air, but we had a couple of seconds of that before we collected our thoughts for an answer: We were planning on having a child, one child, and were at that "thinking about trying" stage, we replied. The question caught us a little off guard, since such discussions were private late-night conversations between the two of us, not something we had told our families, much less gone public. After that call, the show discussion shifted to raising kids in the country, with various callers, most of whom were raised on farms, chiming in with their opinions on the benefits and shortcomings of growing up rurally. Needless to say, Liam was off to a great start, with advice and support coming in from all corners of the state – years before he was even conceived.

Bringing Liam into this world was a decision we took very seriously. Our reason to have a child was firefly-inspired. Every summer in early June the fireflies dance about as soon as the sun goes down. On a clear night, the fireflies partner with the starry velvet sky and we feel as if we're walking inside an enchanted crystal. As time passed, we matured both in our relationship and our livelihood. The fireflies continued to arrive every summer, and we grew in our desire to share this magic, to deepen our connections to nature, to each other and our community, and to the world. Between the two of us, we hoped we could raise a child to be a happy, caring global citizen, leaving this world a better place.

From the outset, we decided to have only one biological child. With world population expanding by millions each year, we couldn't justify bringing any more than one child into this world. Plus, according to estimates by William Rees and Mathis Wackernagel, authors of *Our Ecological Footprint*, if everyone in the world consumed at the level of the average American, we would need four extra planets to supply the necessary resources. Sure, we're trying to raise Liam in a way that he doesn't reflect such statistics, but we couldn't ignore the fact that simply by being born and living in the United States, his impact will be significantly higher than two-thirds of the planet.

In addition to population issues, we had another reason to want only one child. Simply put, we realized the amount of commitment, time, and money a child would take, and felt that one would be all we could handle while still keeping the other aspects of our livelihood in balance. We were looking forward to becoming parents, but knew that this role was not the singular goal of our lives or purpose of marriage. Now, as Liam grows, we envision him blending into and becoming a part of our lives and livelihood. Once he's able to join us in the gardens or participate in our B&B breakfast tangos, we hope that he will choose to do so because it's fun, fulfilling and connecting.

When Lisa was pregnant, we were bombarded with well-intentioned folks warning us about how our lives will change. Of course things change with a baby in the house. We ignored, however, the negativity: we wouldn't be able to travel, our daily routines would be out of control, we'd be perpetually tired, stressed and broke. People told us we'd have to buy a mini-van to schlep around all the kid gear that would put us in debt.

A PROMISE TO OUR CHILD...

Lisa wrote the poem below while pregnant, later using it in the thank you cards for Liam's baby gifts. We pasted it on the front page of Liam's baby scrapbook, as a constant reminder of our philosophy as parents and as a family.

A Promise to our Child ...
May we never lose our own sense of natural wonder,
Watching fireflies dance and caterpillars crawl.
May we nurture in you a passion for innovation,
And not be afraid to sometimes stumble and fall.
May friends, family, fresh food and laughter,
Hold hands around our dinner table.
May crayons, conversations and libraries color your soul.
Help us always be patient, open-minded and playful,
And not confuse your unique essence with society's
    goals.
May you be surrounded by a diverse and loving
    community,
Who teach you to identify stars, debate and be giving.
May we always remember the blessings in becoming
    a parent,
And as a family, share in the magic of living.

No thanks, was our reply — and still is. A key motivation in creating our home-based livelihood and self-reliant lifestyle is that we are able to intimately integrate Liam into our daily lives. We both wanted to be an active part of Liam's life, tag-teaming his care, diaper changes, development and education.

Just as we moved to the farm to surround ourselves with a healthy environment, we realized that, as new parents, we needed to surround our family with other families who reflected similar values; families from whom we could learn, ask questions, share laughter and potty training stories and raise our children playfully together. Fortunately, Brenda and Luis entered our lives as Liam was born. Gracefully balancing a growing family of three, Brenda runs a home-based web business selling silk dress-up clothes, and Waldorf-inspired toys, many of which are created by other work-at-home moms. Committed to homeschooling, extended breastfeeding and attachment parenting, Brenda mentored Lisa, particularly during those newborn months in nursing a gassy Liam, using a sling and, most importantly, keeping a sense of humor and relishing each moment. Brenda initiated a local playgroup, attracting other similar-minded families that connect regularly for playgroups and potlucks, folks who have become good friends, who we otherwise might not have met. Luis and John share a passion for prolific salvaging. At his job in Madison, Luis fervently collected assorted wind turbine supplies for us that would have been otherwise pitched, reducing both landfill waste and our project's price tag. Their tree-year old daughter, Isabella, taught Liam how to climb on the coffee table, jump off the couch and sway in the rocking chair. We share garden bounty and recipes, strengthening our families collectively in community.

We're blending the old and the new when it comes to raising Liam. He's growing up in a world much different, of greater complexity and information, than that of previous generations. Our goal is not to hide him from fast food and battery-operated gizmos. Rather, our focus will be to expose him to the world around us constructively. If we can create a safe learning environment among the llamas and ladybugs, between the willow tree and the strawberry patch, perhaps we can help raise a boy who will grow up as a responsible global citizen, understanding how he is intimately a part of the natural world around him. He'll recognize on his own that the strawberries from the supermarket don't have the same juicy sweetness as those from home. Hopefully he'll notice the grass pushing through the sidewalk crack in the city, look to the skies at night and say "goodnight moon" wherever he may be.

We're committed to creating ways for Liam to have strong, engaged relationships with his grandparents. Our approach to this has reflected our integrated lifestyle: John's mom will often stop by after feeding her llamas and play with Liam for an hour or two while we catch up on a project or power weed in the garden, then

LIAM'S LETTER TO GRANDPA AND GRANDMAS

From the start, we hoped to create a positive, loving relationship between Liam and his grandparents, our parents. We realized the reciprocal joy and love between grandparents and grandchildren. We hoped to create environments where Liam's grandparents could celebrate his life; where we could benefit from their love, wisdom and support, while still maintaining our priorities and commitment to raising Liam as a caring, loving, cooperative and contributing human, despite today's consumption-driven and competitive world. In trying to start on a positive note, we gave the letter below to Lisa's parents and John's mom about a month before Liam was born. The opening and reading of the card turned into quite an emotional experience with happy tears and a shared commitment to the baby.

Dear Grandpa & Grandmas:

Happy Grandparents Day! I'm looking forward to seeing you very soon - in about five weeks (Give or take a couple of days - or weeks. I like surprises!). Thanks for all your love and support these last eight months, especially to Mom and Dad. I know I'm going to be born into a very special family, and I am a lucky baby to have grandparents like you. Thanks for feeding Mom good, healthy, organic food while she is carrying me inside. Good healthy food will continue to make me a strong baby, especially during the next four years when I'm going to be growing A LOT and when Mom is breastfeeding me. Remember all the good healthy food you had when you were growing up? That's the same kind of stuff that will be good for me, but that means we need to be careful reading labels and in where we shop. Mom and Dad also asked me to talk to you about toys. I know the Grandmas and Grandpa (and aunts, uncles, etc.) might like to sometimes bring me presents. I really do appreciate everything (even though it will take a couple of years for me to really tell you so myself!), but the best gift in the world is a hug and cuddle from you . . . or taking me out in the stroller for a walk in the park . . . playing peek-a-boo . . . and as I get older, maybe trips to museums, zoos and other fun educational outings. When you do bring me a toy, please buy something that will help me learn and grow. Mom and Dad talk about all the great toys that you had for them when they were growing up, like art supplies (I want to be creative like my grandparents), wood blocks and Legos, music, books and other things that stimulate my imagination. Please, nothing that requires batteries, is made out of a lot of plastic because I like to chew (i.e., things from China, India, Korea) or has big logos on it (i.e., Winnie the Pooh, Barney, Disney, Nike - there is enough of that stuff around anyway). Thanks, in advance, for your support. Have a great day today and I love you!

we'll share supper together. Lisa's parents live a couple hours away in the northern suburbs of Chicago, so our time with them involves intermittent trips where we blend focused work with spending family time together. We're fortunate to have such enthusiastic help from our parents, participating in Liam's growth and education. It enables us to maintain our work endeavors while not being forced to hire outside help to care for Liam, and it keeps us all tightly connected as family. After us, the first people Liam called by name were his grandparents.

We chose Liam's name for its historic Celtic roots and meaning: great protector. The name reminds us of the characteristics we want to nurture in him: kindness, creativity, courage, compassion, ecological awareness, and vision. What Liam grows up to protect will be his choice: be it global freedom, old growth forests, free speech, his own family and children, or perhaps the 5.5 acres of this farm.

How to

Nurture by Nature

We're rookie parents. But then, what first time parents aren't? While pregnant, Lisa tried to digest a selection of the libraries of baby advice books out there, but we quickly realized that nothing prepares you better for parenthood than learning by doing: that Liam and us together would guide and help each other. Our same philosophies in embracing nature apply to raising Liam. Among the many strategies we've adopted in our care of Liam include the following:

- **24-hour milk bar.** Aside from proven health and bonding benefits (The World Health Organization recommends breastfeeding for two years), breastfeeding is one of the greenest things we can do for Liam. No manufacturing costs of producing synthetic formula, no fossil fuel powered car trips to buy formula, no plastic bottles, no cost, no waste. All natural.

- **Attention and love.** The only thing that spoils with too much handling is ripe fruit. Crying is among the many forms that Liam communicates with us — one that we as parents are compelled to readily respond to, day or night. The notion that a so-called good baby is one who doesn't cry doesn't make sense. It's quite possible that babies that don't cry may have learned that no one will respond to their call for help.

+ **Communication skills.** Liam learns by imitation, trial and error, and in lots of other ways. As parents, we're the show that Liam observes all day long. He sees our ups and downs, as well as his parents snuggling, laughing and pinching each other's butts. By us treating each other with respect, kindness and affection, Liam may hopefully grow to mirror our more positive sides.

+ **Sensual stimuli.** Research has concluded that it is unhealthy — mentally, physiologically and emotionally — for infants and children to watch lots of TV. However, Liam does spend a lot of time learning from a box: Sitting inside his wagon, he studies the world around him; he is engaged and interactive. As soon as the weather warms up, we're outside sharing wagon rides around the farmstead. Speed is not of the essence — the magic is in the ride. We collect smooth rocks, prickly pinecones, crunchy leaves. A grasshopper lands on the wagon edge, fully capturing Liam's attention until the grasshopper hops away, leaping over Liam's head as he squeals with wonder. These simple sensory moments connect Liam to nature, to us, himself and the greater world around him.

+ **Family-focused parenting.** Just as our work and leisure blend, our days blend with a healthy dose of Liam. We don't work and then come home to play with Liam. Rather everything is integrated. John may edit a manuscript while Liam plays with his magnet collection on the metal file cabinets in the office. Liam "helps" Lisa prep a batch of muffins for the next morning's B&B breakfast. Sure, it takes longer and is typically messier to pull Liam's high chair flush with the kitchen counter, give him his own mixing spoon and bowl and have him practice stirring, flour flying everywhere. We sweep the kitchen floor a lot but we have a son enthusiastic about food and cooking. We'll forever remember visions of him dusted in powdered sugar while helping make Valentine's Day cupcakes.

+ **Exploring educational options.** While we try to set aside some money for Liam's possible college or vocational training, we explore options that he might have in his education — when the time comes. Homeschooling, charter schools — especially those based on ecology, community service, project and outcome based portfolios — private schools, and public schools are all options. Ultimately, it will be Liam's decision. Our goals are to nurture his creativity, his curiosity, and his inherent passion for learning, while offering him the social interaction he needs to grow into a happy, caring citizen of the world.

• **Enjoy the ride.** By the time we figure out one baby thing, Liam hits us with something new. Everything, it seems, is a phase. If we spent all our time worrying, analyzing, or reading how-to books, we'd miss the daily joys of smiles, coos and yes, even poopy diapers.

SOURCES AND RESOURCES

La Leche League
   Website: www.laleche.org
   Information and encouragement for breastfeeding, including local support groups.

Mothering Magazine
   Website: www.mothering.com
   The natural family living magazine, featuring helpful articles on raising our son with less of an impact on the earth to biking with kids.

Janet Hunt, *The Natural Child: Parenting from the Heart,* New Society Publishers, 2001.

Bill McKibben, *Maybe One: A Case for Smaller Families,* Plume, 1999.

Zoe Weil, *Above All, Be Kind: Raising a Humane Child in Challenging Times,* New Society Publishers, 2003.

Ask Dr. Sears
   Website: www.askdrsears.com
   Practical pediatric advice from Dr. Bill and Martha, under the attachment parenting umbrella philosophy.

David W. Orr, *Earth in Mind: On Education, Environment and the Human Prospect,* Island Press, 1994.

CHAPTER 7

Leaving a Simple Legacy

Empty Hammocks

Our hammock population density is high. There's the hammock from a trip to Peru, strung between the two maple trees in the shady cool garden cove just west of the pond. The hammock we brought back from our honeymoon in Guatemala lingers across the front enclosed porch. There's the unique pair of hammock-like chairs hanging from the willow tree that, when empty, collapse into a ball of green netting resembling an awkward string bikini; when filled with a relaxed body, though, they're among the more comfortable lounging spots around. However, even during the peak summer season, the hammocks usually hang empty. Guests and visitors might relax in the hammocks, bringing along a stack of reading material only to end up napping. But we can't recall the last time one of us enjoyed a hammock for an afternoon of novel reading.

Nothing against hammocks. It's just that the term "simple living" may first bring to mind hammock novel reading interspersed with infusions of herbal tea. But that's not us, nor does it appear to be representative of the many individuals who embrace and practice simple living. Our goal isn't to have a decaffeinated life journey, but rather one filled with vision, hope, passion and a relentless commitment to leave this world a better place. It's easier and simpler to super-size our soda at the lunch counter than super-size our dreams, but the latter keeps us up at night drawing inspiration from the starry skies, butt-kicks us out of bed in the morning, and espressos our soul.

Complexity seems to have become a dirty word today. But is complexity such a bad thing? Nature is anything but simple. Canning homemade salsa is complex. After growing the tomatoes, onions, garlic and peppers, the vegetables need to be cleaned and deseeded. Remember to put on rubber gloves when touching the peppers. We cook the ingredients and simmer them together for an hour or so. We sterilize the canning jars and lids. Then boil the hot water bath and process each batch of jars for 25 minutes. It's a complex process. But it leads to a great tasting salsa.

We thought we yearned for a simple life. But it turns out that clutter was a bigger problem than complexity. Clutter is composed of the things that we don't really need and that takes time, energy and resources away from the important things. It quietly invades our life until it has staked claim in our closets, relationships, daily schedules, and soul. Clutter stems from consumption of stuff and time: over-committed social and volunteer calendars; over-buying shampoo and winter sweaters; more ornaments than fit on the Christmas tree.

SIMPLICITY, SIMPLE LIVING AND VOLUNTARY SIMPLICITY

According to the non-profit organization Seeds of Simplicity <www.seedsofsimplicity.org>, "simpler living is not backward living, but forward living. Less time spent on material goods means more time spent with family, friends, children, nature and unlocking the real passions and values of your life." Our well-being and that of the planet are inexorably connected.

Voluntary simplicity is the process by which we and millions of others are examining our lives, asking what's important, valuable, and needed; defining for ourselves when enough is enough, then taking steps to change the way we live and work. Simplicity is nothing new. It goes back to the days of Benjamin Franklin's "a penny saved is a penny earned."

Purging is cathartic. Step by step, we work towards living a conscious, more mindful life — a central tenet of simple living — asking ourselves at each crossroad, is this something in our life that we benefit from, need more of, are challenged and grow by? Giving away is just as satisfying as receiving and getting, so long as it's going to a good home or place, not the landfill.

Our de-cluttering efforts have ranged in categories and impact. By creating our livelihood and our income sources based on a commitment to working from home, we have eliminated commutes and the need to dress for work. We ruthlessly remove ourselves from mailing and phone solicitation lists, and have been trying, albeit imperfectly, to channel our family holiday gift giving to focus on the practical or, better yet, the shared experience. We put our TV in the corner library on

SOURCES AND RESOURCES

Simple Living Network
 Website: www.simpleliving.net
 The Simple Living Network is an organization that provides tools and examples for those who are serious about learning to live a more conscious, simple, healthy and restorative lifestyle. The *Web Of Simplicity* guide provides a good overview of the simple living movement, highlights of some of the network's best resources, and provides a general tour of the Simple Living Network.

Seeds of Simplicity
 Website: www.seedsofsimplicity.org
 This non-profit builds a voice for voluntary simplicity as an authentic social justice and environmental movement, and promotes Simplicity Circles, where people join together to offer ideas, support and practical resources, with participants taking concrete action steps to make real change.

Conversation Cafés
 Website: www.theworldcafe.com/ ComConversation.html
 Conversation Cafés are lively, hosted, drop-in conversations among diverse people, giving participants a forum in which to discuss feelings, thoughts and actions in this complex, changing world. The simple structure of Conversation Cafés — and their spirit of respect, curiosity and warm welcome — help people shift from small talk to big talk. Conversation Cafés take place in real public cafés to allow for face-to-face spontaneity and inclusiveness.

Bill McKibben, *Hundred-Dollar Holiday: The Case for a More Joyful Christmas,* Simon & Schuster, 1998.

Jim Merkel, *Radical Simplicity: Small Footprints on a Finite Earth,* New Society Publishers, 2003.

John De Graff, David Wann, Thomas H. Naylor and David Horsey, *Affluenza: The All-consuming Epidemic,* Berrett-Koehler Publishers, 2002.

Duane Elgin, *Voluntary Simplicity: Toward a Way of Life that is Outwardly Simple, Inwardly Rich,* Quill, 1998.

Janet Luhrs, *The Simple Living Guide: A Sourcebook for Less Stressful, More Joyful Living,* Broadway Books, 1997.

John C. Ryan, *Stuff: The Secret Lives of Everyday Things,* Northwest Environment Watch, 1997.

the second floor, so to watch TV we need to decide to watch TV. Cutting out just one hour of TV each day gives us 365 hours, or nine 40-hour weeks, each year to do more of the things we value; we've discovered that scarcity of time is merely an illusion.

Ironically, the more we de-clutter, the more complex our lives tend to become. This complexity isn't negative, though. On the contrary, it drives our passions. Our daily schedules, life goals and responsibilities are tightly intertwined as husband and wife, business partners, parents and best friends. By eliminating unnecessary elements, we have corners and cabinets free and open to take on new challenges. We're open to opportunities to do more of what it is we really feel is our true calling, to follow our bliss. Another way to look at complexity positively is to recognize its dance partner: diversity. By being engaged in simultaneous projects and activities, our lives are enriched, meaningful and self-actualized. Complexity allows our passions, interests and imaginations to mingle.

Managing this complexity and embracing simplicity are perhaps our best defenses against stress. When we're on top of deadlines, when we are in a positive work flow, when we are taking the time to eat well, exercise and sleep, life clicks. However, when one of us has an off day, misses a deadline, or forgets to pay the tax bill, stress arrives. We seem to encounter stress when we are about to leave on a longer trip. We're overloading our circuits, trying to finish up too much at the last minute: fill the chickens' water buckets; search for suitcases and clean underwear; locate Liam's favorite toy. Now we try to start the whole travel preparation process earlier, with much better results.

Life is an evolving, complex give-and-take exercise, filled with daily de-cluttering and mindful moments of simplicity. Every once in a while, we smile at an empty hammock or joyfully, fall asleep in one.

How to

Creative Steps to De-cluttering

Clear out closets. Donate items to charity. Avoid buying what we don't need. These basic mantras of de-cluttering are also simple living favorites, ideas that we, too, have used. We've also found that removing those things that interfere with or diminish our authentic selves can take creative forms like the following:

1. **Use it up.** We're trying to ignore a human tendency to stockpile for a snow-storm that never comes or a renovation project that never happens. Instead, we focus on using things up, clearing the cold cellar, emptying the freezer of last year's frozen bounty. This has turned into a little game each winter when we try to clear out the pantry and eat through all the random items that somehow accumulate in our cupboards. Sometimes it requires some culinary creativity, like what to do with a jumbo box of saltine crackers, or learning how to prepare odd items that somehow turned up on our shelves, such as amaranth grains. Since the garden re-stocks us with fresh produce every season, it doesn't make sense to save preserved fruits and vegetables for more than a year, so we try to eat through everything from last season. Sometimes this use-it-up mentality also allows for some mid-winter indulgences; we have a reason to break open the chocolate truffles someone gave us as a holiday gift that we had been saving for no particular reason. By the time spring rolls around, our cabinets have breathing room and we feel a bit lighter, too.

2. **Focus on one holiday tradition.** Each holiday brings its own long list of to-dos and obligations. Rather than try to do a little bit of everything (ending up stressed and frustrated), our approach has been to pick one tradition that means the most and focus on it. For example, we enjoy sending out holiday cards since it has become our annual form of communication and expression, annually anticipated by our friends. We design our hand-crafted cards to be folksy and personal. One year we glued coneflower seeds from the garden to each card so folks could plant the card — a way to extend our garden to theirs. We often write up an annual Inn Serendipity newsletter, *The Chronicle of Independence*, detailing farm, travel, family and life happenings. This process takes time, but it's something we find rewarding. To make time for its production, we cut back in other areas. We don't go overboard decorating the house or trimming the tree. Purchased gifts are kept to a minimum. Creative card giving and sharing our joys and challenges help maintain our relationships with friends and family.

3. **Support creative recycling and reusing.** Sure, it's always an option to donate used items in good condition to the local charity. But sometimes we end up with things that aren't even resellable at our local thrift shop. We

don't want to see these items in a landfill either. So we've come up with the following alternatives:

- Make greeting cards from old cards. Tear off the front picture side of greeting cards and send them to St. Jude Ranch for Children, a home for physically challenged children who use these cards and a little paper, glue and creativity to make new cards which they sell as a fund-raiser (100 St. Jude's Street, Boulder City, NV 89005-1618 <www.stjudesranch.org>).

- Offer supplies to school and youth groups. Local schools and other youth organizations are often on the lookout for supplies for projects. We had a case of old travel catalogues featuring some of John's photos, which the local junior high school was happy to take.

- Give something a second life. In today's world of gizmos and technology, there's always something that seems to keep breaking down and wearing out. Often, it's a motor or a belt, which by the time we end up replacing them (and footing a repair service fee), we could have purchased a new item for less money. We occasionally do replace things. But instead of sending the broken item to the landfill, we now try to locate a second home for the equipment. For instance, our old dehumidifier proved to be too costly for repair, but much of the motor and other components were in good shape. So we left the machine with the local repair shop to use for spare parts.

4. **Avoid passing along clutter to others.** As we try to de-clutter our lives, we're sometimes guilty of passing along clutter in the form of gifts to friends and family. We've been trying to stop this cycle by focusing on creative gifts that won't take up space and add more stuff to someone else's house. Some things we've tried include taking John's mom to the Arboretum in Madison as a Mother's Day gift to see the spring flowers in bloom and sending homemade cookie care packages to friends who just had new babies. If it was great to receive them in college, why not give them now?

5. **Focus and finish our projects.** Like most people, sometimes house projects drag out, from procrastination, a warped need for perfection, and a variety

of other reasons that seem to sound good at the time. These loose ends cause stress and distractions. The best remedy is about as straightforward as they come: focus on the project at hand and finish it. Sometimes this may mean pushing ahead and getting a rough draft on paper, knowing that editing can be done later. Other times we get overhwelmed by the scale of a project and need to focus on taking little bites, working in small intervals to slowly finish.

Growth Versus Development

We measure our annual applesauce canning production in quart jars: about 12. We measure our annual electricity use in kilowatt hours: around 9,000 kWh (and dropping). About 20 tomato plants yield enough tomatoes to eat in the summer and freeze for winter use. The hens usually each lay an egg a day. We have a budget to track the costs of running our household. About six diapers end up in Liam's diaper pail at the end of the day.

But how do we quantify our quality of life? How do we put a dollar value on day-to-day happiness — on living well? We don't quantify it, at least not by societal notion of standard of living, based on the idea that the more stuff, square feet, money in the bank and luxurious the car, the better. We've realized that the opposite is true: the less we need, the happier we are. Instead of getting caught up in the pressures of expansion, of acquiring more stuff and storage containers to hold everything, we've learned to focus on using and appreciating what we already have. Instead of material growth, we focus on the development of our minds, bodies, spirits, creativity and love.

There are no quantitative standards by which we can measure such a philosophy. Or are there? The income figures we report on our tax forms don't seem to accurately reflect our rich life. Moving to the country resulted in a drastic reduction in our income from our corporate days, matched by a conscious and necessary

...The gross national product does not allow for the health of our children, the quality of their education, or the joy of their play. It does not include the beauty of our poetry or the strength of our marriages; the intelligence of our public debate or the integrity of our public officials. It measures ... neither our wisdom nor our learning; neither our compassion nor our devotion to our country; it measures everything, in short, except that which makes life worthwhile.
— Robert Kennedy, in an address at the University of Kansas, March 18, 1968

reduction in our expenses. Now, our lives have grown exponentially richer with the things we value: family, health, nature, freedom and happiness.

Less equals more, at least it does when it comes to living well. By doing something less often, we more fully appreciate and relish the experience. Part of this comes from the fact that everything is not at our doorstep, twenty-four hours a day. When we choose to engage in something, it takes on greater meaning. When we eat out, typically when we're on the road or in the Chicago area visiting friends and family, it's an experience we enjoy more. We could probably look at last year's calendar and name the restaurants we went to, what we ate and with whom we shared the meal. Our reason to eat goes beyond satiating hunger. It's to savor flavor, conversation and ambiance.

Artist-in-Residence Jason, creating a garden wall with cob.

This less-is-more philosophy has also caused us to rethink our relationships with others. We've grown to focus on deepening our existing friendships and to grow away from distant acquaintances. It no longer is the size of our circle of friends or the number of holiday cards in our mailbox, but the quality of the underlying relationships. That said, we're fortunate to have a strong group of friends and family involved in our lives. It's not to say that we're not open to making new friends. It's just that we've grown cautious not to expand just for the sake of expanding, as though we need to have a full Saturday night social calendar to be normal.

While we do have a lot of comings and goings here, with B&B guests typically staying a night or two, we look for

JOHN IVANKO

situations in which we can share the farm and connect with people for longer periods of time. Sometimes these opportunities come right to our doorstep, literally, through our informal artist-in-residence program. The idea behind the artist-in-residence grew from our desire to share Inn Serendipity more intimately, to provide some refuge and inspiration for kindred spirits in need of time to rethink life goals and launch new ideas; we haven't forgotten that during our own transition we spent our fair share of time on couches, porches and otherwise between permanent addresses.

Typically an artist-in-residence is someone we've connected with in some way, whether it's a friend looking for some downtime or someone who has had a previous extended visit. These artists are not lost sheep, looking for their pasture. Rather, they're folks in various stages of transition, seeking to further change their lives and wanting to foster their artistic sides, however that may manifest. They're in need of a retreat; a place to regroup and refocus. We'll typically host a person as an artist-in-residence for several months during the summer, leaving the relationship at first loosely defined, other than that we provide room and board in exchange for their help around the farm. We've found that this enables their artistic pursuits to evolve and flourish. The artist-in-residence program isn't really a formal program with applications and essay questions; rather, the artist-in-residence idea relies on mutual intuition. We sense that a potential artist's presence would enhance the farm and our lives, and likewise, they'd feel that time spent at Inn Serendipity would nourish their creativity and provide breathing space to plot their next steps.

Jason first came to Inn Serendipity during Strawbale September, when we were working on the greenhouse. He took a week's vacation from his East Coast engineering job to stack bales, stitch walls and apply earthen plaster. The time he spent working with his hands, surrounded by like-minded people and rolling green acres affirmed his decision to depart the corporate world in favor of something under the umbrella of sustainable design, where he could use his engineering talents in a way more in line with his values.

Jason's second journey was the following year, when he stayed through the summer as our artist-in-residence. A thoughtful, gentle twenty-something with a shaved head (better circulation that way, he'd say), Jason steadfastly stepped into his summer experience pulling out nails and recycling old barn boards, adding old windows to the dairy barn for some daylighting, making a cob (straw, sand and clay) garden wall, and practicing guitar on the front porch steps, accompanied by the early evening crickets. His scanner would be buzzing many mornings as he continued to scan his photographs from a recent trip to Turkey. He introduced us to collard greens, attached an ice cream maker to an old exercise bike to create the "vicious cycle," and coached Liam in music appreciation and walking on two feet. Jason strengthened his decision to work in green design that summer, ending up in New Mexico, working with the publishers of *The Last Straw: The Journal of Strawbale and Natural Building*, and furthering his apprenticeship as a straw bale builder and designer. Jason's presence deepened our lives. His craftsmanship, ingenuity and personality enriched that summer season memorably.

Sometimes the richest opportunities for living well come from digging a little more deeply within ourselves. Personal development is limitless - and sustainable. We can enrich our intellect and knowledge through life-long learning; we can take on new challenges. There's always a pile of a reading material sitting on the coffee table in the living room: magazines, newspaper clippings, newsletters and books. We work through an article or two when we get a chance, realizing we'll never fully get through the pile — learning is never finished. We didn't have a vision of the labyrinth, straw bale greenhouse, or life-size chess set when we started on our journey. Such projects evolve with time and space to dream, providing priceless experiences which further perpetuate and enhance a quality of life that rarely shows up on the evening news or as some quantifiable statistic in the pages of the *Wall Street Journal*. It's there nonetheless, nestled between every sunbeam and applesauce jar.

How to

Considering a Diversified Quality of Life Index (DQLI)

Our relaxing lunch of freshly picked salad greens, asparagus, and a few chives with homemade honey-wheat bread is often taken outside on the patio north of the chicken coop. The sun shines warmly and a pleasant breeze, fragrant with lilac, drifts from the southwest. Our chickens scurry about, busily scratching for their own lunches. Our early morning tasks have been completed, giving us a chance to relax. Flexible time and schedules make a big difference in how we view work.

Sitting there on the patio, discussing which new perennials were about ready to blossom, we're not adding much to the Gross National Product (GNP) of the United States (a widely accepted indicator for how America is doing). Harvesting and preparing our own lunch, with the sun brightly shining on the PV system, we're definitely having a negligible effect on GNP. When Liam came along and we devoted our energies and time to his care, that, too, didn't contribute to the GNP. The time spent enjoying our gardens, hanging out with friends, and reading a book from the library doesn't either.

Gross National Product is the total value of the economy's output of goods and services, measured in money. We'd argue that it's measuring a false sense of prosperity. In fact, such atrocities as the September 11th terrorist acts, the *Exxon Valdez* disaster, violent crimes, divorces, the wars on drugs, terrorism and nature, and the vastly expanding prison network all contribute to the GNP; however, these hardly add to the well-being of Americans. Also not accounted for within GNP is the loss of natural capital: soil, forests, water and climate stability.

> We have before us the spectacle of unprecedented prosperity and economic growth in a land of degraded farms, forests, ecosystems, and watersheds, failing families, and perishing communities.
> — Wendell Berry, *In the Presence of Fear: Three Essays for a Changed World*, The Patriotism Series, Vol. 1, Orion Society, 2001.

DIVERSIFIED QUALITY OF LIFE INDEX

Our Diversified Quality of Life Index (DQLI) is measured by various factors including the health of family relationships, enjoyment of work, physical health and well-being, level of satisfaction with life, and opportunity for continued development. Among the essential tenets of DQLI:

- Having a meaningful livelihood that expresses our passion, creativity and soul.
- On-going opportunities for life-long learning and experiences.
- Maintaining mental, physical and holistic spiritual health.
- Opportunities for continuous personal, spiritual, and creative development.
- Control over our schedules.
- Building solid, meaningful relationships with our family and friends.
- The satisfaction and joy that comes with greater self-sufficiency.
- Connecting to the interdependent web of life which provides an abundance of diverse perspectives and experiences.

As if GNP is not enough, add to it the Consumer Confidence Index, an index developed by clever researchers at a publicly traded corporation to measure "consumers' expectations" toward employment and other current conditions which, statistically speaking, influence their willingness to keep spending. Since two-thirds of the US economy, as measured by the GNP, is based on Americans spending money on stuff, the Consumer Confidence Index is a barometer as to how future spending and consumption will fare.

We don't claim to be geniuses, but it seems to us that the Consumer Confidence Index and GNP are measuring the wrong things. Our health, our happiness, our deep connection to the natural world and to our local community are far more important than helping support the continued — and unsustainable — increase in spending.

As a result, when redesigning and reorienting our life, we started experimenting with our ecologically modeled Diversified Quality of Life Index, measured by various factors including the health of family relationships, enjoyment of work, level of satisfaction with life, and opportunity for continued development and community involvement. Our currency is composed of joy, happiness, friendship, satisfying self-reliance, peace.

It turns out that our questioning of the GNP is similar to what the non-profit organization Redefining Progress has been proposing with their Genuine Progress Indicator (GPI), which values things like volunteerism and accounts for loss of natural capital and for the loss of leisure suffered by people working excess hours. According to their scientific methodology, while the GNP has continued to rise, their Genuine Progress Indicator has steadily fallen since the 1970s.

We're both optimistic and hopeful. What matters most to us is what has always mattered — love for all life, meaningful social relationships, and peace. Our life changes have helped us focus on what's important, meaningful and authentic — meaningless when calculating GNP — and probably interpreted negatively by those calculating the Consumer Confidence Index. By achieving an increased sense of happiness, we've come to understand that there's a heirarchy of needs. While we journey toward ever greater self-actualization — becoming all that we can be — our life, the land, and our community is becoming richer. Indeed, money really can't buy happiness.

SOURCES AND RESOURCES

Redefining Progress
  Website: www.rprogress.org
  Partnership organization working to shift economy and public policy toward sustainability.

Arianna Huffington, *Pigs at the Trough: How Corporate Greed and Political Corruption are Undermining America,* Crown Publishing Group, 2003.

David C. Korten, *The Post-Corporate World: Life After Capitalism,* Berrett-Koehler, 1999.

David C. Koren, *When Corporations Rule The World,* Kumarian Press, 2001.

Alan AtKisson, *Believing Cassandra: An Optimist Looks at a Pessimist's World,* Chelsea Green Publishing, 1999.

Bluebirds, Birch and Bass: Creating Wildlife Habitat

Like many of our neighbors, we put up some bluebird boxes. Bluebirds are cavity-nesting birds, which means they build their nest in cavities, or holes, rather than on a tree branch. Since fewer natural cavities exist as a result of decreasing wild areas, the bluebirds were declining. This decline has continued to worsen as a result of myriad other issues (usually human - created).

However, when human-made nesting boxes (built according to cavity-nesting specifications) are placed in the appropriate habitat, a pair of bluebirds will often accept the box and build a nest inside and start a family. The bluebird population has indeed rebounded in many areas of the continent. The habitat at the Inn Serendipity Woods property is ideal for bluebirds, given the open grasslands and lawn, so this is where we focused our bluebirding efforts. We were quickly rewarded with happily nesting bluebirds, as well as chickadees, tree swallows and house wrens in the boxes we installed.

> People have begun to see that life itself is important — not just ourselves, but all life. The older I get, the more I feel the interconnectedness of things all over the world.
>
> — Roger Tory Peterson, world-renowned bird conservationist

By putting up bluebird boxes, we took the first step in our on-going conservation efforts at Inn Serendipity Woods. Why is this so important? What compelled us to later clear weeds and shrubs and plant trees while the pond kept tempting us to lounge in an inner tube? We feel a deeply seated urge for restoration, to help heal the damage that has been done to the land and to the wildlife it supported. Likewise, we feel a responsibility to steward the land, tend to its needs as an active participant, similar to the calling we feel to fix up, repaint and maintain our farm and the cabin.

LAND CONSERVATION & WILDLIFE HABITAT PRESERVATION AND RESTORATION

Inn Serendipity Woods is our on-going conservation, restoration and preservation project, with the goal of creating a private wildlife sanctuary. The opportunity to implement sustainable forestry, or silviculture, restore the forest to its health prior to the timber harvest made by the previous owner, foster greater wildlife diversity, and prevent further degradation along the stream that passes through the property allows us to develop a relationship with the land that's completely different from our relationship to the farm property.

Both our properties are considered farms by the USDA; crops were grown on both for many years, and the agricultural use had degraded the land, especially adjacent to the stream. Ultimately, we plan on ecologically-sound, selective harvests of timber to supply wood to companies that specialize in offering Forest Stewardship Council-certified chain of custody sales of wood products.

These two land conservation activities each serve our long-term conservation goals in different ways and take the following forms:

1. **Continuous CRP (Conservation Reserve Program) to establish a riparian buffer alongside the stream.**

   Acres Involved: 2.5, of which 2.2 acres were cropland and .3 acres were pasture.

   Partners: USDA, Natural Resources Conservation Service (NRCS) and Farm Service Agency

   Duration: 15 years

   Purpose: Our CRP project is aimed at establishing a riparian (streamside) forest buffer, helping to protect soil, air, and water quality and improve fish and wildlife habitat. To this end, we've planted a total of 550 tree seedlings, including northern red oak, white ash, black walnut, black cherry, hickory, silver maple, red maple, sugar maple, swamp white oak, white pine and red pine.

   Steps: We invited the National Resource Conservation Service (NRCS) to make a site visit to determine how much land would qualify under the program. While the NRCS agent was helpful and informative, the numerous forms, filings and procedures were a bit confusing and time consuming for novices

While the cabin and the property have suffered from hard use over the years, it seems in some ways to have once served as a place to enjoy and observe nature. Although we'll never know the full story, we've developed the sense that whoever originally planned the grounds and built the cabin about thirty years ago did so with a master habitat plan. We keep encountering elements on the land that didn't just happen; they must have required some foresight and planning. A unique corkscrew willow sits right next to the cabin and partially shades the deck. A row of pine trees runs along the northern portion of the cabin, providing both privacy and

like ourselves. Perseverance and patience finally enabled us to establish the buffer and receive cost sharing (90 percent of the cost of the saplings) and a nominal rental payment for the land, both of which greatly helped underwrite our conservation efforts.

2. Establish and follow a stewardship forestry plan through the Wisconsin Managed Forest Land Law

Acres Involved: 20

Partners: Wisconsin Department of Natural Resources (DNR) and the Vernon County Forester

Duration: 50 years (ending December 31, 2051)

Purpose: Wisconsin's Managed Forest Land Law aims to encourage the growth of future commercial crops through sound forestry practices which consider the objectives of the individual property owners, forest aesthetics, wildlife habitat, erosion control, protection of endangered or threatened plants and animals, and compatible recreational activities. Our project's aim is to manage the 20 acres of woods for timber, wildlife, aesthetics and recreation. In managing the timber stand, favor is given to native species, especially hardwoods. In terms of wildlife, forests are to be managed for wood duck, screech owl and wild turkey.

Steps: Depending on the state, programs often exist for landowners wishing to sustainably manage forests for commercial value. Participation in such programs offer the ability to reduce local property taxes based upon state legislated rates and terms. As with the Continuous CRP sign-up, the paperwork to sign-up can take time and perseverance. In the case of the Managed Forest Law, the state required a signature from our mortgage company, which ended up taking five stressful months to secure. The mortgage company had difficulty understanding that we were not placing a conservation easement on the property, which reduces property value. In fact, we were setting aside the woods for future commercial timber production, which actually increases the assessed value of the property.

Source: The USDA Continuous Conservation Reserve Program. Website: www.fsa.usda.gov/dafp/cepd/crp.htm

a windbreak. In a meadow behind the cabin sit four rows of grapevines which we're slowly trying to nurture back to health.

Whoever planted the grapevines had a grander vision than producing a couple batches of jelly. Perhaps their dream was to have their own little vineyard to make their own wine. Whatever their original intent, when we see something like a field of overgrown grapevines our minds brim with ideas and our hands start pruning, weeding and tending. We feel a kinship with the original owner, just as we also do with the plants, animals and water, since we're now the caretakers. We have the charge to resurrect and continue his or her good works while adding a few of our own.

In our efforts to repair and restore the cabin property's habitat, diversity has been our on-going mantra. It's one of those simple conservation equations: a richly diverse habitat attracts a diversity of wildlife. We can't import wildlife, but we can actively contribute to the diversity of naturally occurring foods, shelter and, with the pond and stream, clean and healthy water. We've established a riparian buffer alongside the stream to prevent further soil erosion, planting and tending about 550 mostly native hardwood trees so far. These trees will also help us sequester about 100 tons carbon dioxide during their first forty years of growth, according to data collected by the non-profit organization, American Forests.

Approximately one acre in size, the pond at the cabin is an on-going aquatic habitat restoration project. The pond has been stocked with various fish in the past, such as trout and bluegill, but we need to get a better sense of how many and what size. We're working towards a longer-term pond management plan, including restocking it with fish. Our goal is to create both a healthy pond ecosystem as well as allow ourselves to do some fish harvesting for our plate as well.

We find an immense satisfaction and connection to nature when we watch a family of wild turkeys cross the driveway and scurry back into the woods, a red-tailed hawk circling above the birch trees, a male and female bluebird teaching their brood to fly. While our outward goals in habitat restoration are to help and preserve wildlife, we admit we have a personal drive behind this too. By working towards improving the natural world, we're not only helping wildlife, we're helping ourselves. The healthier our surroundings, the healthier we are as people.

How to

Building a Bluebird Trail

In our four years with the North American Bluebird Society, we've come to respect the immense dedication of millions of individuals across the continent who have built, placed and regularly monitored their bluebird nestboxes. Among America's most successful grassroots conservation efforts, bluebird conservation has so far resulted in the successful return of the three species of bluebirds (in some areas west of the Rocky Mountains, however, the western bluebirds are still struggling).

Monitoring a bluebird nest box as part of cavity-nester conservation efforts.

JOHN IVANKO

With their brilliant plumage, bluebirds have captured the imagination and fascination of birders, not to mention poets, philosophers and musicians. It was Thoreau who wrote about the bluebird that carries the sky on his back and Dorothy in "The Wizard of Oz", who sings about bluebirds somewhere over the rainbow.

Because the terrain around the cabin offered wide-open spaces for bluebirds to search out their choice food, insects on the ground, we created a bluebird trail, a series of boxes along a route that we (and our cabin guests) could regularly monitor. A clipboard with record forms help us document nesting activities of bluebirds as well as the other cavity-nesting birds that use the boxes. It's particularly rewarding, since we can open the box and peer inside without interrupting the nesting cycle; bluebirds, like many other songbirds, have a poorly developed sense of smell and will not abandon their nest with such low-level human involvement.

Next in importance to finding an appropriate habitat for bluebirds, according to the North American Bluebird Society, is the careful selection of a nestbox:

- For boxes used by eastern bluebirds and western bluebirds, a hole 1½ inches in diameter should be used to deter starlings from using the box. For the slightly larger mountain bluebird box, a hole 1⁹/₁₆ (3.97 cm) inches in diameter should be used.

- No perches, since they only attract the non-native House Sparrow.

- Easily opened nest box — from the front, side or top — to facilitate regular monitoring and cleaning after each nesting.

- Drainage holes at the bottom of the box to allow rain to drain.

- Vents at the box peak to provide good ventilation.

- Natural wood, especially weather-resistant cedar or redwood, is best. Avoid pressure treated woods, or boxes that are painted dark colors since it's possible that they might overheat their inhabitants in hot weather.

- The box can be made be predator resistant if mounted on a smooth round pipe, about 5 feet (1.5 m) from the ground.

Monitoring of boxes not only records data helpful to improving future nesting success, but if non-native species take over the box, they can be removed. If, somehow, a nestling falls out, it can be replaced into the box, or if something happens to the parents, the nestlings can be placed in other boxes. Regular monitoring allows for lots of troubleshooting, which contributes to the success of the program.

SOURCES AND RESOURCES

National Wildife Federation's Certified Habitat
  Website: www.nwf.org
  The Certified Backyard Habitat or Schoolyard Habitat programs of the National Wildlife Federation provide resources and materials to turn a backyard, schoolyard or farmyard into a mini-wildlife preserve.

National Audubon Society
  Website: www.audubon.org
  Audubon is dedicated to protecting birds and other wildlife and the habitat that supports them, with programs or initiatives from being bird specific to addressing over-population and over-fishing of the oceans.

North American Bluebird Society
  Website: www.nabluebirdsociety.org
  Provides nestbox plans and other helpful introductory fact sheets.

Don Stokes and Lillian Stokes, *Bluebird Book: The Complete Guide to Attracting Bluebirds*, Little Brown & Co., 1991.

Eating Lower on the Food Chain

Each of our B&B guest rooms has a binder of local tourist information, including menus from various restaurants we've personally tried and would recommend. We live in an area where butter, starch and animal products are the culinary norm, but there are a few family-owned spots where guests can get a good meal for a reasonable price, including some meat-free options. So when one of our B&B guests, a Chicago twenty-something vegetarian, returned from dinner complaining that he wasn't able to eat anything but the fries, we were surprised. He handed us a doggie bag with the rest of the rejected meal. We gave him a curious look, peering inside the bag to discover a completely intact hamburger with the fixings.

> God created Eden for vegetarians to run around naked.
>
> — Anonymous

He had ordered a mushroom burger at the type of place that has many such menu options, from cheeseburger to pizza burger. When he ordered the mushroom burger, he expected a grilled portabello mushroom on a bun, like the ones served in Chicago. What he ended up with was a thick, juicy hamburger with some sautéed mushrooms on top. To pick up his spirits and allow him to go to sleep with a full belly, we whipped up an apple crisp to tide him over until our vegetarian breakfast was served the next morning.

We, too, are vegetarians, but not strictly so. When we're home, we eat a vegetarian diet of fruits, vegetables, legumes and nuts, as well as eggs and dairy products. At home we can control what goes in our refrigerator and mouth, so we're able to eat lower on the food chain. Our primary reason in doing so, in addition to reducing our environmental impacts, is for health reasons. The more fruits, vegetables and grains we have in our diet, the better we feel, more energy we exude, and the longer we're likely to live. Such a diet makes sense, too, from a cost perspective, since the bulk of our meals come directly from the garden and a nominal yearly seed investment. Experimenting in the kitchen is a passion of ours and we have an ongoing file of new recipes to try. We indulge in quality dried herbs and spices, which take up a whole cabinet in the kitchen, and we relish cooking with freshly harvested herbs in the summer.

We do, on occasion, enjoy chicken and the annual Thanksgiving turkey which we purchase from a nearby organic farm. When it comes to eating out, we enjoy fish and sometimes other seafood. We try, however, to make more sustainable and informed decisions on the types of fish and seafood to eat.

SUSTAINABLE SEAFOOD

We enjoy seafood and fish from time to time, but we've come to realize that seafood consumption is becoming less sustainable. The oceans, rivers and lakes — and the aquatic life that lives there — are now in severe decline. Fisheries have been overfished and the clean, abundant aquatic world has become clogged with poisons, pollutants and other human-generated waste. Even the effects of global warming are believed to have resulted in the bleaching of the barrier reef systems around the world, threatening their survival. We eat less fish because of mounting evidence that mercury is accumulating in the fat of the fish with possibly harmful affects on human health.

We enjoy Alaskan wild salmon and join the Wisconsin tradition of Friday fish fries - we just try not to indulge too often. The National Audubon Society's *Seafood Lover's Guide* and numerous other sources echo the same chorus: we're eating out the stock of fish and other seafood faster than it can replenish itself. In some cases, it's a matter of incredible waste. For every pound of shrimp harvested in the ocean, for example, seven pounds of other aquatic life is killed in the harvest.

On the infrequent times we do shop for fish or seafood, we look for the seal of the Marine Stewardship Council, the organization that certifies seafood from sustainable fisheries.

The National Audubon Society's Living Oceans Program, often partnering with aquariums and other similar facilities, offers a "Seafood Wallet Card" which provides a quick reference guide for more sustainable and environmentally sound choices when buying or ordering fish and seafood. Visit <www.audubon.org> and print out their *Seafood Lover's Guide*. A Seafood Watch pocket guide can also be downloaded from the Monterey Bay Aquarium <www.montereybayaquarium.org>.

Every growing season, it seems we encounter a new favorite vegetable. One year it was Swiss chard. Another year it was bok choy, which grew in abundance; we made batches of bok choy soup that we froze and ate all winter long. After experiencing pickled beets, we became convinced we didn't like them. Fortunately, we gave them a second chance, and experimented one year with a beet veggie burger recipe. Our beet burger, a patty concoction of shredded beets and carrots, cheese, sunflower and sesame seeds, rice and other grains or legumes, is baked in the oven and tray-frozen for later use. Beets provide the perfect consistency in this patty form. It forever changed our minds about beets, and would have exceeded the expectations of the mushroom burger guy. We also love beets batter fried.

We pride ourselves in preparing hearty and satisfying breakfasts for B&B guests, with such menus as breakfast burritos with seasonal vegetables, potato and rosemary hashbrowns with fresh chives, homemade muffins, fresh fruit in season, and yogurt smoothies. No one has ever walked away from the breakfast table hungry. We've encountered first-time vegetarians who've had a freak encounter with tofu (soybean curd) or a tasteless bean chili. By the end of our breakfasts, we've hopefully instilled in them a new appreciation for the magnificent, hearty and versatile tastes of fruits, vegetables, grains, nuts and legumes.

Still, the label vegetarian breakfast can be misleading to some people who might have had a rhubarb experience of ordering the veggie special at some restaurant only to be left hungry, appalled by the lack of taste and flavor. Restaurants like the Moosewood in Ithaca, New York, The Greens in San Francisco, or L'Etoile in Madison, Wisconsin — and of course the countless Indian, Ethiopian and Middle Eastern restaurants across the continent — are among many that have helped change this misconception about vegetarian food. When we went through our first reprint of the B&B brochure, we added the word hearty to the description of our breakfasts so that the V word wouldn't scare folks away. As it turned out, "serendipity" for some of our guests has come to mean enjoying a meal without any meat.

We most often relax our dietary restrictions when we're travelling. When we're on the road and visiting people, be it in another country or in Monroe, it's more important to us that we are respectful guests rather than strict vegetarians. Many of our friends realize our eating preferences and graciously cook accordingly. But when we're traveling in Scotland where just about every meal includes a meat dish, we prefer to sample a little haggis without regret and chalk it up to cultural experience. If our neighbors invite us to the community pork producer's pork chop supper, we appreciate the invitation and gladly go. In a similar vein, when family meals center around the holiday ham, we prioritize keeping the peace rather than creating a fuss. We grill up some locally procured Wisconsin bratwursts when friends who would appreciate something like that come to visit. Our approach is hardly purist, but sometimes our relationships have higher priority than the main dish. While we may deviate from the vegetarian fare on occassion, we try to make as conscientious a selection of our animal-based foods as possible, which usually means organic, free-range, pasture-fed and, wherever possible, purchased directly from other local farmers.

We're fortunate that the Jordendahl Farm is nearby, offering organic poultry and beef, though we're hardly their top customer by sales volume. For the little meat we do purchase, it's satisfying to buy it directly from the grower and feel confident that the animals were raised and treated humanely. We'll order that

Thanksgiving turkey ahead of time by e-mail and pick it up fresh a couple of days before the holidays.

Our approach to eating helps us combine our desires to eat lower on the food chain, lessen environmental impact and strengthen our local economy and community. Food security and a sustainable economy, after all, are locally intertwined.

Going Vegetarian

When the word leaked out that we were vegetarians, polite smiles were exchanged. Since some of the retirees in the county were on restricted diets (often resembling vegetarian) because their doctor prescribed it, we sometimes sensed that they thought we suffered some dietary disease to be eating so many vegetables. We still manage to stump some restaurants when we ask for a vegetarian option. That a plant-based diet uses less farmland, is less destructive to the soil, and can provide the vitamins, minerals and nutrients we need for our survival makes it a more self-reliant and less costly way to live. Add to that the sheer economy of growing a good portion of our foods needs in our own garden, and we couldn't see a better reason to be vegetarians.

So many of the myths around vegetarianism can be debunked after a bit of careful study. What the meat-centered diet is doing to America is explained at length in several compelling and exhaustively researched books (see Resources, below). Like most Americans, we can appreciate the taste of a good hamburger, especially if the meat was from organically and pasture-raised cattle. But the environmental costs and health effects are too compelling to ignore. Excessive consumption of meat and dairy products are linked to heart disease, cancer, diabetes, arthritis, osteoporosis, clogged arteries, asthma and infertility — all of which are on the rise in the US. While lack of exercise and other variables also contribute to these health issues, our nation suffers from the diseases that come with an affluent lifestyle and the trappings of a meat-based diet.

COOKBOOKS FOR VEGETARIANS

Vegetables sometimes get a bad rap as bland, mushy and boring. We've learned that vegetarian cooking is an acquired skill, and that it's constantly improved if we're willing to try new, tempting recipes.

Some of the cookbooks that are favorites on our shelves include:

- *Hollyhock Cooks: Food to Nourish Body, Mind and Soil,* by Linda Solomon and Moreka Jolar (New Society Publishers, 2003).
- *The New Moosewood Cookbook,* by Mollie Katzen (Ten Speed Press, 2000).
- *The Greens Cookbook,* by Deborah Madison, Edward Espe Brown and Marion Cunningham (Broadway Books, 2001).
- *Whole Foods Companion: A Guide for Adventurous Cooks, Curious Shoppers and Lovers of Natural Foods,* by Dianne Onstad (Chelsea Green Publishing, 1996).
- *Fresh from the Farmers' Market : Year-Round Recipes for the Pick of the Crop,* by Janet Kessel Fletche (Chronicle Books, 1997).
- *From Asparagus to Zucchini: A Guide to Farm-fresh, Seasonal Produce,* by Madison Area Community Supported Agriculture Cooperative (MACSAC), ordered directly by visiting <www.macsac.org>.

SOURCES AND RESOURCES

John Robbins, *Food Revolution: How your Diet can Help Save your Life and Our World,* Conari Press, 2001.

Frances Moore Lappe and Anna Lappe, *Diet for a Small Planet - 20th Anniversary Edition,* Ballantine Books, 1985.

Frances Moore Lappe and Anna Lappe, *Hope's Edge: The Next Diet for a Small Planet,* J.P. Tarcher, 2002.

Eric Schlosser, *Fast Food Nation: The Dark Side of the All-American Meal,* Harper Collins, 2002.

Vegetarian Times magazine
Website: www.vegetariantimes.com
From recipes to healthy eating and wellness, this magazine for vegetarians covers it all.

Health and Wellness

"You know, there's more nitrates in a hot dog than in that glass of water from your well," advised a well-meaning neighbor. We politely smile, looking to change the topic but silently thinking to ourselves, "That's why we don't eat those hot dogs."

We ordered a standard water test administered in Wisconsin by the Department of Hygiene before buying the farm. The water sample analysis identifies levels of potentially harmful chemicals or bacteria in the water, and, in our case found the well water to be high in nitrates, most likely due to years of accumulated fertilizers draining into the aquifer from which the drinking water was drawn.

Drilling a new well solved the problem by tapping into a deeper, uncontaminated water table. It was the only solution as far as we were concerned. But many folks, as our neighbor indicated, didn't see nitrates as such a big deal. They're a widely accepted part of what goes into our bodies, an argument that didn't settle well with us, considering that our bodies are about 70 percent water. We knew water would flow through elements of our possible future life on the farm, from filling the coffee pot and irrigating the raspberry patch to filling Liam's kiddie pool.

We felt that having nitrates in our drinking water was simply not an acceptable option. For us to live well, our water needed to be safe. This evolved into a sticky point during the final rounds of our farm purchase process: we wouldn't buy the farm without a new well, which would cost upwards of eight thousand dollars. The former owners didn't seem to share our concern, but they eventually met us halfway and split the cost of the new well.

Drilling for the new well commenced that following spring, after the ground thawed. Casing for the new well, placed at a different location, went down over 200 feet (60 meters). The depth of this new water table provided a reminder as we settled in: already some of that first 200 feet of land and water underneath the farm was impacted by toxins.

As humans, we also arrived as damaged beings. We had a history of hydrogenated fat in our veins, automotive exhaust in our lungs and stress in our souls. Could we, slowly, restore both the farm and ourselves to better health? Could we, together with the land, regain wellness in the truest sense, a blending of mind, body and spirit, integrated with a life closer to the land and our food, water sources and community?

This discussion of health begs an answer to the underlying question: What is wellness? How will we know when we are well? Health and wellness are personal ideals; ideals that continue to evolve, since our bodies and our environment are always changing. Folks often ask us about our transition to the farm — if we felt uncertainties along the way. Sure, we had a lot of ups and downs, but we never felt unreconcilable doubt or anxiety. While our farm surroundings were new to us, we were comfortably at peace — at home. We felt well in terms of a healthy body, mind and spirit. Our lives were engaged with fresh challenges, yet we felt that happy tingle in our souls when our feet hit the floor each morning, in sync with whatever the day would bring. We had control of our inputs — what food we ate, when we slept, how we organized our time — which resulted in control of our outputs. Individual days accumulated into the life we wanted to lead.

Body

Wellness is not a destination, it's a journey of constant flux and realignment. Our health requires constant attention; we need to learn to identify the early signs of problems, and know when it's time go into system shut down mode and regroup. Living closer to the land, our sensitivity to our own bodies has increased. Just as we see that the droopy cucumber vines need water and the lettuce bed craves a thorough weed to give the plants room to breath, we realize when our bodies need tending to as well. A soothing cup of tea, a roughage-laden bowl of salad greens, or a back rub at the end of a day of harvesting — our bodies send us messages. Identifying and acting on these daily bodily signals helps keep us whole and healthy, and connected to our physical well being.

Sure there are unpredictable flair ups, from crunch deadlines to seasonal allergies. When these come our way, we try to go into prevention mode as best we can. When we feel that tickle at the back of the throat, telling us our bodies are trying to fight some kind of bug, we try to give our bodies a break and take care of ourselves. That means an echinacea tincture in hot water every two hours, sucking on zinc lozenges, drinking lots of liquids and heading to bed early. With our flexible schedule and teamwork, one of us can check out for a half day and come back at 95 percent the next day, rather than fighting a lingering virus or infection at half-strength for weeks.

Each chapter of our life story adds its imprint on our body as well. Giving birth to Liam took Lisa's body through a complete metamorphosis, testifying again to the idea that wellness is a journey. Trying to let her body's needs take the lead during the pregnancy — taking rests and food breaks when it felt right — Lisa took the same approach post-partum, giving her body time and support to come back to full strength. She found nursing to be nature's way of boosting this whole process. Through nursing and eating well, the extra calories burned through extended breastfeeding brought her weight and energy level back to normal nine months after Liam was born.

Mind

Sometimes we need a mental break. We can get so absorbed in a project that our mind starts telling us to pull back and step away for a while. This could mean an evening watching a couple videos, reading something completely unrelated to the project, or taking a snooze. Lisa's in mental break mode when she pores over cookbooks and recipe files as if it were the self-help section at the bookstore. John escapes outdoors to cut wood, weed the garden or dig up potatoes.

These mental breaks are usually a last resort for us; they occur when we've let the well of our creative juices run dry. We've found that a much better alternative is to work ahead as much as possible, avoiding last minute stress. Working ahead and battling procrastination has been a key variable in making our livelihood work. It increases our ability to handle the random stress and unpredictable crises that occur. If one of us needs a half day off, the other can readily step in and cover things. Sick or mental health days simply don't exist in the self-employed world. We shepherd a variety of seemingly unrelated projects: planting crops, taking photos, consulting on marketing plans, weeding perennials, baking muffins for B&B guests, writing books, chasing Liam. We thrive on diversity, and we've discovered that keeping things in balance is dependent upon us staying on top of all those individual projects.

We've learned, too, that trying to keep one step ahead of it enables us to spontaneously take advantage of fun opportunities as they come up; it gives us the chance to accept a last-minute invitation to a fish fry; steal away for an afternoon on a beach along the Wisconsin River; or catch a movie at the theater in town.

Spirit

As an umbrella to everything happening in our lives, we strive to nurture our spirit. We find a strong sense of sacredness close to the land, with the willow tree, the peony patch, and the pond at the cabin, but we've also grown to appreciate the sanctity in the everyday. Our days are colored with routines that on the surface seem mindless: scrubbing the kitchen sink, peeling potatoes, giving Liam a bath. But dig deeper, and the everyday becomes a temple of meditation and reflection.

We've learned to step back from daily habit and relish the peace of the moment, to become truly present. It's often when we are absorbed in these everyday rituals that we lose our sense of time and place. Our spirit is nourished. Canning applesauce provides such a sacred ground. Together we silently peel, slice, cook, mash, pack and seal the jars. This is a routine autumn task, yet going through the process is like meditation. Our minds are still, surrounded by silence and the occasional soft whirl of the hand-cranked apple peeler. A couple of hours later we've racked up not only sixteen quarts of applesauce, but our spirits have harvested peace.

How to

Providing What a Body Needs

Eat an apple a day. Take time for yourself to be at peace and relax. Meditate. Exercise regularly and get lots of rest. Much of this advice comes from the esteemed medical profession, the US Surgeon General, and from Dr. Mom. At the advertising agency, we convinced ourselves that the ulcers and cancer would happen to someone else. We had places to go, careers to advance, and restaurants to try.

Today, a blending of mind, body and spirit nourishes a more healthy life for us. A life lacking this blend tends to result in unhappiness, defined in any number of ways: depression; stress; road-rage; overeating; addiction; consumerism. As it turns out, the wellness movement manifests itself as much in the urban and suburban scenes as it does in the country. The difference within the rural is in its unintentional everyday occurrence. We pause, mesmerized by the sunrise in the morning or amused by the llamas frolicking in the pasture. Everything takes more time in the country. Coffee room conferences become afternoon gatherings under the tree with peanut butter covered celery sticks.

Physical labor pulls at our muscles — moving straw bales, weeding, trimming trees. When we don't get enough outdoor exercise, mostly in the winter, we work out at the gym at the YMCA. In our own ways, the familiarity and regularity of going to the gym keeps us relatively fit and active. Besides providing us with a higher energy level and an occasional connection to folks in town, it's preventative medicine. Other than a rare minor cold, we've not been sick for years. However, we can't escape our own health histories, either. So Lisa deals with her asthma and allergies as best she can, and John is extra careful with his problem back and knee.

We strongly believe in preventative care. We eat organic, whole and healthy foods, exercise regularly, and minimize the amount of stress in our life. Without our good health, the good life is not possible. For helping preserve our bodies, we look to companies that provide toothpaste, haircare and skin moisturizers that are all-natural, responsibly manufactured, and aren't tested on animals or made from animal products. The Body Shop, Aveda, Burt's Bees, Aubrey Organics, Kiss My Face, and Tom's of Maine, while often more expensive, heal our body and help the planet.

When our mind, body and spirit intersect and blend with one another, we experience a flow, an energy, that allows us to be at peace and accomplish more than we ever imagined. Books get written, barns get rebuilt and a child gets raised personally and by both parents. This wholeness allows us to live more meaningful and happy lives. There is always more to do. But everything will eventually get done. It took us five years to remove an abandoned chest freezer, so big that a craft room had been built around the thing by the previous owners of the house. The labyrinth is an ongoing evolution, as is the landscaping around the property; we look for cues from nature and ideas from our visitors as to what to do next.

The farm, this book, and our lives are the manifestations of who we are as creative beings, doing what we love, zestfully. It's measured not by the wealth it produces or how much resources it uses up in its achievement. Nor is failure abhorred. Happiness lives within, and around us, and tends to attract passionate, compassionate and caring people. What we've come to call home has evolved into a place where people enjoy coming for the weekend, or the summer, to try new things, enjoy a meal, or play and experiment. The balance created has nothing to do with our career goals; instead, our health and that of the land tops the list. On the outside of envelopes we send out to friends is a rubber stamped message reading: "Live well, laugh often, love much. Exactly."

SOURCES AND RESOURCES

Alternative Medicine Center
   Website: www.healthy.net
   Explore natural choices for self-managed health care.

Burt's Bees Inc.
   Website: www.burtsbees.com

The Body Shop
   Website: www.the-body-shop.com

Aveda
   Website: www.aveda.com

Tom's of Maine
   Website: www.toms-of-maine.com

Kiss My Face
   Website: www.kissmyface.com

Aubrey Organics
   Website: www.aubrey-organics.com

Freedom To and Freedom From

Farms and freedom have a deep, historic synergy. Until recently, agriculture tended to reflect the symbiotic relationship between farmers and the land they stewarded; the relationship met both food and livelihood needs. For many farmers today, this is no longer the case. The idea of owning land, cultivating crops and providing for one's family compelled many of the original farmers to settle in this area, in accordance with the long-standing American values of freedom and independence, supported by a strong work ethic. We, too, moved in search of freedom, but perhaps of a different kind. We arrived with the hopes of attaining more control over our lives, freedom to live in ways that kept our values and beliefs intact, and to live more independently from the global economy and more interdependently with the local community. An important tenet of freedom is the ability to actively support the social causes and non-profit organizations whose missions we believe in, and to have the time and energy to make a difference.

Beyond using financial resources to support causes, we focused instead on contributions of time and energy. Writing checks and making other in-kind donations are vital to supporting non-profit organizations, but among our goals is to have the capacity to commit ourselves, our time, our hearts and passions to direct involvement. When we were too caught up in our daily corporate routines, we lacked time and energy — falling into the check-writing support category out of convenience, and perhaps, out of guilt.

As our livelihood and lifestyle shifted to one of control over our schedule and freedom to choose how we spent our time, we found ourselves veering more towards non-profit pursuits that address social, economic, and ecological issues. We can devote ourselves more completely to creating a business model that can thrive in a living economy and doesn't destroy the Earth we care so much about. Being involved with non-profit organizations and running our businesses energizes us, connecting us to inspiring people we would probably have not otherwise met and gives us satisfaction no paycheck could ever match.

Our contributions model the themes that permeate the rest of our lives: creativity, diversity and a blending of work and leisure. Our out-of-the-box approach to activism and altruism results in some alternative approaches:

- **Give skills and talents.** Some of our deepest, most enriching experiences have stemmed from situations in which a non-profit organization needed something we could tangibly contribute, like John's photography contributed to the Global Fund for Children. When John was embarking on his photography career, a friend forwarded information about a new non-profit start-up, SHAKTI for Children (later a program of the Global Fund for Children), that focused on creating children's books which foster respect for diversity and encourage children to become productive, caring citizens of the world. John connected with its founder, Maya, and over the years he has developed a relationship and co-authored or contributed photographs to several books. Donating photos at the beginning enabled John to help foster the growth of an organization with a mission he supported.

- **Share passions.** Sometimes an effective way to contribute is by giving our passion: contributing our enthusiasm, energy and experience with a topic. For example, we often donate our time to teach workshops at the Renewable Energy and Sustainable Living Fair, sponsored by the Midwest Renewable Energy Association (MREA). We often lead a workshop on rural living, with a focus on renewable energy, organic gardening and ecologically minded home renovations. We've also facilitated a children's workshop about understanding diversity through use of the creative arts. These topics intimately link to our hearts and experiences, and our passions positively contribute to the success of the Energy Fair.

- **Proffer a unique perspective.** Sometimes valuable contributions stem from innovative out-of-the-box perspectives. We're always on the lookout for situations where we can contribute our skills, experiences, energy, and time toward something that may otherwise not have happened. Often this perspective involves relationship building: connecting people with people. With the parade of people passing through the farm and our lives, we have the opportunity to bring people together who may not have met otherwise. We've found that our role in this process isn't necessarily to introduce specific people that we think should meet. Rather, the contribution we can best make is to create situations where people can informally cross paths, typically over food, a project, or an event such as the open house Inn Serendipity hosts during the National Tour of Solar Homes.

When someone interesting comes to visit, we try to stimulate new connections. When our friend Donald, a retired distillery manager from

Scotland, visited, we hosted a Scotch tasting which included Donald narrating a slide presentation of his homeland and the Scotch whisky making process. Kevin, a folk singer and songwriter from the East Coast, visited during the summer months and we invited neighbors over for music around the campfire. Kevin's songs lean toward activist themes, often about homelessness and war, not exactly the local mainstays of Swiss yodeling and polkas. But sitting under the starry summer night sky passing around the homemade cookies, we all enjoyed the warm camaraderie and melodies. Instigating such eclectic, diverse situations that allow folks to meet gives us a sense of satisfaction, a feeling that in our own small way we're contributing to a closer, more accepting and open-minded world.

> Freedom and responsibility go hand in hand as an essential foundation of a civil society.
> — David Korten

With freedom comes responsibility. Planting roots in a community caused us to feel a greater civic responsibility as residents. Staying put is perhaps one of the more central requirements for sustainable living. Increasingly, we find ourselves drawn to public meetings about issues that influence the quality of life in our community. A bicycle trail planned through Monroe which will eventually weave its way to Madison resulted in us joining more than a hundred area residents to discuss its status and learn to speak our piece and participate.

Democracy is not a spectator sport. We're involved on national as well as local levels, since policies on renewable energy and agriculture — generally decided at a national or statewide level — directly affect our daily experience.

+ **Cultivate compassion.** To feel and offer compassion, to actively understand and help other people directly, is an ongoing, and sometimes complicated, process. The more we learn about the world — the more perspectives and facts we expose ourselves to — the more we realize that our actions have consequences. Every day we are given the opportunity to care through our actions and behaviors, from buying organically grown, fairly traded coffee that pays South American farmers a fair wage, to seeking out products made from recycled materials that have less impact on our already damaged world, to simply reading a range of opinions and perspectives on world issues. Collectively, these actions help us evolve as more compassionate and caring citizens of the planet.

We have opportunities to cultivate compassion directly and locally by taking the time to focus on our friends, family and community. Compassion can be an opportunity for creative expression, developing personal ways to show we care. This often involves the giving of food, sharing the bounty of our harvest or speaking out at public meetings on behalf of the voiceless population: nature and children (who cannot vote). When Chris, aka Pierre, recovers from multiple trips to the hospital, we stop by with apple crisp and conversation. The more we give of ourselves, our time and our efforts, the more enriching and rewarding our lives are and the more whole we feel as humans. Perhaps we're trying to rediscover what it means to be human (as opposed to being a "consumer" or a "worker"). The greatest benefit of our lifestyle and livelihood is our opportunity and freedom to creatively do so.

SOURCES AND RESOURCES

Global Fund for Children (and SHAKTI for Children)
Website: www.globalfundforchildren.org
Website: www.shakti.org
Helping young people develop the knowledge and skills they need to become productive, caring citizens of our global society. SHAKTI for Children is their book publishing venture featuring books that celebrate diversity and community.

National Tour of Solar Homes
Website: www.ases.org
Coordinated by the American Solar Energy Society, this annual national tour held early October offers the opportunity to visit and tour homes and businesses which incorporate a myriad of renewable energy, energy conservation products, and green design elements into their homes or offices.

Global Exchange
Website: www.globalexchange.org
Formed in 1998, this international partnership-building non-profit organization promotes environmental, political and social justice.

Jim Hightower, *Thieves in High Places: They've Stolen Our Country — And it's Time to Take it Back,* Viking Press, 2003.

Leaving a Legacy

Twigs with roots. That's what the trees we planted that first spring looked like to us. We joined the Green County Conservation League when we found out that we would receive 30 one-year-old evergreen seedlings for $1 with our membership. When we picked up the trees in early April, we cleared out the back seat of our car to make room for them, figuring that the trees would take up a bit of space. Wrong. We could hold the 30 trees in one hand. They resembled little six-inch twigs with short roots dangling below, covered in moistened moss and wrapped in brown paper.

We put aside our disappointment at the seedlings' size and quickly planted them on the west side of the property, where we hoped they'd eventually provide a windbreak to reduce our energy heating costs, help shield the field from fertilizer or pesticide drift from the surrounding conventionally-grown fields, and help prevent soil erosion. Those little seedlings looked tiny and frail after we planted them, but the experience became an important first lesson in understanding what it means to build and leave a legacy. Planting those tiny seedlings lacked immediate gratification. They wouldn't reach maturity for several decades but we feel drawn to plant another batch from the Conservation League every spring. Maturity dates aren't important. We are motivated by something greater than ourselves and more enduring than our lifetime. We have embarked on creating our legacy.

Moving to the country jump-started our legacy quest and gave us goals to strive toward in very hands-on ways. Being surrounded by the land, waking up to a house wren's call and being lulled to sleep by the peeping frogs all deepen our desire to leave this world a better place. This drive to create and leave a legacy is so different from our goals in the past. We traded job titles and bank account balances for the opportunity to create something of lasting value. We yearn to be remembered for what we did during our lifetime and hopefully, if we make enough wise choices, how we left things better than when we found them.

For inspiration, we think about Thomas Jefferson's epitaph, the inscription on his gravestone at his Virginia home in Monticello. It reads: "Author of the Declaration of Independence, of the Statute of Virginia for Religious Freedom, and Father of the University of Virginia." He could have listed the many lauded distinctions he achieved in his lifetime, such as President of the United States and US Ambassador to France. But Jefferson instead chose to focus on his legacy, the things he created that would continue long after his life was over.

The concept of leaving a legacy means different things to different people. For many years we didn't give it much thought or concern. We were too busy in our routines and schedules to ponder such deep questions. The concept of a legacy involves acknowledging that we're going to die someday, and who wants to deal with that?

Living closer to the land helped change our worldview. Every day breathing and living in a world far greater than ourselves jolted us from our sleepy existence. Each season we witness new miracles, from the first pussy willow buds in March to the January icicles on the dairy barn that sparkle like a magical crystal. The concept of death takes on new meaning, as we connect on a deeper level with the circle of life. Everything has its season, one life blending into the next.

> Despite all the wide and varied differences that human beings around the world embody, we are in truth more alike than dissimilar. In the core of our being, we yearn to be connected to something real, something substantial, something to believe in - something larger than ourselves. We want to belong, to be a part of something that will endure beyond our lives.
> — Shatoiya and Richard de la Tour, *The Herbalist's Garden*

Crafting our legacy guides our activities, lifestyle and livelihood. For the land, it means enriching the soil, nurturing a diversity of plants and enhancing wildlife habitat. For our community, it means leaving our imprint on this area, such as instigating new approaches to locally based tourism. Economically, it means our small business should operate, to the extent possible, in ways that minimize our impact on the environment and on others. Renewable energy systems, water conservation efforts and green materials have each played a role in our holistic design of living and working. We leave a genetic legacy, of course, with Liam. By providing a supportive community, family, and earth-centered foundations, we hope that he may grow into a caring, loving citizen of the world who follows the beat of his own talents, aspirations and creativity.

Leaving the world a better place involves nurturing a variety of positive relationships in our lives. If we can positively affect those with whom we come in contact — B&B guests, Liam and our family, readers of this book — we're one step closer to leaving our mark. To inspire, and be inspired by our many visitors, guests, friends and family, affirms our pursuit of happiness and bring us closer to our dreams.

We view our legacy, too, from the perspective of what we're not leaving behind, adding to the landfill, or contributing to social inequality. Our many building projects have involved diligence and care in the selection of materials so that their eventual disassembly or disposal need not be as dangerous and wasteful a task as what we inherited. The straw bale greenhouse, is, after all, made mostly of the earth. Every time we buy something that is fairly traded or sweatshop free, we support a new economy based on fairness and greater equality, not on human exploitation. Maybe we've spent one too many days hiking in national parks, following a leave-no-trace mantra. But we do not want to use any energy produced by nuclear reactors, a process that produces a toxic waste that future generations must live with for 10,000 years. We don't want to foster a food supply from seeds that as a life form are patented (and owned) by multinational corporations. To every extent possible, we avoid contributing to the further pollution and poisoning of the air, water, and soil that belongs to everyone — and to no one. And we strive to raise our son in a way that allows him to know when racism, intolerance and overly competitive forces raise their ugly heads, and speak out when they do.

Are we unusual to be talking legacy in our mid-thirties? Statistically, perhaps. While we spend time thinking about, planning, and plotting how we want to leave this world, we're in no way compelled to accomplish everything by the end of the year, or decade. Our culture and lifestyle, and the goods and services we use, were created and perpetuated under a different worldview than the one we're trying to live under today. It will take time for the pendulum of life and our interactions with nature to swing away from consumption, growth, exploitation, and degradation. We have our lifetime to do what we can, however local it may be and in whatever number of minutes, days and years our lives afford us, to achieve our goals. A legacy is not based on quarterly or year-end statements.

Thinking about our legacy is similar to what many Native Americans considered: the impact of our actions on the seventh generation. Our legacy has enriched our life with fun and purposeful activity, increased the joy in everyday living and has motivated and sustained us on a daily basis. As we steward the land, we smile and delight in each firefly that passes by. Liam is a constant reminder of the power of human relationships as he ardently observes, studies and reaches out to connect with the world he sees.

> History will have to recall that the greatest tragedy of this period of social transition was not the vitriolic words and the violent actions of the bad people, but the appalling silence and indifference of the good people. Our generation will have to repent not only for words and actions of the children of darkness, but also for the fears and apathy of the children of light.
>
> — Martin Luther King, Jr.

> It is impossible to care for each other more or differently than we care for the earth.
>
> — Wendell Berry

He is already teaching us about ourselves and the world, reminding us through his actions that the real world around us is far more interesting than the fake one on TV, or at the mall. Each sunset, sliced tomato and swoosh of the wind turbine inspires us to keep going. Every little tree seedling reinforces our connection to generations to come. While our physical being returns to the Earth as dust, our creative and re-creative legacy lives on in the trees, soil, plants, water and community of life.

THE COMMONS

The air and airwaves, water and the aquifers underground, land and its mineral deposits, oil, soil, or forests, and more recently, biodiversity, intellectual property and bandwidth. These would be the assets if the Earth had a balance sheet, essential to the well being of all life. Unfortunately, societies, corporations and people tend not to hold a worldview that respects this understanding. Every time disasters like Chernobyl, the *Exxon Valdez,* or the patenting of life happen, we grow increasingly aware of how our collective commons is altered and degraded, sometimes in irreversable ways.

"The plundering of the commons is a major factor in what is misleadingly called 'economic growth,'" writes Jonathan Rowe in the January-February 2002 issue of *Utne Reader* (adapted from *Yes! A Journal of Positive Futures,* Summer 2001). "It often does not add a good that wasn't there before. Instead, it takes a good from the commons, diminishes or degrades it, and then sells it back to us in commodified form. Pollute our lakes and rivers and then sell us swimming pools and bottled water. Destroy the traditional patterns of village or community life, then sell people cars to get around, treadmills for exercise - and pills to calm their nerves."

Sustainability is directly linked to the preserving, restoring and conserving of the global commons. Sustainable living on a local level is the beacon that can guide common interests, intentions and cooperation.

Source: Tomales Bay Institute, a project of the Earth Island Institute. <www.earthisland.org>

Leaving Biological Legacies

Adapted from the Land Trust Alliance's brochures, *Conservation Options for Private Landowners* and *Protecting Your Land with a Conservation Easement*.

Some may call it our call of the wild: procreation. It's the celebration of love and perhaps among the most sacred and divine of all things we can do as human beings, the making of a new life. With Liam, our biological and genetic legacy will continue to weave its way on this planet in yet-to-be-determined and mysterious ways.

So too, with the land we purchased. We envisioned the cultivation of a livelihood and more sustainable lifestyle that would help restore the land, protect nature, and, — long after we've passed away — thrive and prosper. Looking back on our purchase of the farmstead, perhaps Joy and Del, in their uncanny ways, recognized this.

By working with the Mississippi Valley Conservancy and Gathering Waters land trusts, we began our journey to become better stewards of our cabin property in Hillsboro while sharing it with visitors. To support our mission as well as the Mississippi Valley Conservancy, we enrolled the Inn Serendipity Woods property in their Landowner Registry Program, a voluntary agreement to conserve and steward the land. The Conservancy's Registry Program recognizes owners of land with sensitive species, wildlife habitat, open space, or where active habitat restoration is taking place. It was our first step in the process of permanently protecting our land, or should we say, the land.

We recognize both the responsibility and opportunity that property ownership brings as we embark on wildlife conservation efforts that address native, cavity-nesting bird species as well as species using wetland, grass and forest habitat. Different from other parts of the world, the rights associated with private property ownership in the United States offers the possibility of an owner to define what a parcel of land (or building) can — and can not — be used for. The right to build new homes or buildings, mining, leasing or other income generation possibilities as well as selling or passing along a property to heirs are well established rights of ownership. Increasingly, so is setting forth the terms of land or other property conservation by owners who share a strong belief in conservation, either environmental or historical. Such a commitment is abetted by a provision of the US tax code that can offer a tax deduction and other financial benefits.

As the US population continues to grow, we've found that many people with strong environmental priorities and interest in the outdoors are searching for and owning magnificent open spaces, properties containing scenic vistas, or biologically diverse wildlife refuges, often as second homes. They're helping restore watersheds, preserve wetlands for waterfowl and other species, reestablishing prairies, and doing their part to help keep the air clean. These people, too, are eager to preserve historical heritage and, in the case of the disappearing farmlands, the agrarian landscape — including old barns — that have shaped America.

We're among the many millions of people who aim to leverage land or property ownership and pioneer a new land conservation movement by adding a conservation easement, also known as a conservation restriction, to their holdings. Together we're creating havens for heaven on Earth, turning back the pressures of growth and development without giving up ownership of the property we've worked hard to acquire and care for.

Conservation easements are unique legal documents, crafted to represent the interests of the landowner and characteristics of the property. The easement is a legal agreement between a landowner and a land trust or a governmental agency that limits what and how a property can be used in order to protect, conserve or preserve anything from a large tract of forest to a small parcel of scenic land adjacent to a meandering river. Land trusts are private, non-profit organizations that protect lands possessing scenic, natural, historic or agricultural value as determined by the community they serve and by federal, state or local conservation policy. Land trusts cooperatively monitor these properties into perpetuity and insure that the original conservation terms set forth in the easement are followed.

Among the financial advantages derived from a conservation easement are federal and state income tax deductions, the reduction of estate tax, and possibly, a reduction in local property taxes. To qualify as a donation, the easement must be donated to a qualifying conservation or historic preservation 501(c)3 non-profit organization. The amount of charitable deductions for a conservation easement is determined on a case-by-case basis as the difference between the value of the property with and without the conservation easement. The US Internal Revenue Service allows a charitable deduction if the easement is perpetual and donated exclusively for conservation purposes. Due to the ever-changing tax laws, differences in state laws, and individual circumstances, financial and legal advisors are typically consulted.

Rising land values and the associated taxes, have also spurred this trend. When owners pass away, the estate taxes can force heirs to sell property, which often then goes to developers that, in turn, are known for their ability to pave-over nature, creating sprawling suburbs or warehouse and office complexes.

The size of the property matters little. Rather, to qualify under present US tax rules, the property must have significant environmental conservation or historic value which might address one of the following:

- Important wildlife habitat that features unique natural attributes.

- Protection of a view, such as frontage along a scenic lake or river.

- Significant historical structure or community space, such as a distinguished plantation home or portion of a battlefield.

- Use for public outdoor recreation or education.

A land trust must be identified as being interested in accepting the easement to the property. In most cases, conservation easements do not provide public access unless the landowner so specifies.

For the Inn Serendipity Woods property, our plans, once the mortgage is paid off, is to place a conservation easement on the property and propose that it be accepted by the Mississippi Valley Conservancy, a land trust serving our region. The right to sell or pass along our property remains unchanged.

There are a few shortcomings. Encumbering our property with such an easement can increase the difficulty of securing a quick sale of the property if we needed to do so. There's also no guarantee in reduction of local real estate taxes. We're expecting to pay for the cost of the qualified appraisal from an individual with experience in our region. We've also contributed to the accepting organization's Stewardship Fund, set up to monitor and enforce the legal terms of the easement into perpetuity. Donations to the Stewardship Fund depend on the size of the property and range from several hundred dollars to thousands of dollars.

In addition to conservation easements, there are other flexible and creative conservation methods. Included are land or property donations to a land trust by gift or will, purchase or bargain sales of property, life estates, and limited development arrangements where a portion of the property is wisely developed to finance the conservation of the remaining property.

A conservation easement, and the power of property ownership contained therein, can be a tool for conservation. By defining our values and love of nature through our land, we're insuring that our legacy is left the way we believe it should be — not end up as a parking lot or housing development.

SOURCES AND RESOURCES

Land Trust Alliance
   Website: www.landtrustalliance.org
   Founded in 1982, the Land Trust Alliance is the national leader of the private land conservation movement, promoting voluntary land conservation across the country and providing resources, leadership and training to the nation's non-profit, grassroots land trusts, helping them to protect important open spaces. Their website has a searchable database of land trusts in the US.

American Farmland Trust
   Website: www.farmland.org
   American Farmland Trust is a private, non-profit organization founded in 1980 to protect our nation's farmland. AFT works to stop the loss of productive farmland and to promote farming practices that lead to a healthy environment.

The Nature Conservancy
   Website: www.natureconservancy.org
   The Nature Conservancy is a private, international, non-profit organization established in 1951 to preserve plants, animals and natural communities that represent the diversity of life on earth by protecting the lands and waters they need for survival.

National Trust for Historic Preservation
   Webiste: www.nthp.org
   Focuses on the protection of historical buildings and other places of historic interest.

Independence and Interdependence Day

While we're deeply moved to change our ways by what is happening around the world — global warming, increasing social inequity and exploitation, loss of biological and cultural diversity, environmental degradation, and human overpopulation, among many others — this book is not filled with facts, figures and piles of statistics reaffirming the present course of humanity.

Instead, we've chosen to focus on the practical, the feasible, the personal. Not to ignore the specifics of the state of the world, we've created a website that reflects and summarizes many of the pressing issues, drawing from research analysis from some of the most reliable and accountable sources today. These findings can be found on the website <www.ruralrenaissance.org> for the new program, Rural Renaissance Network (RRN), of the non-profit organization Renewing the Countryside, Inc. The website is designed to disseminate information about the state of the world, and more importantly, about those individuals, organizations, companies and communities that are putting into motion what some may call the future — today.

Change defines life and living. How we evolve, recreate, celebrate and survive is predicated upon our ability to not just weather the changes, for example, by erecting tall walls around our cities that face the possibility of being submerged in the coming Century or two as a result of rising sea levels or severe storms. Rather, we discovered, if not also a bit serendipitously, that by being change agents who seek out and embrace these cycles of life, changes of lifestyle and patterns of living that our life has become all the richer for it.

We can't escape the reality — and opportunity — that a healthy, safe and secure planet is a basic requirement to our own health, safety and happiness. How to go about it is the deeply seated purpose for living, loving and being. It keeps us going, fuels our passion and forms community.

Sources and Resources

The Rural Renaissance Network
   Website: www.ruralrenaissance.org
   An inspiring, dynamic and diverse community of individuals, families, communities and organizations across the continent share a passionate mission for sustainable living, rural revitalization, ecological restoration, greater self-reliance, and aspire to achieve a more creative and meaningful livelihood. From this grassroots reality sprouted the new Rural Renaissance Network program, nested within the non-profit organization, Renewing the Countryside, Inc. The Rural Renaissance Network builds upon many of the themes and topics discussed in this book while offering many other ideas from across the continent and from all walks of life. Both are described below.
   Join the rural renaissance movement and contribute to a vision for a more sustainable tomorrow — one farm, small town, or cabin in the woods at a time.

Renewing the Countryside, Inc.
   Website: www.renewingthecountryside.org
   As a program within the non-profit organization Renewing the Countryside, Inc., the Rural Renaissance Network aims to empower the rural renaissance movement by providing educational resources and how-to information to individuals, families and communities wishing to support "right livelihood" and creative, healthy, ecologically mindful and socially responsible living in rural and small town communities across North America. Among the network initiatives are a dynamic website featuring demonstration homes and businesses with how-to resources, a mentorship program, and educational workshops.

   Through innovative books, calendars, website and other resources, Renewing the Countryside, Inc. brings hope and inspiration to people living in the countryside, raises awareness of urban-dwellers as to how rural people play vital roles in preserving the countryside, educates policymakers of types of initiatives that they can support and showcases individuals, businesses and organizations that are "renewing the countryside" through innovative enterprises and initiatives that combine economic, environmental and community benefits.

   Join a continent-wide effort to renew the countryside and help create a more ecologically viable future.

To help fund the Rural Renaissance Network, contact:

Rural Renaissance Network
Renewing the Countryside, Inc.
2105 First Avenue, South
Minneapolis MN 55404

   For correspondence, or to volunteer as a mentor or demonstration site, contact (please include a self-addressed stamped reply envelope): Rural Renaissance Network P.O. Box 811 Monroe WI 53566 <www.ruralrenaissance.org>

Index

A

activism
    environmental protection, 153–155
    non-profit organizations, 241–244
    purchasing power, 4
    sources, 154, 155, 164, 253
agriculture
    animal feed, 69, 153
    changes to, 69–70
    decline of family farm, 52, 69
    farm business, 100–104, 172–173
    specialty crops, 171, 172
air conditioners, 32
air pollution, indoor, 8, 9
altruism, 241–244
Anderson, Sherry Ruth, 44
animal tested products, 240
appliances, energy-efficient, 29, 30–33
artist-in-residence, 221–222
asbestos, 7, 29
Ausubel, Kenny, 69

B

bank checks, 25
barter and exchange, 170
batteries, 23, 112

Bed & Breakfast (B&B)
    lifestyle, 189–192
    operating, 192, 193–195, 202
Benyus, Janine, 108
biodiversity, 36–38, 69
biomimicry, 108
bioregionalism, 6. *see also* local economy
bluebird conservation, 225–226, 229–230
building and renovations
    greenhouse project, 171–173
    health risks, 7–8, 29
    reuse examples, 14–16
    straw bale construction, 174–176
building materials, 8–11
business. *see* small business

C

campfires, 135–136
canning jars, 92–93
cars, 153, 159–160
Carson, Rachel, 88
Center for a New American Dream, 153, 154

chemical pesticides and fertilizers, 70, 77, 88, 154, 236
chemicals, 7, 8, 88–89
chickens, 59–64, 63–64
children
    decision to have, 205–206
    grandparents, 208
    parenting, 205–211
    a promise to our child, 206
cleaning products, 4, 10, 11
climate change, 18. *see also* global warming
clothing, 24
coffee, 48–50
community building. *see also* friendships
    local economy, 52–54, 128–129, 168–170
    and sharing, 165–167, 242–243
    and technology, 41–42
Community-Supported Agriculture (CSA), 53, 89
composting, 74
computers, 31–32, 41–42
conservation easements, 250–252
Conservation Reserve Programs (CRP), 21, 36
Consumer Confidence Index, 224
consumerism, 3, 16–18
consumers. *see* purchasing decisions
contractors, 14–16, 113–115
cooking, 50–52. *see also* recipes
cooking oils, 4
Co-op America, 10, 11, 24, 38, 49, 195
Cooperative Enterprise Program, 100–104

costs
    and design, 15
    energy credits, 124–125
    "nature's share", 66
    purchasing decisions, 6, 29
    solar power, 113, 120, 123
    wind turbines, 130, 131
cotton, natural, 5, 10, 24
crafting and handiwork, 160–161
creativity
    and cooking, 50–52
    crafting and handiwork, 160–161
    and personal energy, 144–147
cultural creatives, 43–45

D
dehumidifiers, 32
direct marketers, 25
dishwashers, 31
Diversified Quality of Life Index, 223

E
The Earth User's Guide to Permaculture (Morrow), 82
ecological footprint
    consumerism, 16–18
    national comparisons, 3, 16
ecotravel and ecotourism, 200, 201, 202–204
eggs, 62, 63–64
electricity
    basics of, 122
    conservation, 110, 111, 154
    energy credits, 124–125
    global warming, 124
    green energy option, 106
    grid intertie, 122, 124–125, 132

photovoltaic (PV) systems,
 120–125
wind turbines, 129–132
emails, unwanted, 25
Energy Star program, 29, 30
energy use
 appliances, 29, 30–33
 conservation, 109–110, 154
 efficiency, 30–33, 111–112, 154
 personal climate change calculator,
  18
 solar energy, 113, 116–118,
  120–125
 sources, 33, 106, 112, 118, 125
 sustainable living, 105–107
 wind turbines, 129–132
environmental protection. *see also* forest conservation
 activism, 153–155
 extinction rate, 70
 leaving a legacy, 245–252
 wildlife habitat, 22–23, 38, 70,
  225–230

F

fair trade products, 48–50
farm business, 100–104, 172–173
farmers' markets, 53–54, 89
financing, 20–21, 35–36
fireplaces, open, 139
floor finishes, 9–10
floor heating systems, 117–118
flooring, 9–10
food
 coffee, 48–50
 cooking oils, 4

eggs, 62, 63–64
fair trade products, 48–50
healthy choices, 231–234
local, 52–54, 129, 168–170
meat production, 153
milk production, 89
organic, 4, 89–91, 231
packaging, 13
potatoes, 55–57
seafood, 232
shrimp, 153–154, 232
Swiss chard, 158
vegetarian diet, 232–233, 234–235
food preservation
 basics of, 95–97
 salsa example, 214
 satisfaction of, 91–94
 tomato sauce, 94
forest conservation. *see also* wildlife
  habitat
 land trusts, 249–252
 restoration, 33–36, 226–227, 245
 sources, 38
 sustainable production, 10, 36–38
Forest Stewardship Council-certifica-
  tion (FSC), 10, 37, 38
friendships
 of different ages, 125–127,
  155–157, 163
 sharing, 149–152, 161–162,
  165–166, 169
 support through, 75–76, 149–152
furniture, 3, 10

G

garbage, reusable, 14–16

gardening. *see also* nature appreciation
    composting, 74
    food preservation, 91–97, 214
    garden as teacher, 80–82
    organic, 54, 72–75, 77–79
    organic flower business, 101–104
    perennial flowers, 97–99
    permaculture, 82–85
    planting seeds, 65–70
    potatoes lesson, 55–57
    seed types, 71–72
    sources, 67, 72, 79
    water conservation, 142–143
genetically modified organisms
    (GMOs), 72
Genuine Progress Indicator (GPI),
    224
gift giving, 160–161, 169
global trade, 16–17
global warming, 2, 33, 124. *see also* climate change
grants and incentives, 21, 124–125
Green County Conservation League,
    245
green energy option, 106
greeting card recycling, 218
Gross National Product (GNP),
    223–224

H

Hannover Principles for Sustainability,
    6–7
health and wellness, 236–240
health risks
    building materials, 7–8, 29
    and farmers, 70, 73

food examples, 88–89
nitrates, 70, 77, 154, 236
heating
    passive solar design, 32, 111
    solar hot water, 113, 116–118, 172
    woodstoves, 133–139
heat loss reduction, 110
home-based business. *see also* small
    business
    business deductions, 21, 198
    flexibility of, 41–42, 195–196
    managing, 197–198
    and technology, 195–196
Homgren, David, 82
hybrid renewable energy system, 125

I

Inn Serendipity farmstead
    chess set and board, 27–28
    description, 19–21, 57–59
    financing, 185–187
    permaculture zones, 83–84
Inn Serendipity Woods, 34–36, 185,
    225–228
insurance, health care, 21, 197
investments, socially responsible, 184

J

junk mail reduction, 25, 154

L

labor practices, 24
labyrinth, 144, 146, 147–148
land, purchase of, 19–21, 35–36
land and land use
    conservation programs, 36,
        226–227, 245

grants and incentives, 21
    land trusts, 249–252
landscaping, 58, 82–85
lawn mowers, 32–33
legacy, 245–252
Lehman's non-electric catalog, 94
letter writing, 159
Lifestyles of Health and Sustainability
    (LOHAS), 44
lighting, 111–112, 154
livelihood, 177–181, 188, 195,
    199–204
local economy, 6, 52–54, 128–129,
    168–170
Loterie Farm, 201
Lovins, Amory, 159–160

M

mattresses, 5
McDonough, William, 6
Michael Fields Agricultural Institute
    (MFAI), 100, 104
milk production, 89
Mollison, Bill, 82
Monroe (WI), 128
Morning Star Garden, 101–104
Morrow, Rosemary, 82

N

Native Earth Construction, 172
nature appreciation. *see also* gardening
    campfires, 135–136
    chicken-raising experience, 59–64
    connection to water, 139–141
    and cooking, 50–52
    and personal energy, 144–147
    planting weekend, 145–146

seasonal changes, 46–48, 86–88
    sense of place, 57–59
    sunshine, 118–120
networking, 41–42, 242
North American Bluebird Society,
    180, 230

O

organic flower business, 101–104
organic foods, 4, 89–91, 231
organic gardening, 72–75, 77–79
Our Ecological Footprint (Wackernagel
    and Rees), 16, 205

P

paint, 8
paper and paper products, 10, 25,
    160–161, 218
parenting
    and grandparents, 208
    philosophy, 205–209
    strategies, 209–211
passive solar design, 32, 111
passive solar thermal systems, 118
permaculture design, 82–85
pesticides and fertilizers, 70, 77, 88,
    154
phase change salt tube, 118
photovoltaic (PV) systems, 120–125
pond design, 22–23
potato growing experience, 55–57
purchasing decisions
    costs, 6, 29
    local economy, 52–54, 128–129,
        168–170
    product research, 30
    setting criteria, 4–5, 66, 153–155

Q
quality of life, 219–225

R
Ray, Paul H., 44
real estate
 buying a farm, 19–21
 buying wooded property, 35–36
recipes
 Baked Potato Pancakes, 55–57
 Granola, 40
 Raspberry Cordial, 87
 sources, 235
 for tomato sauce, 94
recycled products, 24, 66
recycling, 12–13, 216–219
Redefining Progress, 17, 18
Rees, William, 16, 205
refrigeration and freezing, 30–31
renewable energy. *see* energy use
resources. *see also* websites
 activism, 154, 155, 164, 253
 biodiversity, 69
 building and renovations, 8–11
 ecotravel, 204
 energy use, 33, 106, 112, 118, 125
 fair trade products, 49–50
 farm management, 104
 food preservation, 97
 forest conservation, 25, 38
 gardening, 67, 72, 79
 health and wellness, 240
 household products, 8–11
 insurance, 21, 197
 investing, 184
 labor practices, 24

labyrinth design, 148
land trusts, 252
livelihood, 178, 188, 195
local economy, 53–54, 170
magazines, 45, 164
non-profit organizations, 244
organic foods, 90–91
parenting, 211
permaculture, 85
product research, 30
rural community, 254
seafood, 232
simple living, 214, 215, 225
skin and body care products, 240
small business, 198
straw bale construction, 176
sustainable living, 11, 18, 45, 160, 184
tools, non-electric, 94
travel, 160
vegetarian diet, 235
wildlife habitat, 230
wind energy, 132
woodstoves, 139
reuse
 renovations, 14–16
 second-hand furnishings, 3–4, 13–14
rhubarb experience, 155
rural community
 building, 52–54, 165–167, 168–170
 population growth, 41
 restoration, 41–42, 128–129, 253–254
 sense of place, 57–59
 sources, 254

rural experience. *see* nature apprecia-
    tion

S

Seafood Wallet Card, 232
seeds, 65–70, 71–72
Seeds of Change - The Living Treasure
    (Ausubel), 69
self-employment. *see also* small busi-
    ness
    financial independence, 185–187
    right livelihood, 177–181
Servas, 156, 204
seventh generation philosophy, 12
SHAKTI for Children, 242, 244
shopping. *see* purchasing decisions
showerheads and faucets, 142, 154
shrimp, 153–154, 232
Silent Spring (Carson), 88
simple living. *see also* sustainable living
    and complexity, 213–214, 216
    health and wellness, 236–244
    healthy foods, 231–235
    leaving a legacy, 245–252
    quality of life, 219–225
    sources, 214, 215, 225
    steps to, 216–219
    sterotypes of, 213
skin and body care products, 240
small business
    Bed & Breakfast (B&B), 189–192,
        193–195, 202
    equilibrium economics, 186
    examples, 185–187
    home-based, 21, 41–42, 195–198

self-employment, 177–181,
    185–187
    sources, 198
    specialty crops, 171, 172
    training program, 100–104
    work and leisure, 199–204
SmartWood-certification, 37
social relationships. *see* friendships
solar hot water heating system, 113,
    116–118, 172
solar panels, 120–125
solar shingles, 121–122
solar thermal system, 113, 116–118
sources and resources. *see* resources
specialty crops, 171, 172
stoves, 133–139
straw bale construction, 171–172,
    174–176
Styrofoam, 12, 23
success
    criteria, 108
    quality of life, 222–225
    redefining, 44, 184–185
    wealth, 187
sustainable living. *see also* simple living
    achieving, 26–29, 75–76
    anti-consumer community,
        153–155
    goals, 2, 44
    interdependence, 125–127
    leaving a legacy, 245–252
    lifestyle choices, 1–3, 43–45
    principles, 6–7
    self-employment, 177–181, 188,
        195
    sources, 11, 18, 45, 160, 184

stereotypes of, 39–43
values, 12, 26–27, 57–59, 66,
    181–185
work and leisure, 42–43, 199–204
sweatshop labor, 24, 49–50
Swiss chard, 158

T

technology
    and community, 41–42
    and heating, 133–134
    and learning, 181–182
    and sustainable living, 39–43,
        93–94
telephone, 25
television, 39, 164, 210
Todd, Jonathan, 143
toilets, 143
tools, non-electric, 94
toothbrushes, 24
travel, 158–159, 163, 183, 200–204

U

Umberger, Mary, 41
urban community
    energy conservation, 109
    isolation within, 166–167
    sustainable living, 2, 41–42, 179
utility companies
    green energy option, 106
    grid intertie, 122, 124–125, 132
    wind turbines, 129–130

V

values
    an authentic life, 66
    quality of life, 219–225

self fulfillment, 181–185
sense of place, 57–59
seventh generation philosophy, 12
wabi-sabi philosophy, 26–27
vegetarian diet, 232–233, 234–235
volatile organic compounds (VOCs),
    8, 116
voluntary simplicity. *see* simple living

W

wabi-sabi philosophy, 26–27
Wackernagel, Mathis, 16, 205
washing machines, 31
waste, reducing, 12–13, 108, 140, 153,
    217–218
wastewater, 143
water conservation, 142–143, 154
wealth, 187, 222–225
websites. *see also* resources
    Agricultural Marketing Service
        (farmer's markets), 53
    Alternative Medicine Center, 240
    American Farmland Trust, 252
    American Forest's Personal Climate
        Change Calculator, 18
    American Formulating and
        Manufacturing (AFM), 8
    American Small Business
        Association, 198
    American Wind Energy
        Association, 132
    Appropriate Technology Transfer
        to Rural Areas, 104
    Ask Dr. Sears, 211
    Aubrey Organics, 240
    Aveda, 240

BackHome, 45

Bioneers, 184

Bioshield, 8

The Body Shop, 240

Burt's Bees Inc., 240

Center for Agroecology & Sustainable Food Systems, 79

Center for a New American Dream, 154, 155

Chefs Collaborative, 90

Citristrip, 10

Conservation International, 204

Consumer Assistance (unwanted e-mail), 25

Conversation Cafés, 215

Co-op America (fair trade), 49

Co-op America (responsible shopping), 49

Co-op America's Business Network, 195

Co-op America's Green Pages, 10, 11

Co-op America (sweatshops), 24, 49

Co-op America's Woodwise Consumer Guide, 38

Countryside and Small Stock Journal, 45

Database of State Incentives for Renewable Energy, 125

Earthwatch, 204

Eco Friendly Flooring, 9

Energy Efficiency and Renewable Energy Portal, 118

Environmental Defense, 160

EPA Energy Star, 33

E/The Environmental Magazine, 164

Fair Trade Federation, 49

FEDCO Seed Company, 67

Forest Stewardship Council (FSC), 38

Gaiam Real Goods, 10

Gardens Alive, 79

Global Exchange, 244

Global Fund for Children, 244

Good Life Center, 45

Green Hotel Association, 195

GreenMoney Journal, 184

Green Power Network, 106

Healthy Home, 10

Home Power Magazine, 125

Hostelling International, 160

In Business, 164

Institute for Agriculture and Trade Policy, 104

Institute for Local Self Reliance's New Rules Project, 170

Insure Kids Now, 21, 197

International Ecotourism Society, 204

International Strawbale Registry, 176

Johnny's Selected Seeds, 67

Kiss My Face, 240

La Leche League, 211

Land Trust Alliance, 252

The Last Straw, 176

Lehman's, 94

Local Harvest, 53

Madison Area Community Supported Agriculture Cooperative, 235

Message! Products, 25

Michael Fields Agricultural Institute, 104

Midwest Renewable Energy Association, 112

Monterey Bay Aquarium, 232

Mother Earth News, 164

Mothering Magazine, 211

National Audubon Society, 230, 232

National Organic Program, 90

National Tour of Solar Homes, 244

National Trust for Historic Preservation, 252

National Wildlife Federation, 230

Natural Home, 164

Nature Conservancy, 252

New Road Map Foundation, 188

North American Bluebird Society, 230

Ocean Arks International, 143

Oceanic Society Expeditions, 204

Organic Consumer Association, 90

Peaceful Valley Farm Supply, 67

Recycline, 24

Redefining Progress, 18, 225

Renewing the Countryside Inc., 188, 254

Right Livelihood Award Foundation, 178

Robyn Van En Center, 53

Rocky Mountain Institute, 160

Rural Renaissance Network, 253, 254

Seeds of Change, 67

Seeds of Simplicity, 214, 215

Seventh Generation, 10

SHAKTI for Children, 244

Simple Living Network, 215

Slow Food, 90

Smith & Hawken, 10

St. Jude Ranch for Children, 218

Sustainable Sources, 11

Terra-Green Technologies, 9

Tom's of Maine, 240

TransFair USA, 49

Trees for the Future, 204

United States SERVAS, 204

Utne Reader, 164

Vegetarian Times, 235

Veriditas: The World-Wide Labyrinth Project, 148

Windustry, 132

Working Assets, 25

Worldwatch Institute, 11

World Wildlife Fund, 38

Yes! A Journal of Positive Futures, 164

wildlife habitat. *see also* forest conservation

bluebird conservation, 225–226, 229–230

designing, 22–23

extinction rate, 70

sources, 38

windows, 110

wind turbines, 21, 129–132

wood, sustainable production, 10,
        36–38
wood finishes, 9–10
woodstoves
    choices, 139
    as hearth, 133–136
    Lopi Endeavor, 137–138
workshops, rural living, 187, 242

Y

youth hostels, 158–159